DICKINSON

DICKINSON

The Anxiety of Gender

by Vivian R. Pollak

Cornell University Press

ITHACA AND LONDON

Copyright © 1984 by Cornell University Press

All rights reserved. Except for brief quotations in a review, this book, or parts thereof, must not be reproduced in any form without permission in writing from the publisher. For information, address Cornell University Press, 124 Roberts Place, Ithaca, New York 14850.

First published 1984 by Cornell University Press.
Published in the United Kingdom by Cornell University Press Ltd., London.

International Standard Book Number 0-8014-1605-1
Library of Congress Catalog Card Number 83-45941

Printed in the United States of America

Emily Dickinson's poems are reprinted by permission of the publishers and the Trustees of Amherst College: From *The Poems of Emily Dickinson,* edited by Thomas H. Johnson. Cambridge, Mass.: The Belknap Press of Harvard University Press. Copyright 1951, © 1955, 1979 by the President and Fellows of Harvard College. From *The Complete Poems of Emily Dickinson,* edited by Thomas H. Johnson. Copyright 1914, 1929, 1935, 1942 by Martha Dickinson Bianchi; copyright © renewed 1957, 1963 by Mary L. Hampson. By permission of Little, Brown and Company. From *The Life and Letters of Emily Dickinson,* by Martha Dickinson Bianchi. Copyright 1924 by Martha Dickinson Bianchi. Copyright renewed 1952 by Alfred Leete Hampson. Reprinted by permission of Houghton Mifflin Company.

Emily Dickinson's letters and prose fragments are reprinted by permission of the publishers and the Trustees of Amherst College from *The Letters of Emily Dickinson,* edited by Thomas H. Johnson. Cambridge, Mass.: The Belknap Press of Harvard University Press. Copyright 1914, 1924, 1932 by Martha Dickinson Bianchi. Copyright © 1958 by the President and Fellows of Harvard College.

Emily Norcross Dickinson's letter to Emily Dickinson, May 1844, Box 3, Dickinson Family Papers, Houghton Library, Harvard University, is reprinted by permission of the Houghton Library.

Lines from Sylvia Plath's poem "Edge" are reprinted from *The Collected Poems of Sylvia Plath,* edited by Ted Hughes, by permission of Harper & Row, Publishers, Inc.; and from *Ariel* by Sylvia Plath. London: Faber and Faber. By permission of Olwyn Hughes. Poem Copyright © 1963 by Ted Hughes.

Chapter 4 contains material that previously appeared in my article "Thirst and Starvation in Emily Dickinson's Poetry" in *American Literature,* volume 51, March 1979, reprinted here by permission of the editors.

*Librarians: Library of Congress cataloging information
appears on the last page of the book.*

*The paper in this book is acid-free and meets the guidelines
for permanence and durability of the Committee on Production
Guidelines for Book Longevity of the Council on Library Resources.*

For Bob

CONTENTS

PREFACE

Most of Emily Dickinson's poetry, and all of it that matters, originates in frustration. Perhaps half of her 1,775 short poems revolve around a single question that remains fundamentally unanswered. Why, Dickinson asks herself, does the "nearest Dream" recede "unrealized"? Within the rest of her poems, happiness is not at issue and the questions Dickinson asks are more difficult to pinpoint, but many of these intellectually challenging texts also reflect her belief that, as a woman whose quest for sexual identity has been terminally thwarted, she is nature's victim. In calling this book *The Anxiety of Gender*, I mean to suggest that Dickinson's identity crisis was, broadly speaking, a crisis of sexual identity, that her poetry associates love and social power, and that, as the laureate of the dispossessed, Dickinson is also the laureate of sexual despair.

Portraying herself as absurdly self-defeating and as hopelessly victimized by a pathologically hostile environment, Dickinson wishes to discover whether she is at fault or whether the fault inheres in her world. Though it is apparent that her finest poems obviate this distinction between individual psychological errors and collective social mistakes, most of Dickinson's poetry sustains it. The moral neutrality of her greatest utterances is exceptional. Side with me, she says, whoever I am: erotically bereaved, a self-reliant solitary, or merely weird—a case of permanently arrested development. Consequently, to know Dickinson is to know her antagonists, which have

9

often been described as nature, God, time, and death. As a biographical critic, I recognize that Dickinson's ability to link her unique personal concerns to a larger drama of human identity depends on this vocabulary of abstraction. My consistent assumption, however, is that Dickinson's attitudes toward nature, God, time, and death were the products of her social experience.

Clearly, my attempt is to describe Dickinson's indebtedness to life, rather than her indebtedness to other writers. Though I should like to think that this book reflects some sensitivity to the literary models with which Dickinson identified and from which she deliberately distanced herself, my aim is to describe how her poems remystify the reality of her experience. Thus, without denying Dickinson's interest in the experience of other writers or her attentiveness to the collective vocabulary of her culture, I am most deeply involved with her reading of human relationships. In the beginning was the family.

The findings of two radically different biographers, Richard Sewall and John Cody, have made this book possible. Earlier biographical critics were severely impeded by inadequate information and, in some instances, by a lack of psychological sophistication. Together, Sewall and Cody have greatly advanced our understanding of Dickinson's life, and my intellectual debt to them is profound. Unlike Sewall, however, I do not believe that Dickinson's literary vocation was her generative obsession; unlike Cody, I do not believe that Dickinson's poems necessarily reenact actual events.

My debt to feminist criticism is equally profound. Many of the questions I ask have been posed by others, but I hope that the structure and scope of this analysis may help to explain why Dickinson is the only American woman poet of her era with whom modern readers continue to identify. Furthermore, by examining Dickinson's attitudes toward the sexual conventions of her culture, I seek to dispel the misconception that her language is excessively or even exclusively self-referential. These attitudes, I believe, contribute to our understanding of Dickinson's vitality in our time, and her decision, if such it was, to capitalize on her self-perceived abnormality seems to me essential to Dickinson's achievement.

This achievement cannot be organized into neat historical periods, for reasons that I consider briefly in the following introductory chapter. Ideally, a work that aspires to read Dickinson's poems within the context of her life would depend on precisely dated texts and would reflect a development. But most of her texts cannot be precisely dated, and there is an important sense in which Dickinson's poetry does not develop, since the identity crisis on which it depends remains unresolved and thus leads to static experience. I have sought to compensate for these stubborn realities by concentrating on the internal sequence of events within poems, rather than on their perhaps irrelevant immediate occasions. And so I do not always specify the probable date of composition of her poems. For my purposes, when texts were written is not always relevant. What is relevant is the history to which they allude.

This book's history has been quickened by the following scholars who read and commented on drafts of individual chapters: Nina Auerbach, Sharon Cameron, Joanne Feit Diehl, Lillian Faderman, Elsa Greene, George Monteiro, David Porter, Barton St. Armand, and Richard Sewall. Robert Regan cheerfully read and discussed with me a draft of the entire manuscript. Jonathan Morse was exceptionally generous in helping to improve the manuscript in its final stages: he read revisions of revisions. I am also grateful to Cheyney University for a sabbatical leave and to the American Philosophical Society and the National Endowment for the Humanities for financial support. Finally, I should like to acknowledge the personal support of my husband, Robert Pollak, the other members of my family, and my friends.

VIVIAN R. POLLAK

Merion, Pennsylvania

DICKINSON

INTRODUCTION

"I had a terror—since September—I could tell to none—and so I sing, as the Boy does by the Burying Ground—because I am afraid—" Dickinson wrote to Thomas Wentworth Higginson in April 1862. After a brief digression into her reading tastes she continued, "When a little Girl, I had a friend, who taught me Immortality—but venturing too near, himself—he never returned—Soon after, my Tutor, died—and for several years, my Lexicon—was my only companion—Then I found one more—but he was not contented I be his scholar—so he left the Land" (L261).[1] Resuming this theme several months later, she explained, "My dying Tutor told me that he would like to live till I had been a poet, but Death was much of Mob as I could master—then—And when far afterward—a sudden light on Orchards, or a new fashion in the wind troubled my

1. All texts for Dickinson's letters are from *The Letters of Emily Dickinson*, ed. Thomas H. Johnson, 3 vols. (Cambridge: Harvard University Press, 1958). The letter "L" precedes such citations to differentiate letters from poems. "PF" stands for prose fragments, in *Letters of Emily Dickinson* 3: 911–29. All texts for Dickinson's poems are from *The Poems of Emily Dickinson*, ed. Thomas H. Johnson, 3 vols. (Cambridge: Harvard University Press, 1955). The parenthetical numbers refer to the chronological numbering in this work.

The Manuscript Books of Emily Dickinson, ed. R. W. Franklin, 2 vols. (Cambridge: Harvard University Press, 1981), was published after most of my book had been completed. In several key instances, however, I have footnoted the textual variants that are suggested by this facsimile edition. In general, Franklin's work supports Johnson's quantitative analysis of the shape of Dickinson's career.

attention—I felt a palsy, here—the Verses just relieve—" (L265).
Having emphasized that poetry was, to her, autotherapeutic speech,
she nevertheless went on to caution Higginson, one month later,
"When I state myself, as the Representative of the Verse—it does
not mean—me—but a supposed person" (L268).

The extent to which the life of Emily Dickinson can be used to
organize the perceptions and experience of her "supposed person"
has been a central concern of Dickinson criticism from its inception.
On the one hand, she herself suggests that her art was a response to
the psychosexual anxieties of her life, anxieties interfused with the
disintegrating religious culture of her place and time: Amherst,
Massachusetts, in the mid-nineteenth century. Her poems, she implies, can be organized around a single theme: a contest between
immortality and death mediated by human agencies. She acknowledges that, as a woman poet, her imagination of an absolute is influenced by the presence or absence of a strong male figure. She has
found such people two or perhaps three times, only to lose them. As
a consequence, she uses her art as she would wish to use other
human beings: as an instrument of self-control. On the other hand,
Dickinson warns Higginson, as she has come to warn us, against
biographical literalism. "My life," she insisted some years later, "has
been too simple and stern to embarrass any" (L330). Of course a
statement such as this implies a repressed life which, if exposed in its
riotous complexity, would discomfort many.

Within the same letter in which she was emphasizing the unevent-
fulness of her past, Dickinson also explained, "You were not aware
that you saved my Life. To thank you in person has been since then
one of my few requests." Clearly, these two statements are difficult
to reconcile. The letter was written in 1869 to Higginson, a critic
whom she had not yet met. Thus one element of her thinking is
unmistakable. Through his letters, she implies, he rescued her from
despair, though inadvertently, at a time when her personal anxieties
were almost unbearable. Receiving this extraordinary document,
with its seemingly contradictory histories, Higginson might have recalled her "terror—since September," in 1861–62. Perhaps he
hoped that a face-to-face interview would enable him to comprehend this enigmatic event. Their interview occurred in the summer of 1870, but Dickinson said nothing further about the crucial
episodes in her drama of fragmented identity to which she had
previously alluded. After this visit, Higginson recorded the singularly disturbing effect of two seemingly irreconcilable impres-

sions: "I never was with any one who drained my nei
much. Without touching her, she drew from me. I am
live near her. She often thought me *tired* & seemed ver
of others" (L342b). Tacitly rebuking Higginson's efforts
tize their relationship, Dickinson menaced *him* with tl
solicitousness of her presence. Though she believed t ... ... nau
saved her life, Dickinson repaid him, perhaps inadvertently, by
draining his.

Despite the efforts of generations of biographers, Dickinson's
"terror—since September" has never been conclusively identified
with a specific erotic bereavement. What has been identified is her
tendency to eulogize men whose deaths, real or typological, liberated her from the threat of their presence. Dickinson's male muses
are, then, best understood as symbols of her lifelong ambivalence
toward the patriarchal values of her cultural tradition, which, for a
female self, held out the promise of a Master, the threat of being
mastered. And yet, as Allen Tate was among the first to insist, "Poetry does not dispense with tradition; it probes the deficiencies of a
tradition. But it must have a tradition to probe."[2] How was it, then,
that Dickinson succeeded in converting a potential disadvantage—
the faintness of her line of poetic foremothers—into a formidable
critique of patriarchal power? What was the relationship between
Dickinson's identity as a woman and her identity as a poet? To what
extent does her art of autobiography probe the deficiencies of an
alien text of female nature? What are the stylistic consequences of
her attitudes toward masculinity and femininity? Is it possible to ask
such questions without imposing the categories of late twentieth-
century thought on a mid-nineteenth-century consciousness enamored of the particular?

When, in 1871, Dickinson engaged in her habitual pastime of
ranking writers, she employed a critical vocabulary of strength and
weakness based on a predictable biological archetype:

> Mrs Hunt's Poems are stronger than any written by Women since
> Mrs—Browning, with the exception of Mrs Lewes— (L368)

Insofar as Emily Dickinson thought of herself as a major poet, she
may not have thought of herself as a woman poet. Insofar as Emily

2. Allen Tate, "Emily Dickinson," *Collected Essays* (1932); reprinted in *Emily Dickinson: A Collection of Critical Essays*, ed. Richard B. Sewall (Englewood Cliffs, N.J.: Prentice-Hall, 1963), p. 24.

Dickinson thought of herself as a woman poet, she may not have thought of herself as fulfilling her own critical demands:

> "If I read a book [and] it makes my whole body so cold no fire ever can warm me I know *that* is poetry. If I feel physically as if the top of my head were taken off, I know *that* is poetry. These are the only way I know it. Is there any other way." (L342a)

Can a sensibility that conflates creation and destruction and that, in certain moods, could perceive poetry as a psychological rape, represent anything other than the uniqueness of its own aberrations? "Women talk: men are silent: that is why I dread women" (L342a). Nevertheless, these are among the questions this book addresses, arguing as it does that gender was Dickinson's generative obsession.

By examining the biographical relationships that impinged most directly on her sexual class consciousness, I seek to explain both Dickinson's sense of her own deficiencies and her sense of the deficiencies of her culture. John Lynen explains: "Emily Dickinson is a baffling poet because she seems to bear little or no relationship to the historical period within which she worked. She stands apart, as indifferent to the literary movements of her day as to its great events. . . . The poems will not even seem convincing as the product (much less the portrayal) of entirely personal experiences if we cannot visualize those experiences as ones which transpired in an actual epoch."[3] Thus, though her most driven years as an artist included and may indeed have coincided with the period of the American Civil War—almost half of her 1,775 poems appear to have been written from 1861 to 1865—she has almost nothing to say about its precipitating causes, its events, or its consequences. Instead, she flaunts a schismatic style which announces that she has seceded from "their story" into hers. Deploying her extensive vocabulary of military, legal, political, scientific, economic, and religious imagery, she directs our attention to an interior, invisible, and nominally self-contained world, to "The Battle fought between the Soul / And No Man—" (594), to "that Campaign inscrutable / Of the Interior" (1188), affirming gleefully, sardonically,

> The Only News I know
> Is Bulletins all Day
> From Immortality. (827)

3. John Lynen, "Three Uses of the Present: The Historian's, the Critic's, and Emily Dickinson's," *College English* 28 (November 1966): 129.

To the extent that Dickinson appropriates a collective past, she does so only to place herself at center stage, rewriting secular and sacred script so that she may herself take the leading role. Given this exhibitionistic art of insistent self-display, self-advertisement, our interest in the person behind the poems is intensified. This person addresses us in a language that is both pre- and postconfessional.

Consider, for example, the following speech, written in about 1862, Dickinson's most furiously productive poetic year. Consider how directly this poem implicates the reader in Dickinson's definition of madness as the creation of a new personality in a new time, a time without a future:

> The first Day's Night had come—
> And grateful that a thing
> So terrible—had been endured—
> I told my Soul to sing—
>
> She said her Strings were snapt—
> Her Bow—to Atoms blown—
> And so to mend her—gave me work
> Until another Morn—
>
> And then—a Day as huge
> As Yesterdays in pairs,
> Unrolled its horror in my face—
> Until it blocked my eyes—
>
> My Brain—begun to laugh—
> I mumbled—like a fool—
> And tho' 'tis Years ago—that Day—
> My Brain keeps giggling—still.
>
> And Something's odd—within—
> That person that I was—
> And this One—do not feel the same—
> Could it be Madness—this?   (410)

What happened? we ask. Or, as the Reverend Charles Wadsworth put it, "I can only imagine the affliction which has befallen, or is now befalling you. Believe me, be what it may, you have all my sympathy. . . . I am very, very anxious to learn more definitely of your trial" (L248a).

Dickinson's life has been the subject of a formidable quantity of biographical research, but it is well known that many of the *facts* of her life, including the exact dating of her manuscripts, have continued to elude the literary historian. It is equally well known that

Dickinson's poems have been mishandled by literary detectives intent on proving theories which, if true, would tell us very little about why her poetry matters. It is perhaps less well known that Dickinson criticism is still permeated with the unfortunate assumption that her poems are unsecured by any consciousness of events, including those of her own life. Moreover, her life itself has often been described as a nonevent, whose only event was her vocation, language. Evidently, certain features of Dickinson's style, in and out of poetry, encourage us to perceive her as "Exterior—to Time—" (448), since she fought furiously to transform herself into a "supposed person," a person without a history. And when she wrote "Explore thyself! / Therein thyself shalt find / The 'Undiscovered Continent'— / No Settler had the Mind" (832), she did not mean that the process of observation is influenced by one's social context. Rather, she meant that the process of observation is culture-free. Dickinson's intensely concentrated style both celebrates this attitude and encourages it in her readers. "It would be hard to name another poet in the history of the English language," Northrop Frye observes, "with so little interest in social or political events." Richard Howard concurs. "It is true: there was only one event, herself."[4]

Thus, though Dickinson has often been read as an autobiographical poet, she has also been read as a poet who created an "archetypal" rather than a personal biography of her consciousness.[5] Similarly, she has been approached as a poet without a subject matter by at least two critics who perhaps believed her when she stated that "Subjects hinder talk" (L397), an assumption that, had she entertained it consistently, would have effectively debarred her from communicating anything other than the desire to communicate.[6] Despite the tension between autobiographical and antiautobiographical elements in Dickinson's style, Dickinson's subject was herself; her language probes the consequences of an attitude toward culture and

4. Richard Howard quotes Northrop Frye in "A Consideration of the Writings of Emily Dickinson," *Prose* 6 (Spring 1973): 95. The original source is "Emily Dickinson," in *Fables of Identity: Studies in Poetic Mythology* (New York: Harcourt, Brace and World, 1963), pp. 193–217.

5. Robert Weisbuch, *Emily Dickinson's Poetry* (Chicago: University of Chicago Press, 1975).

6. In his essay "Emily Dickinson's Notation," *Kenyon Review* 18 (1956), R. P. Blackmur contended, "All her life she was looking for a subject, and the looking *was* her subject—in life as in poetry." Reprinted in *Emily Dickinson*, ed. Sewall, p. 82. In *Dickinson: The Modern Idiom* (Cambridge: Harvard University Press, 1981), David Porter argues that "Dickinson had no subject, least of all reality" (p. 129).

toward gender that views these interrelated manifestations of identity as problematics. This attitude toward culture—that it is a problem to be transcended, that traditionlessness is the best tradition—is a familiar one in romantic and postromantic American literature. It was accentuated and exaggerated in Dickinson as a consequence of her anxiety of gender. This observation returns *me* to *my* theme. An art that tries to be haunted with the composite workings of an anonymous, universalized mind is also haunted with the human history of a particular female nature discovering in its encounters with sexual tradition the limits of traditionlessness.

Liberating her language from the moral didacticism and evasive sentimentality which, her early poems and letters suggest, were the traditional styles available to her during the 1850s, Dickinson was later to boast, and justifiably, " 'It is finished' can never be said of us" (L555). Describing a life in process, the only tradition to which she adhered consistently was a tradition of inconsistency, since it was her intention and her fate to undermine orthodoxies, whatever their point of origin. Describing a life in process, she also described a life whose processes have been suspended. Reacting against her culture's subordination of its women, she also reacted against her culture's failure to subordinate its women sufficiently. Thus she frustrates readers who wish to see her unambiguously as a role rebel, since the roles against which she is rebelling are duplicitous and double. Furthermore, many of Dickinson's finest poems seek to transcend the social causes of psychological states by dispensing with the concept of social role playing altogether. Though this is, as Cora Kaplan astutely observes, a project which cannot finally be realized, she concludes, "Such poetry accentuates the way in which the female psyche has a recalcitrant tendency to remain recognisable in its supposedly weaker aspects, despite a variety of ostensible improvements in women's social and political status."[7] Quite oppositely, Sandra Gilbert and Susan Gubar describe Dickinson as enacting and eventually resolving "both her anxieties about her art and her anger at female subordination,"[8] whereas Margaret Homans suggests that

7. Cora Kaplan, "The Indefinite Disclosed: Christina Rossetti and Emily Dickinson," in *Women Writing and Writing about Women*, ed. Mary Jacobus (New York: Barnes and Noble, 1979), p. 64.
8. Sandra M. Gilbert and Susan Gubar, *The Madwoman in the Attic: The Woman Writer and the Nineteenth Century Literary Imagination* (New Haven: Yale University Press, 1979), p. 583.

"her work is as complex and profuse as it is, at least in part, because she is able to put behind her problems of identity that make Dorothy [Wordsworth] and [Emily] Brontë linger over the same themes and issues in poem after poem."[9] Challenging the belief that Dickinson's poetic innovations are "precursors of a new world vision," Eleanor Wilner's subtle argument holds that "Emily Dickinson uses innovation to break the convention of her day, in order to force the mind, not forward, but back. Her attempt was imaginatively to repossess and reconstruct an old order, and if to do so, she was led to innovations which later were to serve the cause of modernism, this is historical irony, rather than intention."[10]

The tension between Dickinson's respect for the conservative values of her culture and her active animosity toward any social relationship which impeded her own will to power was of incalculable value for her art; this conflict defines the cast of her feminist intelligence. Staunchly committed as she was to a politics of personal autonomy, Dickinson was equally committed to a politics of mutual interdependence, though her imagination of interdependency was riddled with the threat of a complete loss of control over herself as a self-identifying being. Moreover, her ambivalence toward the possible identities her immediate environment afforded was so thoroughgoing as to preclude a comprehensive definition of the issues over which her battle for identity was joined. Hence her art exhibits no clear-cut psychological development; she has no early, middle, and late manner.[11] Instead, Dickinson achieved limited resolutions

---

9. Margaret Homans, *Women Writers and Poetic Identity: Dorothy Wordsworth, Emily Brontë, and Emily Dickinson* (Princeton: Princeton University Press, 1980), p. 165.
10. Eleanor Wilner, "The Poetics of Emily Dickinson," *ELH* 38 (March 1971): 145.
11. In *Major Writers of America*, ed. Perry Miller, *et al.*, 2 vols. (New York: Harcourt, Brace and World, 1962), 2:10, Northrop Frye remarks, "She seems, after her early valentines, to have reached her mature style almost in a single bound." In *The Voice of the Poet: Aspects of Style in the Poetry of Emily Dickinson* (Cambridge: Harvard University Press, 1968), pp. 56–57, Brita Lindberg-Seyersted observes that "it has sometimes been asserted that there is no discernible line of development in Dickinson's poetry. There are obviously no radical or abrupt changes, but rather, as has been evidenced in our material, a shifting of emphasis from the very emotional and personal to a more 'philosophical' and more universal tone. Quite certainly the trend of change seen in the proportion of 'I' poems accounts for some of the change of tone: from a preponderance of 'I' poems in the early poetry, through a gradual, but not steady, decrease of 'I' presence in the poems of the 1870s, toward what seems a balance between the very personal and the more general attitudes." Thus Lindberg-Seyersted qualifies without overturning earlier formulations of this problem by Austin Warren in "Emily Dickinson," *Sewanee Review* 65 (Autumn 1957): 565–86, and by Charles Anderson, in *Emily Dickinson's Poetry: Stairway of Surprise* (New York: Holt, Rinehart

to limited conflicts by blocking out some of the competing impulses that drove her. Because of her inability to integrate these resolutions, each poem begins again as if anew. These restless improvisations were nevertheless grounded within a single formal archetype (the hymn-ballad quatrain) whose stylistic logic she then proceeded to undermine. In personal terms, the price Dickinson paid for her excessive independence was unquiet solitude. In literary terms, the reward was a style whose attentiveness to the workings of the maladjusted mind remains unsurpassed.

Although it is neither desirable nor possible to approach Dickinson's poetry as an ordered diary of social events, it is both desirable and possible to distinguish between the trivial and fundamental ellipses of a surpassingly elliptical style. Jay Leyda suggests that "a major device of Emily Dickinson's writing, both in her poems and in her letters, was what might be called the 'omitted center.' The riddle, the circumstance too well known to be repeated to the initiate, the deliberate skirting of the obvious—this was the means she used to increase the privacy of her communication; it has also increased our problems in piercing that privacy."[12] More significant than the "omitted center" is what might be called the "hidden source." The riddle, the circumstance too little known to be repeated to the self, the deliberate skirting of the essential—this too was the means she used to increase the privacy of her self-portraiture; it has also increased our problems in evaluating her psychological ambitions. Her hidden source is proximately designated as nature or God or as an absent friend or lover, but it is also, as she tells us again and again, "Ourself behind ourself, concealed—" (670), the unconscious. Hence the extent to which Dickinson either comprehended herself or wished to do so warrants further investigation, John Cody's deeply inventive psychobiography notwithstanding.[13]

Just as Dickinson's poems invite us to complete the text of her life

---

and Winston, 1960). Similarly, Inder Nath Kher in *The Landscape of Absence: Emily Dickinson's Poetry* (New Haven: Yale University Press, 1974) rejects the proposition that "Dickinson's poetic career can be studied period by period or 'developmentally' " (pp. 5–6).

12. Jay Leyda, *The Years and Hours of Emily Dickinson*, 2 vols. (New Haven: Yale University Press, 1960), 1: xxi.

13. In *After Great Pain: The Inner Life of Emily Dickinson* (Cambridge: Harvard University Press, 1971), John Cody attributes Dickinson's self-distrust to unresolved childhood conflicts. He was the first biographer to emphasize the significance of Dickinson's relationship to her mother.

and in so doing push us back to a source she knows and knows not, so too they frequently present us "with states of feeling that are severed from the geography that would explain them."[14] Both the degree of this severance and the effect of it remain at issue. Because many of her scenes are, as Robert Weisbuch has demonstrated, illustrative rather than mimetic, within many poems external contexts exist abstractly.[15] Their uniqueness has already been been generalized out of existence. This loss of individuality then functions as the speaker's goad to utterance. Dickinson's poems re-create their external occasions by focusing on the speaker's response to them. Insofar as the feeling portrayed is comprehensible, some crucial element of social geography is implied. Insofar as the feeling portrayed is incomprehensible, no such background exists.

One of the specific occasions that has disappeared in Dickinson's style is the occasion of sex. This loss sometimes constitutes her goad to speech. Deconstructing social myths of female nature (the belief that women are or should be sexually accessible to men, for example), Dickinson also deconstructs her deconstruction. Seeing comparatively, she sees herself in terms of what she is not: a harebell, hallowed, Paradise, a moat of pearl, a persuasive spokeswoman for virginity:

> Did the Harebell loose her girdle
> To the lover Bee
> Would the Bee the Harebell *hallow*
> Much as formerly?
>
> Did the "Paradise"—persuaded—
> Yield her moat of pearl—
> Would the Eden *be* an Eden,
> Or the Earl—an *Earl*?   (213)

Dickinson's textual femininity manifests itself here in a cult of virginity which comes to include both men and women and which is then generalized into a more pervasive cult of separation and of self-control. Since our language is effectively devoid of secular images of male virginity, the word "Earl" is yoked into service. But this is a

14. Sharon Cameron, *Lyric Time: Dickinson and the Limits of Genre* (Baltimore: Johns Hopkins University Press, 1979), p. 15.

15. In *Emily Dickinson's Poetry*, Robert Weisbuch, an antibiographical critic, argues persuasively that Dickinson's language can be interpreted from multiple perspectives; that is, he shows that her language is generalizable.

prurient poem. Since when do bees *hallow* harebells? Because it reveals a mind working to combat its own prurience, such language
arouses prurience in the reader. What is wrong with the poem is that
its occasion has not been sufficiently lost; this is also what is right
with it. The poem's reason for being is to free Emily Dickinson from
the specific circumstances within which her sexual frustration is
meaningless. The poem's achievement is that it both endorses and
disparages the terms of its own self-debate. It shows why her battle
against nature is as meaningful as her participation in it. The ways in
which Dickinson's poems lose their occasions as her style reaffirms
the significance of history in abstracting language from it shall be a
constant point of reference for my analysis. "To disappear enhances—" (1209).

Most comprehensively, the lost occasion in Dickinson's poetry is
the occasion of pleasure unambiguously conceived, pleasure that
does not arouse a corresponding anxiety of loss. In many poems,
this loss occurs at the level of conscious wish formation and is embedded within the manner and the matter of her art. Dickinson
understood her sexuality as both a social and a biological limitation;
her poems reveal a mind intent on testing the consequences of a
partial severance from this historical given. I am using the word
"severance" to signify a repression of history through the re-cre-
ation of an alternative scene which probes the consequences of this
repression. Her poems also reveal a mind intent on testing the duration of this severance, in quest of hedonic links. Saying yes to that
strain of the American romantic sensibility that exaggerated the
value of personal autonomy, Dickinson said no to the undefended
condition into which any Ahab is thrust once the headlands disappear. That she came to view the intense suffering into which her
isolation propelled her as a funeral in the brain is not surprising.
That she also viewed intense pleasure as a knot in the skein of her
consciousness is rather more so:

> It was the limit of my Dream—
> The focus of my Prayer—
> A perfect—paralyzing Bliss—
> Contented as Despair—   (756)

This equation of perfection and paralysis permits us to understand
that, among the many kinds of freedom from "Circumstances— /

And a Name—" (382) she wished to appropriate for herself, the freedom to begin again was the axis around which the whole enter-prise whirled, circumferentially. It was a very American "Route of Evanescence / With a revolving Wheel—" (1463), this notion that, even in Amherst, one could light out for the territory without leav-ing behind the cornerstone of an architectonic whole.

Dickinson's poems seldom speak about experiences that, as she conceives them, are exclusively female. Rather, they define a self that views its social isolation as a suicidal compact with despair, as an ecstatic compact with the unexpected, and as a morally ambiguous composite of the two. In her superb and superbly blocked imagina-tion of social reality, psychological gratification depends, in part, on the body and its sexual appetites. Having come to dread her own sexuality—dread which is the obverse of love—Dickinson sought, through language, to free herself from it. She also had an unerring eye for those circumstances in which neither sexuality nor names mattered: the circumstance of being a corpse, for example. Naive readers of her poetry have always been shocked by the moral ambi-guity of her attitude toward this circumstance: "Match me the Silver Reticence—/Match me the Solid Calm—"(778).

Repeatedly, Dickinson reminds us of the advantages of death. She also reminds us of the advantages of bereavement. These disturbing attitudes are secondary manifestations of her anxiety of gender. Her dread of being mastered impelled her into a flight from the norma-tive biological and social roles available to women in her time and place: marriage and motherhood. This dread was generalized into an ambivalence toward any enduring, incremental, reciprocal social relationship. It also impelled her into a style in which she did not "speak things like the rest" because she did not see things like the rest.[16] *What* Dickinson saw was an essential component of her stylis-tic history. Like any history truly told, her field of vision was com-posed of commonly predetermined and uniquely accidental actions, enthusiasms, and griefs.

Of course the possibility exists that the anguish, guilt, and hostility she reveals constitute superb literary poses, particularly since such poses are precisely those which maximize the illusion of confessional veracity. People do not, we naively assume, pose at pain. In the case

16. Emily Dickinson, as cited in Richard B. Sewall, *The Life of Emily Dickinson*, 2 vols. (New York: Farrar, Straus and Giroux, 1974), 1: 273.

of Dickinson, an unpublishing writer, this illusion is fortified by our inability to specify the "margin" of her discourse: the extent to which, writing for herself, she was also conscious of writing for others; the extent to which, writing for others, she impersonated an unobserved self.[17] But even if it could be established, as it cannot, that her "impersonations" of a pain-ridden self were highly self-conscious literary attitudes, we would still wish to know why, among the many possible houses she could have chosen to inhabit, she returned so insistently to the House of Pain. In the case of Dickinson, the simplest explanation is also, I think, the truest.

Dickinson did not pose at pain. Rather, she believed that language has the potential to order emotions that are inherently disordered, that to comprehend an experience is to alter its effect, and that many experiences can never be adequately comprehended. This latter assumption freed Dickinson to create a poetic self who is arguably the most complex character in American literature. The experience of having desires that were imperfectly gratified through her major relationships, including her relationship to language, is the central fact of Emily Dickinson's life. To delineate those desires is not to trivialize her life or to perceive it "with a banality that misses the complex truth of the woman."[18] Rather, to delineate those desires is to acknowledge the reality of Dickinson's anxiety of gender, whose obverse attitude was an arrogance toward social experience unparalleled in nineteenth-century American literature. She often perceived the social world as a masculine construct whose "Area" was "no test of depth" (L811). The depth of her art, a woman's art of inner space, mirrors, distorts, and clarifies the psychological and

17. Barbara Herrnstein Smith discusses the "conventional ambiguity" of some art works, including Dickinson's, in *On the Margins of Discourse: The Relation of Literature to Language* (Chicago: University of Chicago Press, 1978), pp. 48, 54–55. The conventions governing our response to Dickinson's poems as fictive utterances and the fictive context we infer from them have been, to appropriate Smith's language, "inadequately signaled. Consequently, the appropriate classification of a given composition may be mistaken or doubtful." The "sincere" autobiographical effect of Dickinson's poetry is reinforced by our knowledge that she wrote for herself, for individual private audiences, and for posterity. Ironically, her art of autobiography is enhanced by the "conventional ambiguity" Smith describes.

18. Porter, in *Modern Idiom*, objects to readings of "Dickinson's poems of desolation" (p. 169) that depend upon her loss of a lover. He considers this mode of analysis sexist. Other critics have raised this objection. See Elsa Greene, "Emily Dickinson Was a Poetess," *College English* 34 (October 1972), 63–70, and Suzanne Juhasz, "'A Privilege So Awful': The Poetry of Emily Dickinson," in *Naked and Fiery Forms: Modern American Poetry by Women, A New Tradition* (New York: Harper & Row, 1976), pp. 7–32.

political tensions of her world of experience. It also provides her with a world elsewhere: the world of her style, which defended her against the condition of not knowing and against the condition of knowing too much.

Since other scholars have investigated the influence of Dickinson's sexual anxieties on her style, it may be useful, at this point, to say something further about the relationship of my work to theirs. Biographical critics have tended to emphasize the uniqueness of Dickinson's family background, of her religious convictions or doubts, of her relationships to other women, of her relationships to the men who were her Masters, of her "terror—since September," and of her frustrated literary ambitions.[19] Feminist critics have tended to deemphasize the uniqueness of specific periods or relationships in Dickinson's life and to concentrate instead on linking her attitudes toward female power and powerlessness with the sexual norms of her society and of her literary tradition.[20] Whereas biographical critics, including the Freudian Cody, have been particularly effective in analyzing Dickinson's exceptional social isolation, feminist critics, some of whom are neo-Freudians, have been particularly effective in analyzing Dickinson's exceptional sensitivity to the sexual rhetoric of her culture and to the subordinate status of women within it. Thus, much recent biographical criticism has emphasized the uniqueness of Dickinson's experience of gender, whereas much recent feminist

19. See, for example, Cody on Dickinson's family, in *After Great Pain;* William R. Sherwood on religion, in *Circumference and Circumstance: Stages in the Mind and Art of Emily Dickinson* (New York: Columbia University Press, 1968); on her relationships to other women, see Cody, in *After Great Pain;* Rebecca Patterson, in *The Riddle of Emily Dickinson* (Boston: Houghton Mifflin, 1951), and in *Emily Dickinson's Imagery,* ed. Margaret H. Freeman (Amherst: University of Massachusetts Press, 1979); Lillian Faderman, in "Emily Dickinson's Letters to Sue Gilbert," *Massachusetts Review* 28 (Summer 1977): 197–225; Sewall on her "masters" and for a survey of the scholarship on this subject, in *Life of Emily Dickinson* 2; on her "terror—since September," Thomas H. Johnson, *Emily Dickinson: An Interpretive Biography* (Cambridge: Harvard University Press, 1955); Theodora Ward, *The Capsule of the Mind: Chapters in the Life of Emily Dickinson* (Cambridge: Harvard University Press, 1961); Cody, in *After Great Pain;* on her frustrated literary ambitions, Ruth Miller, in *The Poetry of Emily Dickinson* (Middletown, Conn.: Wesleyan University Press, 1968).
20. See, for example, Adrienne Rich, "Vesuvius at Home: The Power of Emily Dickinson," *Parnassus* 5 (Fall–Winter 1976): 49–74; Albert Gelpi, *The Tenth Muse: The Psyche of the American Poet* (Cambridge: Harvard University Press, 1975); Gilbert and Gubar, *Madwoman in the Attic;* Homans, *Women Writers and Poetic Identity;* Joanne Feit Diehl, *Dickinson and the Romantic Imagination* (Princeton: Princeton University Press, 1981).

criticism has emphasized the influence on Dickinson of a normative cultural model of sexual difference. Similarly, whereas biographical critics have tended to focus on the historical formation of Dickinson's anxiety of gender, feminist critics have tended to focus on her strategies for transcending it.[21] Consequently, whereas biographical critics have been comparatively uninterested in the vitality of Dickinson's sexual class consciousness, feminist critics have been comparatively uninterested in the vitality of those biographical relationships that were of central importance to her. My aim is to reconcile these divergent approaches to Dickinson by examining the ways in which she identified herself with some other women and the ways in which she identified herself as an unprecedented or inexplicable anomaly.

In Part One of this book, I examine Dickinson's life during her formative years as a poet from 1850 to 1862. Chapter 1, "The Family Romance," investigates the psychological climate of her home. Its major finding is that the sexual politics of the Dickinson household replicated a world view in which men initiated actions and women responded to them. Thus Dickinson reacted against a social text that conferred virtue on her rather than power. She had a mother who did not "care for thought" (L261), a father who did not care to have his thoughts challenged. Through her relationships with other women, Dickinson sought to redress this balance of power. These relationships, which I examine in chapter 2, were themselves fraught with the social and erotic tensions that initially caused her to withhold her assent from God the Father and his human surrogates, though not in that order. Throughout this analysis and subsequent chapters, I assume that Dickinson's inconsistent religious attitudes were a secondary manifestation of her conflicted attitudes toward her family, toward the society in which she lived, and toward authority as such. Thus the recipient of the notorious "Master" letters, examined in chapter 3, is viewed as a father surrogate whose inaccessibility became the cornerstone of her psychological design.

21. Among biographical critics, John Cody has explored this subject most extensively, whereas the feminist critic Adrienne Rich emphasizes Dickinson's freedom from self-doubt and rather continuous mastery of her domestic environment. In her essay "Vesuvius at Home," reprinted in *Shakespeare's Sisters: Feminist Essays on Women Poets*, ed. Sandra M. Gilbert and Susan Gubar (Bloomington: Indiana University Press, 1979), Rich writes, "Given her vocation, she was neither eccentric nor quaint; she was determined to survive, to use her powers, to practice necessary economies" (p. 101).

In Part Two of this book, I extend the themes of the first and propose a comprehensive structure for the life cycle of her persona. The sequence of the critical chapters is as follows. Chapter 4, "The Birth of Consciousness: The Consciousness of Exclusion," establishes that Dickinson's poetry is centrally concerned with the origins and consequences of her social isolation. Because of her ambivalence toward the possible relationships her immediate environment afforded, she set herself goals, grandiose and indeterminate, that were consistently inaccessible. There emerges in response to this association between social experience and psychological frustration an ethic of "sumptuous Destitution" (1382), in which less is more. Seeking to distance herself from a world intent on shutting her up in prose, she was forced into a stance of extreme self-reliance in which the distinction between conscious volition and unconscious compulsion was increasingly blurred. Describing her loss of social identity as freedom and as fate, Dickinson never wholly liberated herself from the suspicion that she was engaged in an anxious rationalization of a uniquely neurotic plight.

In the next two chapters I consider in more detail the relationship between verbal compression and instinctual repression, contextual ambiguity and psychological conflict, that her poems establish. Chapter 5, "Sisterhood," examines Dickinson's imagination of relationships with other women. I argue that, in part because of her relationship with Susan Gilbert during her formative years, Dickinson wished to but could not conceive of female friendship as an effective resolution to her status anxieties. Because the circumstances surrounding the cluster of poems examined here can be amply documented through her correspondence, I am able to focus on the kinds of distancing devices Dickinson employed to alter the affect of the narrative she censored. Chapter 6, "The Wife—without the Sign," treats her major love poems as a perpetuation of her quarrel with tradition. Increasingly, the scattered plot elements of her elliptical marriage fiction are seen as composing a war against nature and time.

Within this incremental framework of unresolved and fundamentally irresolvable sexual conflict, grounded as it was in Dickinson's ambivalence toward her precursors (I refer, of course, to her parents); intensified as it was by the hermetic repetitions of her daring gamble on self-reliance; exacerbated as it was by her perception, paranoid in degree though not in kind, that her culture castrated its gifted women,[22] chapter 7, "Anti-Quest, or the Awful Vacuum," provides a new context for reading those poems on pain and death which are Dickinson's most shockingly original achievements. In them, the artist-maker is locked in mortal combat with the artist-patient, as she reorders those desperately disordered funerals in the brain which occur when she plunges into the whirlpool of negative identity. Brutally accurate in their power of close observation, these poems assault us as, one surmises, Dickinson was assaulted, by the return of the repressed.

Having demonstrated that Dickinson's experience consisted of an inner civil war between the two selves she perceived herself to be—conventional woman dependent on the power structure which had in some measure nurtured her, unconventional poet hammering away at its most cherished texts—in the concluding chapter I re-emphasize that the rift between these two characters, "Daisy" and "Loaded Gun," was never fundamentally bridged. In chapter 8, "'Some—Work for Immortality—': The Female Artist as Private Poet," I examine Dickinson's election of a private vocation as still another attempt to propitiate "The Man within," a character who, even as he threatened to destroy, also promised to complete her nature.

Throughout, I have sought neither to sanctify nor to sensational-ize Emily Dickinson. I have never been able to decide whether, as Gilbert and Gubar suggest, her art might have been better had she written under "less constraining circumstances,"[23] or whether, as she herself so often contended, under such circumstances she would never have written at all. Nor, finally, have I ever been able to decide whether, had her temperament been more flexible, these circum-stances might have seemed to her ampler, more various. To the extent possible, I have tried to ignore such unanswerable questions in order to distinguish between those elements of her style that are functionally random and those random elements of her style that undermine the authority of her voice. Because the convoluted com-

---

22. Rebecca Patterson concludes her excellent study of Dickinson's male personae with the statement, "In a sense not yet appreciated, she was the victim of an age that mutilated its gifted women." See "Emily Dickinson's 'Double' Tim: Masculine Identi-fication," *American Imago* 28 (Winter 1971), 362. An updated version of this essay appears as chapter 1, "The Boy Emily," in *Emily Dickinson's Imagery*. Cody also dis-cusses Dickinson's castration fears in *After Great Pain*. For a broader discussion of vocational paranoia and creative envy, see Harold Bloom, *Poetry and Repression: Revi-sionism from Blake to Stevens* (New Haven: Yale University Press, 1976).

23. Gilbert and Gubar, *Madwoman in the Attic*, p. 557.

plexity of her life warranted a fresh approach, I have found it essential to make an initial separation between the patterns of her experience as revealed primarily through her letters and the patterns of her experience as revealed primarily through her poems. My hope is that this procedure has served to explain the absence of demonstrable turning points in the life and art of Emily Dickinson as a perpetuation of those historical conflicts which, in shaping her vocation, also undermined its incremental coherence.

This book is, then, the story of what turned Dickinson's life inward, an examination of the stylistic consequences of this introversion, and an assessment of its degree. I should like to put to rest the notion that, because her style emphasizes her uniqueness, she has no sexual class consciousness. Within the divisions of her psyche, Dickinson discovered our own.[24]

24. Four recent books reflect the diversity of feminist approaches to Dickinson. I mention them only in passing because it is too late for me to incorporate or dispute their argument: Barbara Clarke Mossberg, *Emily Dickinson: When a Writer Is a Daughter* (Bloomington: Indiana University Press, 1982); Suzanne Juhasz, *The Undiscovered Continent: Emily Dickinson and the Space of the Mind* (Bloomington: Indiana University Press, 1983); Suzanne Juhasz, ed., *Feminist Critics Read Emily Dickinson* (Bloomington: Indiana University Press, 1983); Wendy Martin, *An American Triptych: Anne Bradstreet, Emily Dickinson, Adrienne Rich* (Chapel Hill: University of North Carolina Press, 1984).

PART I

The Life

THE FAMILY ROMANCE

Imagine the following setting. It is 1850. Emily Dickinson has been home from Mount Holyoke Female Seminary for two years. Her initial relief at escaping from this strictly regimented community of women consecrated to patriarchal religious values has yielded to dissatisfaction with a daughter's duties (her mother's ill health and her sister Lavinia's absence at boarding school imposing extra housekeeping burdens on her), and she is casting around for a life vocation. Although she had almost experienced a religious conversion sometime in her early teens and could say that she had "never enjoyed such perfect peace and happiness as the short time in which I felt I had found my savior" (L10), she is not, by local standards, pious. Thus missionary work has no appeal for her. Teaching she views as a distinctly marginal occupation, unnecessary for those fortunate girls like herself whose homes, so she maintains, are unbroken. Not a joiner, she refuses to attend the meetings of the local female charitable society. Her absence, she notes with pleasure, puzzles the public "exceedingly." As she well knows, the usual conclusion to this exemplary American girlhood is marriage, the marriage she half expects and is half expected to make. Writing to her friend Abiah Root in 1845 she had boasted, "I am growing handsome very fast indeed! I expect I shall be the belle of Amherst when I reach my 17th year. I don't doubt that I shall have perfect crowds of admirers at that age. Then how I shall delight to make them await my bidding, and with what delight shall I witness their suspense while I make my final decision" (L6). But in 1850, these "perfect crowds of admirers" had not yet manifested themselves, nor had a single perfect candidate as yet subjected himself to the suspense of this superbly self-aggrandizing design.

Instead, the only candidates unmistakably awaiting Dickinson's bidding were words, which she associated, half-mockingly, with satanic wrong-thoughts. Right-thoughts were those of which God, his ministers, her parents, some of her friends, and she herself approved; wrong-thoughts were those that dispersed this coherent moral context—selfishly, and for a song: "The path of duty looks very ugly indeed—and the place where *I* want to go more amiable—a great deal—it is so much easier to do wrong than right—so much pleasanter to be evil than good, I dont wonder that good angels weep—and bad ones sing songs" (L30).

1850, a year of exceptional religious tension in Amherst, is also the year we first hear Dickinson in verse. In a satiric comic valentine sent to a confirmed bachelor, her father's dour law clerk Elbridge G. Bowdoin, she linked piety and marriage. The poem, a burlesque sermon, begins emphatically, "Oh the Earth was *made* for lovers, for damsel, and hopeless swain, / For sighing, and gentle whispering, and *unity* made of *twain*. / All things do go a courting, in earth, or sea, or air, / God hath made nothing single but *thee* in His world so fair!" (1).[1] And by 1850 if something has begun to go right for literature, for the woman there are portents of difficult times ahead. For by 1850, her proclamation that "Amherst is alive with fun this winter. . . . Sleigh rides are as plenty as people. . . . Parties cant find fun enough. . . . beaus can be had for the taking—maids smile like the mornings in June—" (L29) is already couched in a hyperbolic rhetoric which hints at an opposing strain, pulling her away from the future into an idealized past. "Beaus can be had for the taking": the very ease of the enterprise subtly undercuts the value of the achievement. Indeed, much of her emotional energy is concentrated on preserving the "Home, Sweet Home" already undermined by her father's austerity, her mother's incipient depressive illness, her brother's tentative testing of the larger world beyond Amherst. Concurrently, she redoubles her efforts to preserve the band of "sisters"

1. For a fuller discussion of parody in her earliest work, see my article "Emily Dickinson's Valentines," *American Quarterly* 27 (March 1974): 60–78.

already separated—by physical distance, marriage, death—whose companionship had buffered her against an encroaching sense of self as "one of the lingering *bad* ones" (L36), child not of the Jesus Christ to whom her friends had turned, but of a darker, more menacing spirit whose "play" could prove "piercing earnest," waiting to ambush her "Somewhere—in Silence—" (338).

But it is still 1850 and in a lengthy letter to her friend Jane Humphrey written in the spring when she is nineteen, Emily Dickinson confesses to an erotic awakening. She describes it as a sleep and a dream and carefully separates her response from the situation that occasioned it. Already stealth obscures the event. Already the literary event that transpires reverses the power dynamics of the event depicted:

I would whisper to you in the evening of many, and curious things . . . and have asked no advice from any—I have heeded beautiful tempters, yet do not think I am wrong. Oh I have needed my trusty Jane—my friend encourager, and sincere counciller, my rock, and strong assister! I could make you tremble for me, and be very much afraid, and wonder how things would end—Oh Jennie, it would relieve me to tell you all, to sit down at your feet, and look in your eyes, and confess what *you only* shall know, an experience bitter, and sweet, but the sweet did so beguile me—and life has had an aim, and the world has been too precious for your poor—and striving sister! The winter was all one dream, and the spring has not yet waked me, I would *always* sleep, and dream, and it never should turn to morning, so long as night is so blessed. What do you weave from all these threads, for I know you hav'nt been idle the while I've been speaking to you, bring it nearer the window, and I will see, it's all wrong unless it has one gold thread in it, a long, big shining fibre which hides the others—and which will fade away into Heaven while you hold it, and from there come back to me. I hope belief is not wicked, and assurance, and perfect trust—and a kind of a twilight feeling before the moon is seen—I hope human nature has truth in it—Oh I pray it may not deceive—confide—cherish, have a great faith in—do you dream from all this what I mean? Nobody *thinks* of the joy, nobody *guesses* it, to all appearance old things are engrossing, and new ones are not revealed, but there *now* is nothing old, things are budding, and springing, and singing, and you rather think you are in a green grove, and it's branches that go, and come. I shall see you *sometime* darling, and that sometime *may* not be distant, try to grow fast, and live really, and endure, and wait in patience—and reward *cannot* be distant. Be strong Jennie in remembrance, don't let 'bygones *be* bygones'—love what you are taken from and cherish us tho, so dim. Dont put us in narrow graves—we shall *certainly rise* if

you do, and scare you most prodigiously, and carry you off perhaps!
'This is the end of earth.'

Very affectionately your friend
Emily E Dickinson.   (L35)

Unless Jane concluded that Emily was always posing, what she
made from these threads would have been a romance. She would
not have concluded, as some modern readers have done, that
Dickinson was announcing her career in poetry. Instead, she would
have wondered who had inspired this tantalizing text, and her
thoughts might have reverted to Benjamin Franklin Newton and to
the possibility of a secret engagement. In January, Dickinson had
written to her, "I had a letter—and Ralph Emerson's Poems—a
beautiful copy—from Newton the other day. I should love to read
you them both—they are very pleasant to me." She had also explained, "I can write him in about three weeks—and I *shall*" (L30),
perhaps because one or both of her parents were discouraging her
correspondence with Newton, her father's former law clerk. Or if
Jane's speculations did not extend to a secret engagement, she might
have imagined something more tentative, such as an engagement to
be engaged, sealed by a series of rapturous embraces. Or if Jane had
had the subsequent text of Dickinson's life before her, she might
have imagined that Dickinson preferred invented romances to actual ones. But in 1850, this fact was less palpable.

In letter 36, for example, written to her friend Abiah Root,
Dickinson describes a real romance which has been frustrated. Possibly the friend who asked her to ride in the woods shortly before her
mother's troubling illness began is the undenominated other of the
letter just cited:

> I heard a well-known rap, and a friend I love *so* dearly came and
> asked me to ride in the woods, the sweet-still woods, and I wanted to
> exceedingly—I told him I could not go, and he said he was disap-
> pointed—he wanted me very much—then the tears came into my
> eyes, tho' I tried to choke them back, and he said I *could*, and *should*
> go, and it seemed to me unjust. Oh I struggled with great tempta-
> tion, and it cost me much of denial, but I think in the end I con-
> quered, not a glorious victory Abiah, where you hear the rolling
> drum, but a kind of a helpless victory, where triumph would come of
> itself, faintest music, weary soldiers, nor a waving flag, nor a long-
> loud shout. I had read of Christ's temptations, and how they were
> like our own, only he did'nt sin; I wondered if *one* was like mine, and

whether it made him angry—I couldnt make up my mind; do you think he ever did?

Dickinson has, then, described two romantic temptations to two different correspondents: a temptation risked and a temptation resisted. The temptation resisted induces tears and anger, thoughts of battle, of Christ, and of injustice. To resist such a temptation is to martyr oneself. Though she does not ask Abiah's advice about the wisdom of her decision to refuse a ride with a dearly loved friend, she asks her whether Christ ever sinned. Thus the sin she describes is an emotion rather than an action, the emotion of anger. Her anger depends on an action not taken. She also asks Abiah whether Christ was indecisive: "I couldnt make up my mind; do you think he ever did?" The struggle and the disappointment she describes appear excessive, given the immediate circumstances which aroused it. Apparently this episode had symbolic value for Dickinson. Apparently her ties to her home interfered with the ordinary pleasures of young womanhood. One sees here the possibility that one or both of her parents actively discouraged the ordinary rituals of courtship and that some of the myths about Dickinson's love life—that she would have had more of it had it not been deliberately disrupted by her parents—identify one frustration with which Dickinson had to contend as a young woman: the excessive control to which she was subjected by her elders.[2]

In 1850, however, Dickinson does not describe either of her parents as deliberately impeding her freedom. Instead, she describes a religious culture that potentially impedes her freedom of thought ("*God* is sitting here, looking into my very soul to see if I think right tho'ts" [L31]), housekeeping that actually impedes her freedom of action, and, in May 1850, a mother whose exceptional illness worries her:

> I have always neglected the culinary arts, but attend to them now from necessity, and from a desire to make everything pleasant for father, and Austin. . . . We are sick hardly ever at home, and dont

2. It is also possible that Dickinson exaggerated her caretaking responsibilities to avoid a stressful social encounter. Having magnified her obligation to her parents, she could then blame them for infantilizing her. Lavinia Dickinson, however, stated on a number of occasions after her sister's death that their parents did not wish them to marry. See Richard B. Sewall, *The Life of Emily Dickinson*, 2 vols. (New York: Farrar, Straus and Giroux, 1974), 1: 59–61. Sewall describes Lavinia as an unreliable source.

know what to do when it comes. . . . When I am not at work in the
kitchen, I sit by the side of mother, provide for her little wants—and
try to cheer, and encourage her. I ought to be glad, and grateful that
I *can* do anything now, but I do feel so very lonely, and so anxious to
have her cured. (L36)

Somewhat more ambiguously, her first valentine describes an archetypal father who actively promotes marriage, for his son. In any
case, nothing tangible emerges (beyond her letters) from the twin
temptations Dickinson describes.

Nevertheless, if Dickinson subsequently encountered any kind of
rejection in the relationship she described to Jane Humphrey, she
may have been even more guarded in the future. So that, for example, writing to her closest male friend Henry Emmons, a member of
the Amherst College literary set to which she had easy access, she
contented herself at age twenty-three with a prim one-liner, "Please,
Sir, to let me be a *Valentine* to Thee!" (L155).

Dickinson was often tense in the presence of potential suitors, and
there are some indications that by her mid-twenties she preferred
the companionship of men whose romantic interests were otherwise
engaged. Joseph Lyman, for example, who had been a suitor of
Lavinia's but who used Emily Dickinson, with whom he corresponded, as his touchstone of a superior woman throughout his life,
observed to his fiancée in 1856, "Emily you see is platonic—She
never stood 'tranced in long Embraces mixed with kisses sweeter,
sweeter than anything on Earth.'" (The quotation is from Tennyson's *Maud*.) Developing this theme some two years later he remarked, "Emily Dickinson I did like very much and do still. But she
is rather morbid and unnatural."[3] Though Lyman's precise intention in using these adjectives is probably irretrievable, these two
comments, when juxtaposed, suggest that by 1858 he perceived
Dickinson as sexually repressed. Describing Dickinson as "the most
appreciative lady friend" he ever had, as someone who encouraged
his professional ambitions and who had confidence in his future
success, he also described her as unlikely to marry. Thus, from
Lyman's point of view, the contrast between the two Dickinson sisters was striking. Lavinia was, he explained, excessively seductive but

3. Joseph Lyman, as quoted in *The Lyman Letters: New Light on Emily Dickinson and
Her Family*, ed. Richard B. Sewall (Amherst: University of Massachusetts Press, 1965),
pp. 35, 65.

not intellectually gifted; Dickinson was a stimulating, even flattering companion but sexually remote.

During the 1850s these two sisters were evidently responding to their common family background in very different ways. Though neither of them ever married, Lavinia was markedly flirtatious in her youth, and rejected at least one proposal of marriage. Our concern, however, is with the poet rather than with her "practical sister" to whom she looked in later life for what she herself described as parental care. Dickinson's eventual designation of Lavinia as a surrogate mother reflects her need to distance herself from her actual parent.

"I never had a mother," the poet told Higginson bitterly during their 1870 interview. "I suppose a mother is one to whom you hurry when you are troubled" (L342b). And in an 1874 letter to Higginson she reiterated, with a pun, "I always ran Home to Awe when a child, if anything befell me. He was an awful Mother, but I liked him better than none" (L405). Even though Dickinson's letters of the 1840s and early 1850s cast doubt on these statements—the Mount Holyoke student of letter 20, for example, does not yet perceive herself as psychologically orphaned—Dickinson eventually found it necessary to believe that her mother had always been an inadequate caretaker. An orphaned persona, she appears to have reasoned, is guilt-free. Even after her mother's death in 1882, she explained to her friend Elizabeth Holland, "We were never intimate Mother and Children while she was our Mother." Then she added, "but Mines in the same Ground meet by tunneling and when she became our Child, the Affection came—" (L792). Thus, though it is not clear that Emily Norcross Dickinson rejected her daughter when she was a child or subsequently, it is clear that during much of her adult life Dickinson rejected her mother, or wished to. Moreover, the vehemence of Dickinson's assertion that she "never had a mother" suggests that the reality was significantly more complex. The uncomplicated story she told Higginson and Elizabeth Holland has its perverse inner logic, just as it reflects some of her mother's actual weaknesses as a nurturer and as a role model. Those weaknesses warrant closer inspection.

In fact very little of substance is known about Emily Norcross Dickinson, except that it is impossible to separate her history from that of her husband who eventually devoured, whether willingly or unwillingly, whatever modest propensity for self-assertion she had originally possessed. The daughter of a prosperous farmer, Joel Norcross, and his wife Betsy (or Betsey) Fay, she was the third of nine children and grew up in Monson, Massachusetts, about twenty miles south of Amherst. She attended a girls' boarding school in New Haven, Connecticut, in 1822–23, where she received a commendation for good behavior and diligent application. In the winter of 1826, about three years after her return to Monson, she met Edward Dickinson, a graduate of Yale College, who was probably visiting relatives in the town. He proposed in a letter written on 4 June 1826, and they became engaged in the late summer or early fall. Despite his impatience to be wed in early 1827, she postponed their marriage for more than a year, until May 1828. During their engagement, which lasted almost two years, she was a sluggish correspondent and unenthusiastic about visiting him in Amherst. Characterizing himself in a letter of March 1828 as "naturally quick & ardent" in his feelings, "sometimes unyielding and obstinate," he characterized her as "kind—benevolent—patient in trouble—able to endure sickness." "You will deprive yourself of comfort & repose to render a friend more comfortable," he continued. "I do not flatter, My Dear, when I say that I find in you just what I have long wished to find a lady to possess." Throughout their courtship, he was unmistakably the pursuer, she the pursued. Nevertheless, the goals he proposed for their union also reflected his emotional self-restraint: "Let us prepare for a life of rational happiness. I do not expect, neither do I desire a life of *pleasure*, as some call it—I anticipate pleasure from engaging with my whole soul in my business . . . and with my dearest friend. . . . May we be happy, useful and successful."[4] On the eve of their marriage, she was homesick. He was twenty-five; she was twenty-four.

Though the relative social status of these two before their marriage is difficult to determine, in marrying Edward Dickinson, Emily Norcross was marrying a man who, even during his youth, was obviously on his way up. In marrying him, she was distinguishing herself within the conventional terms of her culture, by hitching her wagon to a future star. Because her extant courtship letters to him are stilted and vague, it is difficult to determine which of his personal characteristics attracted her, though she refers in passing to his "courage" and "perfect punctuality." In these letters, she apologizes

4. Edward Dickinson, as quoted in Sewall, *Life of Emily Dickinson*, 1: 50, 47.

repeatedly for neglecting him and portrays herself as preoccupied by household responsibilities, in part because of illness in her family, including the illness of her mother. Occasionally, she refers summarily to "engagements" which prevent her from answering his letters. While to some extent avoiding her fiancé, she nevertheless found time to accompany her father on a two- or three-week visit to New York and to socialize with her friends. Despite her protests to the contrary, these accumulated apologies raise the possibility that she was genuinely neglecting him. Edward Dickinson, however, praised her "steady habits," trusted her judgment, and found her apparently undemanding, easy-going personality soothing. Furthermore, he believed that she would help him to realize his professional ambitions by creating a secure domestic environment which would relieve him of personal cares. Probably he was reassured by her malleability as a daughter and by her deference to her father's opinions.

Mrs. Dickinson had three children within four years: William Austin was born in 1829, Emily Elizabeth in 1830, and Lavinia Norcross in 1833. A story, perhaps apocryphal, has it that on the eve of the birth of her famous daughter she defied her husband's wishes for the first and only time by inducing a paper hanger to redo her bedroom. She was not active in community affairs and appears to have had no close friends within the town, although she exchanged visits with her own relatives.

Following the birth of Lavinia, Mrs. Dickinson's health was poor.[5] Thus, at the age of two and one-half, Emily Elizabeth Dickinson was sent to her Aunt Lavinia's in Monson for a stay of some five or six weeks. This aunt, her mother's only living sister, sent back the following accounts of her charge:

> Just after we passed Mr Clapps—it thundered more & the thunder & lightning increased—Elizabeth called it *the fire*—the time the rain wind & darkness came we were along in those pine woods—the thunder echoed. . . . the horse when the rain came with such fury shook his head & galloped on—did not like it much—it soon grew

5. In *After Great Pain: The Inner Life of Emily Dickinson* (Cambridge: Harvard University Press, 1971), p. 50, John Cody argues that Mrs. Dickinson may have been suffering from a postpartum depression. He links her vulnerability to depression to her family history: three of her siblings died during her youth and a fourth died while she was pregnant with Austin; her mother died at the age of fifty-one during the next year (1829); and her father announced his decision to remarry in December 1830, shortly before the birth of the poet.

r, but continued to rain some & the thunder & lightning con-
ed also. . . . Elizabeth felt inclined to be frightened some—she
d "Do take me to my mother"

Emily is perfectly well & contented—She is a very good child & but
little trouble—She has learned to play on the piano—she calls it the
moosic She does not talk much about home—sometimes speaks of
little Austin but does not moan for any of you—

She speaks of her father & mother occasionaly & *little Austin* but does
not express a wish to see you—Hope this wont make you feel bad—
She is very affectionate & we all love her very much—She dont
appear at all as she does at home—& she does not make but very
little trouble—[6]

A number of observations can be made here. First, one notes that
these letters are articulate, even vivid. Mrs. Dickinson did not come
from a tongue-tied family. Second, one notes that names are important and not yet fixed: "little Elizabeth (as we call her here)." That is,
Aunt Lavinia perceives the possibility of a confusion of identities
because of the presence of two Emilies in one family. Third, one
observes Dickinson's precocity: she plays the piano, in some fashion,
at age two and a half; her speech is considered remarkable. Fourth,
and most important, Dickinson was perceived as troublesome at
home, presumably by her mother; however, she forms new attachments easily. To suggest, then, as Cody has done, that Dickinson
already exhibits the characteristics of the love-starved child is to
identify one possible dimension of a significantly more fluid situation.[7] Her behavior may have been unnaturally adaptive because of
her insecurity at home. She may also, quite naturally, have transferred her affection for her mother to her aunt.

Dickinson's struggle to define her identity was also informed by
the fact that she was the middle child: she had a brother one and a
half years her senior; a sister two years her junior. It appears that
her brother was her father's favorite child; her sister, her mother's.
If Dickinson felt slighted within her family during her childhood
and adolescence, she responded in part by singling out others as
close friends, just as she had ingratiated herself with her Aunt Lavinia when her mother was unable to care for her, following her

6. Lavinia Norcross, as quoted in Jay Leyda, *The Years and Hours of Emily Dickinson*,
2 vols. (New Haven: Yale University Press, 1960), 1: 20–22.
7. Cody, *After Great Pain*, pp. 50–51.

sister's birth. During the year 1850, for example, Dickinson addresses each of her correspondents as the focus of her undivided attention. Her strange statement of 1873, "Subjects hinder talk" (L397), is already anticipated in a letter to Abiah Root, written in January 1850: "I wondered when you had gone why we did'nt talk more—it was'nt for want of a subject, it never *could be* for *that*. Too many perhaps, such a crowd of people that nobody heard the speaker, and all went away discontented" (L31). Subjects represent people; people hinder talk. Even at age nineteen, Dickinson describes herself as crowded. She desires privacy; privacy represents the undivided attention of an inspiriting Other.

Until 1850, Dickinson's letters describe her mother as an excellent cook and capable housekeeper, an unassuming woman who took pleasure in home, family, and horticulture. Since Mrs. Dickinson was exceptionally diffident about taking pen in hand, not because of any particular difficulty with the English language but because she usually found that she had "nothing to say"—a trait already in evidence before her marriage but more pronounced in later years—the quality of her inner life is difficult to gauge. A neighbor visiting her in 1843 recorded that "she was as usual full of plaintive talk."[8] Beginning in 1850, Mrs. Dickinson's health began to decline for no apparent reason. She was a semi-invalid during most of 1856–58, when her housekeeping responsibilities were assumed by her daughters, although there was also hired help. By 1860 a cousin observed that her health was improved, though she was unable or unwilling to attend her sister in her last illness at this time; instead, her daughter Lavinia went to Boston for an extended stay. In 1863, a neighbor wrote a friend: "Mrs. Edward Dickinson sent [Dr. Stearns, president of the college] a most elegant Boquet . . . she . . . admires him, & is now quite herself."[9]

In 1864–65, when the poet was herself seriously ill and depressed, she described her mother, together with their Irish housekeeper, as "so kind" (L302), but it was Lavinia whom she wished to meet her at the train station on her return from Cambridge for medical treatment.[10] Her instructions on this point were clear: "You will get me

---

8. Ann Shepard, as quoted in Leyda, *Years and Hours of Emily Dickinson*, 1: 81.
9. Mary Shepard, as quoted in Leyda, *Years and Hours of Emily Dickinson*, 2: 81.
10. Cody believes that Dickinson's eye problems were psychosomatic. Certainly the writings of her physician, Henry Willard Williams, acknowledge the relationship between eye problems and psychological stress, in some instances. In "'Eyes Be Blind,

at Palmer, yourself. Let no one beside come" (L296). Her mother's attempts to cheer her up at this time are, on one occasion, acknowledged, but she also forms part of a concerned family circle that inadvertently exacerbated Dickinson's discomfort: "They say I am a 'help.' Partly because it is true, I suppose, and the rest applause. Mother and Margaret are so kind, father as gentle as he knows how, and Vinnie good to me, but 'cannot see why I don't get well.' This makes me think I am long sick, and this takes the ache to my eyes." If she wrote her mother during these months when she was living away from Amherst, these letters no longer exist. During this interval when her eyesight was a cause of great anxiety to her, two of Dickinson's letters (295, 308) express concern about her mother's physical condition. Dickinson's subsequent references to her mother during the middle and late 1860s indicate that Mrs. Dickinson was well-intentioned but platitudinous. In August 1866, for example, Dickinson commented on an exchange between her mother and Austin's child Ned: "Grandma 'hoped' characteristically 'he would be a very good Boy.' 'Not very dood' he said, sweet defiant child! Obtuse ambition of Grandmamas!" (L320).

Thereafter, she virtually disappears from view until her husband's death in 1874 (he was stricken while making a speech on the floor of the Massachusetts legislature and died a few hours later). In 1875, on the first anniversary of her husband's death, she suffered a paralytic stroke from which she never fully recovered.[11] Although she had been a church member since 1830, her religious imagination

---

Heart Be Still': A New Perspective on Emily Dickinson's Eye Problem," *New England Quarterly* 52 (September 1979): 400–06, Martin Wand and Sewall contend that "it now seems clear that her eye trouble, at least, was physiological": "In lay language she was 'walleyed'; in medical terminology, she had '*exotropia*.'" A puzzling aspect of Wand and Sewall's intriguing thesis is that no one who saw Dickinson ever commented that her eyes turned out. Wand and Sewall also believe that her mother and sister suffered from the same hereditary condition. Again, the nonphotographic evidence here is scant to nonexistent, despite Dickinson's comment in L308, "I hope Mother is better, and will be careful of her Eye." As described by Dickinson, her specific problem was photophobia: an aversion to sunlight. If this problem was purely physiological in origin, why it flared up so acutely in 1864 and 1865 remains to be explored. During the rest of her life Dickinson's eyes do not appear to have troubled her, although eye disorders were an occupational hazard for nineteenth-century writers.

11. Readers of Frederick Crews may wish to attribute greater significance to this anniversary stroke than I attach to it. See his discussion of neurotic responses to the death of a consciously revered person in *The Sins of the Fathers: Hawthorne's Psychological Themes* (New York: Oxford University Press, 1966), p. 55.

was limited, and she was discomforted by any sign of nonconformity in her children. On her death Dickinson wrote to the Norcross cousins, "She was scarcely the aunt you knew. The great mission of pain had been ratified—cultivated to tenderness by persistent sorrow, so that a larger mother died than had she died before" (L785). Though Dickinson's late letters speak with great dignity and eloquence of her devotion to this enfeebled parent, in the end it was Lavinia whom Mrs. Dickinson most trusted. Her last words were, to cite the poet, " 'Dont leave me, Vinnie' " (L779).

As a teenager, Emily Dickinson identified with her mother, but as an adult she needed to disengage herself psychologically from her. This disengagement was in certain respects thwarted by Mrs. Dickinson's colorless personality. Richard Chase concludes, "If she was not Emily's kind of recluse, she was yet a recluse in her own style, the style of thousands of self-effacing Victorian wives."[12] Yet self-effacing Victorian wives need not have called attention to their self-effacement, as Mrs. Dickinson so abundantly did. Her lack of zest cannot be attributed solely to the ethos of her era. Though narrow-minded, Mrs. Dickinson lacked confidence in her own judgment. Her self-distrust was sometimes expressed in her overconcern for others and during her periods of prolonged inertia in the 1850s, in her abject dependency on her family.

Dickinson never comments directly on her parents' marriage, but her ambivalence toward marriage for herself was undoubtedly influenced by the marriage she had observed most closely and for the longest duration. During the 1850s, Dickinson witnessed her mother's transformation from an "amiable" young woman, capable of asserting herself as mothers must do to protect their offspring, into a less amiable trivia expert who sought to express her unarticulated dissatisfactions with her marriage and her life through illness. Thus the change in Dickinson's attitude toward her mother during this decade reflected both the heightening of Dickinson's need for psychological autonomy and the deterioration in her mother's personality.

In the eyes of her children, Emily Norcross Dickinson was overshadowed by a formidable husband, but on his death she mourned, "I loved him so." She seems to have left virtually all major household decisions, including those that impinged most directly on the chil-

12. Richard Chase, *Emily Dickinson* (New York: William Sloane, 1951), p. 12.

dren's welfare, in his hands.[13] When we hear her voice directly in letters, her tone is flat, subdued, emotionally inexpressive—as it was in May 1844 when she wrote to her daughter Emily who was suffering from melancholia because of the death of a school friend. Dickinson had been sent to her Aunt Lavinia's in Boston to recuperate:

Dear Emily
I leave all my affairs this morning to say a few words to you, presuming you are happy to hear from home often. We were a little disappointed in not getting a letter from you on Saturday but concluded that you was so much occupied that you could not find time to write. We hope you are well and enjoying your visit finely. We are lonely without you and shall be very glad to see you safe home again. I suppose Father and Mother and Cous. Emily are with you. I thought of them much those two pleasant days they were out on their journey, hope they are all comfortable. We are all well, and evry thing moves about as usual with us. I see some of your young friends evry day or two. They make many inquiries for you, and wish to be remembered to you. I suppose Father has written to you with reference to the time he thinks it best for you to return. I shall not therfore say anything about it. Your plants are doing well. Lavinia takes very good care of them. I am in haste and must close. We all join in love to you, and our dear friends.

From your dear Mother[14]

Unlike her daughter, Emily Norcross Dickinson "felt safest

13. But see L8 (25 September 1845) in which Dickinson explains, "You asked me if I was attending school now. I am not. Mother thinks me not able to confine myself to school this term. She had rather I would exercise, and I can assure you I get plenty of that article by staying at home. I am going to learn to make bread to-morrow." Similarly, in describing her parents' decision to interrupt her schooling at Mount Holyoke in 1848 for a month, because of concern for her health, she makes it clear this was a joint decision (L23). In describing her plans for the future, however, she explains, "Father has decided not to send me to Holyoke another year, so this is my *last term*. . . . Father wishes to have me at home a year, and then he will probably send me away again, where I know not. . . . " The issue here is not whether Mrs. Dickinson's anxieties ever coincided with her husband's—they obviously did—but what happened when their styles of parenting and of living conflicted. Dickinson's letters never describe a quarrel of any sort between her parents.
14. From the manuscript collection of Houghton Library, Harvard University, Cambridge, Massachusetts. This letter contains perhaps twenty-five words that are underlined in whole or, most commonly, in part. Given the erratic length of these markings, I have not attempted to reproduce them. Other visual features of the manuscript, such as commas that are difficult to distinguish from periods and lowercase letters that are difficult to distinguish from capitals, reflect Mrs. Dickinson's curiously emphasized tentativeness.

among tangible things."[15] Thus, one of the recurrent motifs of her letters and of Dickinson's accounts of her nonspeech is that she is too busy to write, just as she was too busy to ascertain what "Father" had decided about her daughter's return. Though she represents herself as willing to take time out from her routine to write under unusual circumstances, ordinarily, one gathers, she kept herself exceptionally busy—at least until her breakdown, following a move from one house to another, in late 1855. Someone predisposed to feeling slighted could easily read this letter as expressing impatience. To such a reader, this letter might say, "I don't wish to be interrupted, but am willing, though grudgingly, to be interrupted by you, especially when you are unwell." The portrait that emerges here is that of a woman who was harried and self-absorbed.

During the 1840s, Emily Norcross Dickinson may have emulated her husband's zeal for personal industry; that is, under his influence she may have become an overly conscientious housekeeper. But by 1851, Dickinson had begun to suggest that her mother was poorly organized: "Mother never was busier than while we were away—what with fruit, and plants, and chickens, and sympathizing friends, she really was so hurried she hardly knew what to do" (L52). By 1862, Dickinson was covertly expressing her resentment toward her mother in her poetry. The literary revenge she extracted from those "Gentlewomen" whom she described as too substanceless for rape, too constricted for salvation (401), was partly inspired by a mother whose initially compliant personality had become an anxious one. And by 1862, Dickinson's poetic identity depended on her belief that she was the victim of maternal neglect even during her childhood. By 1875, perhaps after her mother's stroke, she was able to take a more charitable view of her mother's ill-defined personality, but Dickinson's "timid" Eve remains a formidably problematic figure:

> The Garment of Surprise
> Was all our timid Mother wore
> At Home—in Paradise. (1335)

The poet's reaction against her culture's definition of "true womanhood" was conditioned both by her resentment of her mother and

15. Leyda, *Years and Hours of Emily Dickinson*, 1: xxxix.

by her resentment of her mother's subordination to her father. Whether justly or unjustly, she perceived herself as having been neglected by her mother; certainly, her mother had not heard and was incapable of appreciating her *exceptional* voice. Nevertheless, she was sufficiently identified with her mother, who had heard one of her voices, the voice of a child, and had to some extent heeded it, to perceive that her mother's voice was muffled by the voice of her Master. Amiable young women may become "wives forgotten"; "wives forgotten" may themselves, obscurely, encourage female offspring who are exceptionally attentive to the power dynamics of mid-nineteenth-century American marriages.

Though not overtly rebellious as a child, Dickinson was probably venturesome and restless. Sometime after her mother's death, she explained,

> Two things I have lost with Childhood—the rapture of losing my shoe in the Mud and going Home barefoot, wading for Cardinal flowers and the mothers reproof which was more for my sake than her weary own for she frowned with a smile   (PF117)

Note that Dickinson associates "the mothers reproof" with love. Diffident, gentle, and in her own self-designation "compassionate," Mrs. Dickinson is unlikely to have been a strong disciplinarian. She "frowned with a smile." This is a winning image, but Dickinson's adult fascination with adversity can be traced back to her earliest extant letters. Suppose, then, that Dickinson was overindulged as a child, particularly since her health was somewhat frail. Suppose, too, that Dickinson was not shut up in closets when she misbehaved as a little girl (613) and that what was missing on her mother's part was not tenderness but firmness. Dickinson may have interpreted her mother's permissiveness as disguised hostility, which it may to some extent have been. But as Emily Norcross Dickinson explained in a letter to her fiancé written on 14 September 1827, the management of her own affairs was enough for her "without interfering with others." A "mother" is someone "to whom you hurry when you are troubled" *and* someone who keeps you out of trouble. Clearly, Mrs. Dickinson did not inspire "awe."

Richard Sewall, however, credits Emily Norcross Dickinson with having created a home her daughter never left: "Oddly enough, although it is seldom seen this way, the greatest tribute that Emily paid her mother lay perhaps in the fact that she never wanted to leave the home that Mrs. Dickinson helped create."[16] Emily Dickinson did, on many occasions, wish to leave her home. During her twenties and early thirties, when she was unable to cross the bridge between adolescent and adult sexuality, she retreated into a physical space that perpetuated some of the conditions of her childhood. As her social isolation intensified and as she began to create awesomely adverse conditions for herself, her hostility toward her mother was more difficult to control. Finally, she was isolated within her home, as her comments to Higginson during their 1870 interview indicate. By then, Dickinson may have unconsciously blamed her mother for her agoraphobia. Even as a teenager, however, she perceived herself as having been imperfectly socialized, which explains why she was "always in love" with her teachers. She looked to them for a better balance of too little and too much tenderness. At Mount Holyoke in 1847–48, she was homesick; in Amherst in 1870, she was "Homeless at home" (1573).

Emily Norcross Dickinson's gentle style nevertheless informed the harsher style of her daughter, who concluded that her mother was a false teacher and that the world was not a gentle place. Paternity emerges as a key concept in the poetry; with several exceptions, maternity is strikingly absent. Under Emily Norcross Dickinson's tutelage, Dickinson learned to destroy her teacher. In the process, she also damaged one of the sources of her self-esteem and overcompensated for her anger toward her mother by her unremitting physical presence.

Since Dickinson's scapegoating of her mother is perhaps the least attractive element of her character, let me reiterate Dickinson's observation that "when she became our Child, the Affection came." Real adversity—her father's death and her mother's paralyzing stroke—to some extent liberated Dickinson from her neurotic need to create it. Since this need was by 1875 integral to her style, this transformation in her disturbed relationship to her mother appears to have had little influence on her poetry.

As perceived by Dickinson, the sexual politics of her parents' marriage reinforced a world view in which male dominance was the norm. The accuracy of this perception of the Dickinsons' marriage has never been seriously challenged by any other observer. "What father *says*, 'he means,'" Dickinson wrote to her brother in 1852

16. Sewall, *Life of Emily Dickinson*, 1: 89.

(L82). Higginson in 1870 found him "thin dry & speechless," adding, "I saw what her life has been" (L342b). Having unquestionably met the head of the household, he did not find it necessary to comment on Mrs. Dickinson's failure to present herself. What I have attempted to show, however, is that Mrs. Dickinson exhibited progressively fewer of the characteristics of the "sweetly submissive" Victorian wife and progressively more of the characteristics of a woman who was confused and unhappy. Although it is perhaps farfetched to think of her as a covert role-rebel, it seems likely that a deeply buried conflict between husband and wife was beginning to surface in 1850. It is less likely, however, that either party understood its sources or even acknowledged its existence.

The Dickinsons' marriage survived Emily Norcross Dickinson's midlife crisis, but in the end Dickinson spoke of her father's "lonely Life and his lonelier Death" and often described her reclusion as an attempt to gratify him. Though it is easy to dismiss this explanation as a pathetic rationalization of a neurotic plight, Dickinson's desire to take her mother's place impeded her sexual development. In an 1866 letter, she wrote, incestuously, that "Shame is so intrinsic in a strong affection we must all experience Adam's reticence" (L318). In an 1846 letter she had explained, "I have lately come to the conclusion that I am Eve, alias Mrs. Adam. You know there is no account of her death in the Bible, and why am not I Eve?" (L9). If Emily Dickinson had "never had a mother," her privileged relationship to her father would have been actualized, or so she unconsciously believed. Ironically, her hostility toward her mother must be partly attributed to her jealousy of her.

Edward Dickinson suffered, even as he benefited, from his wife's inability to challenge him directly, but of the immediate members of his family only his son Austin ever posed any overt threat to his authority. True, on one occasion Dickinson is reported as "screaming to the top of her voice" to get her father to stop beating a horse;[17] on another, as smashing a plate on a stone in the garden after her father objected to a chip in it.[18] But her typical pattern was to withdraw from the watchful eye of her "paralyzing papa."[19]

---

17. Lavinia Dickinson, as quoted in Sewall, *Life of Emily Dickinson*, 1: 63.
18. Millicent Todd Bingham, *Emily Dickinson's Home: Letters of Edward Dickinson and His Family* (New York: Harper & Bros., 1955), p. 112. She refers to this episode as a "well-known anecdote."
19. John Berryman, "Your Birthday in Wisconsin You Are 140," *Delusions, Etc.* (New York: Farrar, Straus, and Giroux, 1972), p. 26.

When she was seven years old, he wrote that he wanted her to be "one of the best little girls in Town." This ambition never wavered. And that he did keep a watchful, easily irritated eye on his children's behavior when he was at home is clear, both from his letters and from hers. Despite her remark of 1862 implying that she was neglected and had always been neglected by him ("Father, too busy with his Briefs—to notice what we do—" [L261]), Edward Dickinson's passion for order included his passion for ordering the lives of his family. Though he spared no effort in his attempts to advance their welfare as he saw it, he was, as an obituary notice indicated, an intimidating presence. Severe with himself, he was also severe with others; uncomfortable with feelings and with the spontaneous expression of thought, his discomfort sometimes infected those around him, including the poet.

The following vignette, for example, armed in "Mirth . . . the Mail of Anguish—" (165), captures the essence of their strained interaction on those occasions when his "real life" and hers "collided." There are extenuating circumstances, of course, as there always are: "Father has been shut up with the rheumatism, since Saturday—is rather better today, and hopes to be out tomorrow—the rest of us are as well as could possibly be expected! Our *minds* are not well, *mine* especially, has quite a number of symptoms—and I apprehend a *result!* On the whole, however; we bear it with a good deal of fortitude." In March 1852 she wrote to Austin,

> I would have given most anything to have had you here, last evening—the scene was indeed too rich, to be detailed by my pen, and I shall ever regret that the *world* has lost such a chance to laugh. Let me add as I go along, that father's frame of mind is *as usual* the *happiest*, developing itself in constant acts of regard, and *epithets of tenderness!*
>
> Soon after tea, last night, a violent ring at the bell—Vinnie obeys the summons—Mr. Harrington, Brainerd, would like to see me at the door. I come walking in from the kitchen, frightened almost to death, and receive the command from father, "not to stand at the door"—terrified beyond measure, I advance to the outside door— Mr. H. has an errand—will not consent to come in, on account of my father's sickness—having dismissed him hastily, I retreat again to the kitchen—where I find mother and Vinnie, making most desperate efforts to control themselves, but with little success—once more breathe freely, and conclude that my lungs were given me, for only the best of purposes. Another ring at the door—enter Wm. [Cowper] Dickinson—soon followed by Mr Thurston! I again crept into the sitting room, more dead than alive, and endeavored to *make*

conversation. Father looked round triumphantly. I remarked that "the weather was rather cold" today, to which they all assented—indeed I *never witnessed* such *wonderful unanimity.* Fled to my mind again, and endeavored to procure something equally agreeable with my *last happy remark.* Bethought me of Sabbath day, and the Rev. Mr Bliss, who preached upon it—remarked with wonderful emphasis, that I thought the Rev. gentleman a very remarkable preacher, and discovered a strong resemblance between himself & Whitfield, in the way of remark—I confess it *was rather* laughable, having never so much as seen the *ashes* of that gentleman—but oh such a look as I got from my rheumatic sire. You should have seen it—I never can find a language vivid eno' to portray it to you. . . .

Austin, my cup was full—I endeavored to shrink away into primeval nothingness—but sat there large as life, in spite of every effort. (L79)

Do we see in this episode the seeds of Dickinson's agoraphobic future and hold Edward Dickinson to some extent accountable for it? Had she learned to hide herself at home to shield herself from his censure, well before her "cowardice of strangers" became uncontrollable? Unmistakably, his presence inhibits her with her male contemporaries. (Brainerd Harrington was an Amherst College senior; William Cowper Dickinson was a tutor, who had been the valedictorian of his class; his friend Thurston was probably the Benjamin Thurston who graduated in 1852.) Nevertheless, in displeasing her father, she appears to have gratified her mother, who found this excruciating courtship scene comical. As far as I have been able to discover from the admittedly scant accounts of her behavior, this is the only time when Emily Norcross Dickinson is described as laughing. What aroused such mirth? The sight of her daughter "terrified beyond measure"? This seems unlikely. The comical element here is not Dickinson's embarrassment but her father's. When she comments on the weather, she provokes a wonderful assent. When she alludes to George Whitefield, she is rebuked for it. The person made to look foolish here is Edward Dickinson, but this female satire on him is achieved without conscious premeditation on Dickinson's part and at great cost to herself. Of course the possibility exists that Emily Norcross Dickinson (and Lavinia) were reacting solely to Dickinson's excessive timidity and that they responded in a light-hearted manner, as girls together do. Somehow, I doubt it. In any event, Edward Dickinson bears the brunt of this timidity here, as he probably did on many other occasions. It could not have been pleasant for this eminently respectable public man to be subjected to this combination of apparent compliance with his commands, this actual defiance of them. Because of his displeasure and discomfort, it was not until "Father . . . adjourned to the kitchen fire" that, Dickinson explains, "Vinnie and I, and our friends enjoyed the rest of the evening."

Had Dickinson not become the "Queen Recluse" of Amherst, and of American poetry, this episode would not retrospectively have taken on the importance I am attributing to it. Later, in about 1862, in one of her most obviously hostile autobiographical poems, describing herself as a corpse, Dickinson wonders "which would miss me, least" (445). Her thoughts revert immediately to Father and to his passion for regularity. If Father was the member of her household whom she most obviously resented, he was also the parent she most obviously respected. Indeed, his obituary notice, "His failing was he did not understand himself; consequently his misfortune was that others did not understand him," might also have been hers.[20] Was to meet a stranger to test the depth of her loyalty to Father? And was this agonizing bout of shyness all the more terrifying because, in addition to resenting his vigilance, she also pitied his awkwardness? Despite Edward Dickinson's political career, personal popularity within his community and to some extent within his family continued to elude him. His father's zeal for evangelical enterprises was, in Edward's lifetime, expressed as a comparable zeal for financial success and community service, probably in that order. That is, Edward Dickinson's community service was directed primarily toward the economic concerns of Amherst life, though not exclusively. He was, for example, a trustee of the Northampton asylum for the insane. The minister who preached his funeral sermon observed that he unwisely concealed "the gentleness which was in him," asking, "Had he the Puritan notion that sentiment betrayed weakness, or was it his training in that elder school whose primal precept was repression. . . ?"[21]

In an undated letter to Lyman, written sometime before 1872, Dickinson wrote, "My father seems to me often the oldest and the oddest sort of a foreigner. Sometimes I say something and he stares in a curious sort of bewilderment though I speak a thought quite as

20. Samuel Bowles, as quoted in Leyda, *Years and Hours of Emily Dickinson,* 2: 224–25.
21. J. L. Jenkins, as quoted in Leyda, *Years and Hours of Emily Dickinson,* 2: 226–27.

old as his daughter . . . . Father says in fugitive moments when he forgets the barrister & lapses into the man, says that his life has been passed in a wilderness or on an island—of late he says on an island." In 1874, she explained to Higginson,

> The last Afternoon that my Father lived, though with no premonition—I preferred to be with him, and invented an absence for Mother, Vinnie being asleep. He seemed peculiarly pleased as I oftenest stayed with myself, and remarked as the Afternoon withdrew, he 'would like it to not end.'
> His pleasure almost embarrassed me and my Brother coming—I suggested they walk. Next morning I woke him for the train—and saw him no more.
> His Heart was pure and terrible and I think no other like it exists.   (L418)

Within this carefully ordered household of talented and burdened New Englanders, Dickinson lived out one of her lives.

In 1850, however, there was still a great deal of history to come. Confronted with the necessity for sexual self-definition, for choosing between and marrying inner images of her mother and her father, in 1850 Dickinson was just beginning to speak of herself as a child and to memorialize a dead master. Toward the close of that year, she wrote a letter to her pious friend Abiah Root, who would become a minister's wife. The feminine ideal Abiah represented— that of a woman harmoniously linked to her environment through religion—both fascinated and dismayed the "*selfish*" Emily. In this prophetic letter (39), filled with posturing graveyard rhetoric, she began by describing the death of "the departed Humphrey" (Leonard Humphrey had been the principal of Amherst Academy in 1846–47) in language that subordinated her specific memories of him to a more pervasive sense of bereavement:

> I write Abiah to-night, because it is cool and quiet, and I can forget the toil and care of the feverish day, and then I am *selfish* too, because I am feeling lonely; some of my friends are gone. . . . the hour of evening is sad—it was once my study hour—my master has gone to rest, and the open leaf of the book, and the scholar at school *alone*, make the tears come, and I cannot brush them away; I would not if I could, for they are the only tribute I can pay the departed Humphrey.
> *You* have stood by the grave before; I have walked there sweet summer evenings and read the names on the stones, and wondered

who would come and give me the same memorial; but I never have
laid my friends there, and forgot that they too must die; this is my
first affliction, and indeed 'tis hard to bear it. To those bereaved so
often that home is no more here, and whose communion with
friends is had only in prayers, there must be much to hope for, but
when the unreconciled spirit has nothing left but God, that spirit is
lone indeed. I don't think there will be any sunshine, or any singing-
birds in the spring that's coming. I shall look for an early grave then,
when the grass is growing green. . . . I will try not to say any more—
my rebellious thoughts are many. . . . I wish I were somebody else—

After gently reproving her friend for neglecting her, she introduces
the twin images of senectitude and childhood, implicating Abiah in
her fantasy of a single-sex world uninvaded by the "Son of Man":

I dream of being a grandame, and banding my silver hairs, and I
seem to be quite submissive to the thought of growing old; no doubt
you ride rocking-horses in your present as in young sleeps—quite a
pretty contrast indeed, of me braiding my own gray hairs, and my
friend at play with her childhood, a pair of decayed old ladies!
Where *are* you, my *antique* friend, or my very dear and young one—
just as you please to please. . . . When I think of the friends I love,
and the little while we may dwell here, and then "we go away," I have
a yearning feeling, a desire eager and anxious lest any be stolen
away, so that I cannot behold them. I would have you here, all here,
where I can *see* you, and *hear* you, and where I can say "Oh, no," if
the "Son of Man" ever "cometh"!

Comparing herself to still another pious Abby, who would marry a
missionary, she emphasizes her desire to remain a child:

I see but little of Abby; she cannot come to see me, and I walk so
far not often, and perhaps it's all right and best. Our lots fall in
different places; mayhap we might disagree. We take different views
of life, our thoughts would not dwell together as they used to when
we were young—how long ago that seems! She is more of a woman
than I am, for I love so to be a child—Abby is holier than me—she
does more good in her lifetime than ever I shall in mine—she goes
among the poor, she shuts the eye of the dying—she will be had in
memorial when I am gone and forgotten. Do not think we are aught
than friends—though the "silver cord *be* loosed" the "golden bowl" is
not broken. I have talked thus freely of Abby because we three were
friends, because I trust we three *are* friends, and shall meet in bliss
together, because the golden links, though dimmed, are no less gold-
en, and I love to hold them up, and see them gleam in the sunshine;

you and I, too, are more alike than Abby and I are sometimes, and the name of each is dear and is cherished by the other.

Won't you say what you think of Abby—I mean of her heart and mind—when you write me. I think it is a license which friend may take with friend, without at all detracting from aught we like or love. And tell me of *some one else*—what *she* is thinking and doing, and whether she still remembers the loves of "long ago," and sighs as she remembers, lest there be no more as true—"sad times, sweet times, two bairns at school, but a' one heart"—*three* bairns, and the tale had been truer.

Despite her humor and conventional religious rhetoric, Dickinson barely restrains her anger at her social displacement. Seeking to create an asexual identity for herself, she was simultaneously attempting to seduce Abiah away from the generic "Son of Man" looming on the near horizon. Her formal education over, her vocational anxieties intensified by her experience of "woman's sphere," the home, Dickinson began invoking the parodic image of the perpetual child to express her alienation from her mother's model of "true womanhood," to dissociate herself from her "*selfishness*," and to repress the newly awakened eroticism that she has already begun to convert into a preoccupation with death. Midway through this letter, interrupting her exaggerated paeans to female friendship, Dickinson had explained,

I do not care for the body, I love the timid soul, the blushing, shrinking soul; it hides, for it is afraid, and the bold obtrusive body— Pray, marm, did you call *me*? We are very small, Abiah—I think we grow still smaller—this tiny, insect life the portal to another; it seems strange—strange indeed. I'm afraid we are all unworthy, yet we shall "enter in."

But it was not to be Abiah Root with whom, in the coming years, Dickinson sought to realize her dream of a sisterhood secured against the intrusions of the body, depicted in the passage just cited as a lower-class servant. What began as a diffuse sentimental cult of female friendship was to take on a more ominous psychological cast as Dickinson ultimately got both more and less than she had bargained for. The erotic tensions against which, in 1850, she was already seeking to defend herself with her child persona were to be more difficult to subdue than she had supposed.

SUSAN GILBERT

"With the exception of Shakespeare, you have told me of more knowledge than any one living," Dickinson wrote to her sister-in-law Susan Gilbert Dickinson toward the close of her own life. "To say that sincerely is strange praise" (L757). During the winter of 1851–52, Dickinson's friendship with Sue had become the vehicle for a set of rich and intensely gratifying fantasies. Her relationships with Jane Humphrey, Abiah Root, and Emily Fowler had anticipated some of its component features, just as her subsequent attachments to Elizabeth Holland and perhaps Kate Anthon were to reiterate them, though in a significantly attenuated form. Among these features were her fantasies of subsequent meetings, which included hurried kisses and whispered good-byes; the exclusion of those routine obligations represented by "the worthy pastor"; the creation of a new sacred text, which would also release the sly and derisive laughter enjoyed by the members of a superior, secret society; a freedom of verbal invention to celebrate its mission; and the transcendent pleasure of having effectively circumvented the authority of a monolithic community of elders, while remaining physically present within it. No dancing girl in a pasha's harem, no slave in an antebellum mansion, and no homosexual in a resolutely heterosexual society could have conceived a finer scheme.[1]

1. William R. Taylor and Christopher Lasch, in "Two 'Kindred Spirits': Sorority and Family in New England, 1839–1846," *New England Quarterly* 36 (March 1963): 23–41, argue that New England religion was no longer responding adequately to the

Sue was a genteel orphan, an Amherst girl living with her sister and brother-in-law who had decided on a sudden impulse, against the wishes of her relatives, to abandon her subservient position in their household and the restrictions of small-town life for the big city.[2] She headed for Baltimore where she taught in a girls' boarding school and returned to Amherst in July 1852, having played out this careerist experiment to her own satisfaction. In the spring of 1853, she entered into a long and difficult engagement to the poet's brother. Thus, unlike Dickinson's relationships with the other women just mentioned, this friendship was increasingly entangled in the Dickinson family context within which it necessarily transpired.[3]

Conducting this passionately subversive courtship at a safe distance via the mails, in April 1852 Dickinson writes, in her characteristic fusion of Christian rhetoric and feminine rebellion,

> So sweet and still, and Thee, Oh Susie, what need I more, to make my heaven whole?
> Sweet Hour, blessed Hour, to carry me to you, and to bring you back to me, long enough to snatch one kiss, and whisper Good bye, again.
> I have thought of it all day, Susie, and I fear of but little else, and when I was gone to meeting it filled my mind so full, I could not find a *chink* to put the worthy pastor; when he said "Our Heavenly Fa-

---

needs of intellectual women. They examine the influence on female friendship of this deficiency. More recently, Carroll Smith-Rosenberg's "The Female World of Love and Ritual: Relations between Women in Nineteenth-Century America," *Signs* 1 (Autumn 1975), 1–29, has been extremely influential. Building on the analysis of Taylor and Lasch, she argues that "an intimate mother-daughter relationship lay at the heart of this female world" and concludes that "the supposedly repressive and destructive Victorian sexual ethos, may have been more flexible and responsive to the needs of particular individuals than those of mid-twentieth century" because it encouraged "a wide latitude of emotions and sexual feelings" located on a continuum between "committed heterosexuality" and "uncompromising homosexuality."

2. Sue's mother, Harriet Arms, had died in 1837. Her father, Thomas Gilbert, was the owner of a tavern in Amherst when he died in 1841. Leyda refers to him as "improvident"; Cody calls him an alcoholic. Educated at Utica Female Academy, Sue was reared by an aunt in Geneva, New York. Her sister Harriet Cutler, with whom she lived beginning in 1850, was the wife of a prosperous Amherst merchant. When Sue married, two of her brothers presented her with a substantial gift of five thousand dollars. Exactly how ashamed she was of what Leyda called "her miserable childhood" remains problematic.

3. In *After Great Pain: The Inner Life of Emily Dickinson* (Cambridge: Harvard University Press, 1971), John Cody argues that Dickinson's unresolved oedipal dilemma was reenacted "to her own near destruction" (p. 154) through her relations with Austin and Sue. He describes three major components of Dickinson's relationship with Austin: she viewed him as her child, her sexual representative, and her lover. See chapters 4 and 5.

ther," I said "Oh Darling Sue"; when he read the 100th Psalm, I kept saying your precious letter all over to myself, and Susie, when they sang—it would have made you laugh to hear one little voice, piping to the departed. I made up words and kept singing how I loved you, and you had gone, while all the rest of the choir were singing Hallelujahs. I presume nobody heard me, because I sang so *small*, but it was a kind of a comfort to think I might put them out, singing of you. (L88)

What kind of revolution is Dickinson fomenting? None at all, since her revolution, a revolution in consciousness, has already occurred. Knowledge is power, and to reveal a secret is to diffuse her knowledge of it. In 1852, however, Dickinson's knowledge depends on one other person, in this instance Sue, who is both the source of her power and her secret sharer. Although this element of Dickinson's conception of power (that it depends on one other person) never entirely disappears from either her prose or her poetry, during the 1850s her letters gradually deemphasize the social context within which knowledge is accrued. During the 1850s, in and through her relationship with Sue (though not exclusively), Dickinson's sense of her own social powerlessness was accentuated, and her conception of the sources of power was subtly transformed into an esthetic within which power could neither be accrued nor shared. Its sources then were either nonexistent or wholly internal. This condition within which "Reverse cannot befall / That fine Prosperity / Whose Sources are interior—" (395) had, as she was to observe repeatedly, something in common with being dead:

> The Soul selects her own Society—
> . . . .
> Then—close[s] the Valves of her attention—
> Like Stone—   (303)

However, I am anticipating the most extreme version of this esthetic; during the 1850s, Dickinson's style continued to develop and to preserve this tension between selecting her own society and selecting one other person around whom this esthetic of knowledge as power could be organized. By April 1852, Sue was becoming this person.

Nevertheless, Dickinson was pursuing mutually antagonistic goals. She was simultaneously attempting to create a female counterculture with Sue and to integrate her into the Amherst family circle. Attempting to reconcile the claims of the One and the Many, she had no intention either of abandoning her home and the economic and social security it afforded or of shirking her responsibilities to a family that, whatever its degree of internal dissension, was characterized by tenacious loyalty to its members. Intentions, Dickinson discovered, do not always determine events. Thus throughout their correspondence she maintained a precarious poise between overt professions of homosexual love and a distancing background of local gossip, literary chat, religious disputation particularly as it impinged on social conditioning, and fervent flights of poetic fancy soaring upward toward another world where all these "problems of the flesh" would be less troublesome. What already appears, then, as a tendency toward otherworldliness in fact implies a multiplicity of desires which this vocabulary of social disengagement sustains. In denying the power of social attitudes, Dickinson's prose also refuses to clarify them.

Susan Gilbert combined social graces with an undercurrent of turbulent unpredictability which in later life made her an outstanding hostess and a duplicitous friend. She was worldly, brilliant (her strength was mathematics), poised, and attractive to men. Before her romance with Austin, son of the town's leading citizen, there were rumors that she was about to become engaged to Edward Hitchcock, Jr., son of the Amherst College president. Even after her marriage, her friendship with the magnetic Samuel Bowles caused raised eyebrows. She was thus an unlikely partner for the kind of exclusive, single-sex relationship Dickinson was intermittently constructing in their correspondence. Hence Dickinson's identification with Sue as secret sharer was also an oblique identification with herself as a socially powerful woman.[4]

Particularly during the initial stages of her correspondence with Sue, Dickinson repeatedly emphasized her desire to "romanticize" her own life "down, down, in the terrestrial" by writing love letters to her. As she herself remarked, she had few stories to tell. Her letters make it clear that by stories she meant romances and that by

4. With the exception of her sister Lavinia, Dickinson had no close friends who remained unmarried during the 1850s. Emily Fowler married in 1853, Abiah Root in 1854, Jane Humphrey in 1858. Elizabeth Holland was already married when Dickinson met her in 1853. Kate Scott Turner Anthon was a widow in 1859 when Dickinson met her, as was Helen Hunt Jackson with whom Dickinson probably began corresponding in the late 1860s. It appears that after Sue's marriage Dickinson avoided the company of women who, like herself, had never married. Again, the exceptions here are family members, her cousins Louise and Frances Norcross, who were significantly younger than she was and whom she to some extent mothered.

romances she meant tales of courtship. (She was an inveterate asker after the news of her friends' romances and sometimes anticipated them when they did not already, to her knowledge, exist.) Since she herself had few, if any, suitors capable of poeticizing her existence, she fabulated a romantic tale with herself and Sue as the principal actors. These letters depended, as letters, on Sue's physical absence; Sue's physical absence heightened the drama of Dickinson's loneliness and also buffered her against making excessive demands on her friend in person. Within this style it is, of course, difficult to distinguish between suppressed homosexuality and suppressed heterosexuality, and Dickinson herself found it increasingly difficult to make this distinction. Initially, she could perceive this correspondence and this relationship as "a rehearsal in girlhood of the great drama of woman's life," namely marriage. However, what Longfellow in *Kavanagh*, a novel Dickinson self-consciously employed as a model for female friendship, could describe as a rehearsal was, for Dickinson, less obviously such. Occasionally, she describes herself as anticipating a romance. More commonly, she writes as though she intends to observe this "great drama" in the lives of her friends while remaining single and celibate herself.

In letters to several other women during the early 1850s, Dickinson made it clear that she viewed their marriages, impending or actual, as impediments to her continued intimacy with them. Even in 1859, she wrote to Elizabeth Holland, "Am told that fasting gives to food marvellous Aroma, but by birth a Bachelor, disavow Cuisine" (L204). J. G. Holland, who had been absent from home for some time, had just returned, as Dickinson knew from reading the *Springfield Republican.* Her comment reflects both her interest in the Hollands' marital romance and her commitment to celibacy, which she viewed as innately unfeminine. Participating vicariously in Sue's romances in 1851–52, Dickinson already recognized that these alternative relationships, when pursued beyond a certain point, would exclude her. Therefore in June 1852, shortly before Sue's return to Amherst, it was not yet true that "No Romance sold unto / Could so enthrall a Man / As the perusal of / His Individual One—" (669). But in June 1852, the nondrama of Dickinson's romance had not yet, unmistakably, transpired:

> You and I have been strangely silent upon this subject, Susie, we
> have often touched upon it, and as quickly fled away, as children

shut their eyes when the sun is too bright for them. I have always hoped to know if you had no dear fancy, illumining all your life, no one of whom you murmured in the faithful ear of night—and at whose side in fancy, you walked the livelong day; and when you come home, Susie, we must speak of these things. How dull our lives must seem to the bride, and the plighted maiden, whose days are fed with gold, and who gathers pearls every evening; but to the *wife*, Susie, sometimes the *wife forgotten*, our lives perhaps seem dearer than all others in the world; you have seen flowers at morning, *satisfied* with the dew, and those same flowers at noon with their heads bowed in anguish before the mighty sun; think you these thirsty blossoms will *now* need naught but—*dew*? No, they will cry for sunlight, and pine for the burning noon, tho' it scorches them, scathes them; they have got through with peace—they know that the man of noon, is *mightier* than the morning and their life is henceforth to him. Oh, Susie, it is dangerous, and it is all too dear, these simple trusting spirits, and the spirits mightier, which we cannot resist! It does so rend me, Susie, the thought of it when it comes, that I tremble lest at sometime I, too, am yielded up.   (L93)

Though this now-famous letter is often cited as an example of Dickinson's phobic sexuality, one of its most sharply pronounced attitudes is that marriage represents an encounter with a primal source of natural energy for which she herself, like her sexually insatiable "flowers," yearns. She describes marriage as a risk-fraught venture; she acknowledges that women are often neglected by their husbands; engagements and honeymoons are, she contends, not infrequently followed by an anticlimax or even by exceptional anguish; some wives, she knows, envy unmarried women. Despite these reservations (and I see nothing neurotic about them), she describes a compulsion to risk this experiment. Within this style, "peace" is not a sufficient goal; exceptionally powerful experience is. Marriage is such an experience, though it is apparent that Dickinson has no particular "man of noon" in mind and that her Sun God is an emblematic rather than an actual figure. What is perhaps neurotic about such language is its exaggeration of male power; given such exaggeration, few, if any, actual men will represent it. Given such exaggeration, this ideology—experience at any price—is unlikely to be translated into action. Rejecting actual men, she craves a super man. The marriage depicted is not a partnership, but a form of phototropism in which a "flower" who cannot control her nature is irresistibly attracted by a "Sun" who either cannot or will not control his. In June 1852, however, the suspense of this encounter is still pleasurable, nor is this biological determinism absolute. It might still happen that a woman who *could* control her nature as Sue, for example, appears to have been able to do might encounter a more human figure—someone, for example, like Dickinson's brother Austin, who was himself intent on such self-control.

Yet if in early June Dickinson advanced this set of arguments for and against marriage, in late June she calls Sue her "absent Lover." Mimicking the style of "Ik Marvel," whose *Reveries of a Bachelor* she is obviously exploiting, she explains,[5]

> Oh Susie, my child, I sit here by my window, and look each little while down towards that golden gateway beneath the western trees, and I fancy I see you coming, you trip upon the green grass, and I hear the crackling leaf under your little shoe; I hide behind the chair, I think I will surprise you, I grow too eager to see you, I hasten to the door, and start to find me that you are not there. And very, very often when I have waked from sleep, *not quite* waked, I have been sure I saw you, and your dark eye beamed on me with such a look of tenderness that I could only weep, and bless God for you.
>
> Susie, will you indeed come home next Saturday, and be my own again, and kiss me as you used to? Shall I indeed behold you, not "darkly, but face to face" or am I *fancying* so, and dreaming blessed dreams from which the day will wake me? I hope for you so much, and feel so eager for you, feel that I *cannot* wait, feel that *now* I must have you—that the expectation once more to see your face again, makes me feel hot and feverish, and my heart beats so fast—I go to sleep at night, and the first thing I know, I am sitting there wide awake, and clasping my hands tightly, and thinking of next Saturday, and "never a bit" of you.
>
> Sometimes I must have Saturday before tomorrow comes, and I wonder if it w'd make any difference with God, to give it to me *today*, and I'd let him have Monday, to make him a Saturday; and then I feel so funnily, and wish the precious day would'nt come quite so soon, till I could know how to feel, and get my thoughts ready for it.
>
> Why, Susie, it seems to me as if my absent Lover was coming home so soon—and my heart must be so busy, making ready for him. (L96)

Although Dickinson stated in the first of these June letters (93) that she had never mentioned marriage before, in fact she had already implied that she resented any future marriage Sue might make. Hearing that Sue was keeping a diary, probably from Sue's sister Mat who was still in Amherst, she had immediately responded,

5. "Ik Marvel" was the pseudonym of Donald Grant Mitchell (1822–1908), to whom Dickinson refers in letters 56, 75, and 113.

"I want you to get it bound—at my expense—Susie—so when he takes you from me, to live in his new home, I may have *some* of you. I am sincere" (L88).

Although Sue continued to reciprocate Dickinson's affection after her return from Baltimore, in time she began to disengage herself from an excessively complicated friendship; Dickinson, however, became increasingly dependent on her for company and for emotional support. Even after Sue's engagement was officially announced in the spring of 1853, Austin Dickinson was away from Amherst much of the time completing his legal training, and Susan wavered in her feelings toward him, so that the threesome maintained a temporary equilibrium. Emily had encouraged the courtship at least to the extent of serving as go-between for their letters when they were attempting to conceal their involvement from prying eyes. Subsequently, she continued to reassure Austin about the family's ready reception of Sue and about Sue's devotion to him. Concurrently, however, she was reminding Austin of his special obligation to her and complaining of loneliness:

> I cant help wondering sometimes if you think of us as often as we all do of you, and want to see us *half* as much. I think about this a great deal, and tho' I dont talk with Vinnie or Sue, about it, yet it often troubles me. I think we miss each other more every day that we grow older, for we're all unlike most everyone, and are therefore more dependent on each other for delight.   (L114)

Until the summer of 1854, the two women continued to spend much of their time together: sewing in the afternoons, walking and talking, keeping each other company on Saturday evenings, and the like. When the Dickinsons went to Washington to visit Edward, excluding Emily because of her desire to remain at home, Susan moved in with her, along with John Graves, Dickinson's cousin. Throughout the period of the engagement, they attended church together, read Austin's letters out loud to each other, accompanied each other when doing errands in town, visited in each other's houses, exchanged books, and, to hear Dickinson tell it, considered and reconsidered any snippet of information about Austin from any quarter. By the summer of 1854, this friendship was thoroughly enmeshed in Austin's relationship with Sue and in hers with him. In September 1854, for example, Susan had left Amherst and wrote

Austin asking why she had not heard from Emily. She apparently accused him of having discouraged his sister's correspondence with her. Feelings between Austin and Sue were extremely strained at this time; she probably suspected that Austin was punishing her through his sister. He replied testily,

> As to your deprivation of "Spiritual converse" with my sister—I Know Nothing—I was aware that you had been in correspondence for some time, but had never had an intimation that the correspondence was at an end—
>
> I have full confidence in her good sense—as guide in this respect—So you will not suspect me of having interfered with your epistolary intercourse with her—
>
> Her choice of friends and correspondents is a matter over which I have never exerted any control—
>
> Knowing therefore that you will not suspect me of having interfered with your epistolary relations & assuring you of my sentiments of regard for yourself—my respect and admiration for the President of the United States and the Gov Gen of Canada—I remain yours truly—Wm A Dickinson[6]

The events that clearly realigned this triangle occurred during the summer of 1854, when Austin returned from Harvard Law School. Sue fell ill with what was diagnosed as "Nervous Fever," and when she had recuperated sufficiently left Amherst for seven months. Dickinson's letter of late August, the first since Sue's departure on 4 August, alludes to a quarrel between them and conveys the bleakness of her mood:

> Susie—
> I have been very busy since you went away, but that is'nt the reason I've not written to you, and we've had a great deal of company too, but *that* is not the reason—I was foolish eno' to be vexed at a little thing, and I hope God will forgive me, as he'll have to many times, if he lives long enough.
> Thro' Austin, I've known of you, and nobody in this world except Vinnie and Austin, know that in all the while, I have not heard from you. Many have asked me for you, and I have answered promptly that you had reached there safely, and were better every day, and Susie, do you think, H. Hinsdale came to our house several days ago; came just to ask for you, and went away supposing I'd heard from

6. Austin Dickinson, as quoted in Jay Leyda, *The Years and Hours of Emily Dickinson*, 2 vols. (New Haven: Yale University Press, 1960), 1: 316.

you quite often. Not that I told her so, but spoke of you so naturally, in such a daily way, she never guessed the fact that I'd not written to you, nor had you thus to me.

Never think of it, Susie—never mention it—I trust your truth for that, but when you meet, and I meet—we'll try and forgive each other. There has not been a day, Child, that I've not thought of you, nor have I shut my eyes upon a summer night, without your sweet remembrance, and tho' full much of sorrow has gathered at your name, that ought but peace was 'tween us, yet I remembered on, and bye and bye the day came. I do not miss you Susie—of course I do not miss you—I only sit and stare at nothing from my window, and know that all is gone—Dont *feel* it—no—any more than the stone feels, that it is very cold, or the block, that it is silent, where once 'twas warm and green, and birds danced in it's branches.

I rise, because the sun shines, and sleep has done with me, and I brush my hair, and dress me, and wonder what I am and who has made me so, and then I wash the dishes, and anon, wash them again, and then 'tis afternoon, and Ladies call, and evening, and some members of another sex come in to spend the hour, and then that day is done.

After a few paragraphs of local gossip, including her own "charming farewell ride" with Henry Emmons, who had just graduated from the college, she interjects, "It's of no use to write to you—Far better bring dew in my thimble to quench the endless fire—" (L172).

Three months later, realizing that Sue's feeling for her was unlikely ever to burn as brilliantly as she had once thought it might, she writes,

Susie—it is a little thing to say how lone it is—anyone can do it, but to wear the loneness next your heart for weeks, when you sleep, and when you wake, ever missing something, *this*, all cannot say, and it baffles me. I would paint a portrait which would bring the tears, had I canvass for it, and the scene should be—*solitude*, and the figures— solitude—and the lights and shades, each a solitude. I could fill a chamber with landscapes so lone, men should pause and weep there; then haste grateful home, for a loved one left. . . . I want to think of you each hour in the day. What you are saying—doing—I want to walk with you, as seeing yet unseen. . . . "They say that absence conquers." It has vanquished me. (L176)

Even in this letter of late 1854, Dickinson describes herself as baffled by a sense of loneliness which, though intensified by Sue's absence, is not adequately explained by it. A face-saving stance? Perhaps. But Dickinson seems to be identifying a reaction she herself does not comprehend. Lamenting Sue's absence, she also laments the absence of a "something," a "Missing All," that Sue merely approximates. Evidently, the feelings of desolation she describes are usually suspended in Sue's presence. Dickinson, however, is suggesting a loss of contact with reality as she perceives it. The depression she describes seems excessive to her, even given the fact that Sue, her dearest friend, has to some extent abandoned her. Similarly, her desire to walk with Sue "as seeing yet unseen" suggests a desire to spy on Sue because of the jealousy she stresses throughout their correspondence. Again, this jealousy often appears to her disproportionate to the circumstances that have aroused it.

Even before this friendship was subjected to the tensions of competing with Austin for Sue's affection and to the tensions between Austin and Sue, Dickinson was interjecting a discordant note into their correspondence. In February 1852, while Sue was still in Baltimore, she had concluded a lengthy paragraph of sentimental literary posturing by saying:

> I think of you dear Susie, *now*, I dont know how or why, but more dearly as every day goes by, and that sweet month of promise draws nearer and nearer; and I view July so differently from what I used to—once it seemed parched, and dry—and I hardly loved it *any* on account of it's heat and dust; but *now* Susie, month of all the year the best; I skip the violets—and the dew, and the early Rose and the Robins; I will exchange them *all* for that angry and hot noonday, when I can count the hours and the *minutes* before you come—Oh Susie, I often think that I will try to tell you how very dear you are, and how I'm watching for you, but the words wont come, tho' the *tears* will, and I sit down disappointed—yet darling, you know it all— then why do I seek to tell you? I do not know; in thinking of those I love, my reason is all gone from me, and I do fear sometimes that I must make a hospital for the hopelessly insane, and chain me up there such times, so I wont injure you. (L77)

Thus, though Sue is the agent of her self-control, she is also the agent of its undoing. Moreover, Dickinson's perception of herself as a threat to her friend is echoed in other letters, though seldom this explicitly. Sue provides Dickinson with a subject matter; in some way, she also inhibits its expression. In response to this frustration, which Dickinson associates not just with Sue but with "those I love," she proposes to construct "a hospital for the hopelessly insane" and to chain herself up in it, "so I wont injure you." Most commonly,

however, she expresses a self-perceived sense of excessive sensitivity
to any sign that Sue is neglecting her. Less self-consciously, she
translates this sense of neglect into thoughts of death—her own and
that of others. This sense of having been slighted she explained to
herself and to Sue as the mood of a passing moment, but she also
remarked, in March 1853 while Sue was visiting relatives in Manchester, New Hampshire:

> Dear Susie, you are gone—One would hardly think I had lost you to
> hear this revelry, but your absence insanes me so—I do not feel so
> peaceful, when you are gone from me—All life looks differently,
> and the faces of my fellows are not the same they wear when you are
> with me. I think it is this, dear Susie; you sketch my pictures for me,
> and 'tis at their sweet colorings, rather than this dim real that I am
> used, so you see when you go away, the world looks staringly, and I
> find I need more vail— (L107)

Sue's mission was nothing less than to reconcile Dickinson to the
monotony of continuous household drudgery, to compensate
Dickinson for her maternal deprivation, to interpret reality for her,
and to fend off Dickinson's gathering sense of herself as a misfit and
of the world as a hostile place. Sue's mission was to transform, to
romanticize, and to poeticize Dickinson's life "down, down, in the
terrestrial." Sue was to inspire her, to be her muse, and to enable her
to transcend her disappointment at not having yet taken her place
"in that Paradise of which the good man writes":

> Oh my darling one, how long you wander from me, how weary I
> grow of waiting and looking, and calling for you; sometimes I shut
> my eyes, and shut my heart towards you, and try hard to forget you
> because you grieve me so, but you'll never go away, Oh you never
> will—say, Susie, promise me again, and I will smile faintly—and take
> up my little cross again of sad—*sad* separation. . . . I dont know how
> I shall bear it, when the gentle spring comes; if she should come and
> see me and talk to me of you, Oh it would surely kill me. . . . Susie,
> forgive me, forget all what I say, get some sweet little scholar to read
> a gentle hymn, about Bethleem and Mary, and you will sleep on
> sweetly and have as peaceful dreams, as if I had never written you all
> these ugly things. Never mind the letter Susie, I wont be angry with
> you if you dont give me any at all— (L73)

This text supports Lillian Faderman's insight that Dickinson's letters
to Sue are clearly distinguishable from those intended for women

"with whom she was merely good friends."[7] This address to Sue is both unprecedented and unreplicated in her correspondence with other women. The opening lines of this quotation, written while Sue was still in Baltimore, elevate frustrated sexual desire into a major theme. This theme disappears as soon as it is expressed; once again, Dickinson represents herself as bereaved, though perversely.

Few lovers could have accomplished this multifaceted mission, and Sue was not predisposed to attempt it. Her letters were usually less frequent than Dickinson might have wished, and their meetings occurred in a social environment that made it abundantly clear, even to Dickinson, that they both had centers of reality other than their relationship to each other. Nevertheless, Dickinson was counting on Sue to provide her with a respite from a thoroughly unpoetical life, which she tactfully described as less heroic than her friend's:

> Never mind the letter Susie, I wont be angry with you if you dont give me any at all—for I know how busy you are, and how little of that dear strength remains when it is evening, with which to think and write. Only *want* to write me, only sometimes sigh that you are far from me, and that will do, Susie! Dont you think we are good and patient, to let you go so long; and dont we think you're a darling, a real beautiful hero, to toil for people, and teach them, and leave your own dear home? Because we pine and repine, dont think we forget the precious patriot at war in other lands! (L73)

Sue had been complaining of the dullness of her pupils, but for someone whose mission in life consisted, or so it appeared when she was not writing, in washing dishes and clearing the table, school-teaching might appear a singularly romantic occupation. School-teaching was probably the only paid occupation open to Dickinson in 1852. She was not, as I have already suggested, temperamentally predisposed to attempt it, nor did her economic situation impose on her the necessity to do so. The temptation to earn a living and to leave home existed, but she was "held in check by some invisible agent" and turned back "without having done any harm" (L42). Because of her father's possessiveness, the harm, it appears, would have been directed primarily against her family: "After tea I went to

---

7. Lillian Faderman, "Emily Dickinson's Letters to Sue Gilbert," *Massachusetts Review* 28 (Summer 1977): 205. Some of this material is excerpted in *Surpassing the Love of Men: Romantic Friendship and Love between Women from the Renaissance to the Present* (New York: William Morrow, 1981).

see Sue—had a nice little visit with her—then went to see Emily Fowler, and arrived home at 9—found Father in great agitation at my protracted stay—and mother and Vinnie in tears, for fear that he would kill me" (L42) (8 June 1851, to Austin).

Although the precise chronology of many letters is uncertain, and virtually all of Sue's letters to both Austin and Emily were subsequently destroyed, it appears that Emily's interest in Sue intensified once she realized that Austin was seriously pursuing her.[8] This combination of personalities and familial roles was more fateful than accidental. Dickinson's identification with Austin, only one and one-half years her senior and temperamentally more like her than the less complex Vinnie, had always been very strong. During the 1850s, while he was teaching in Sunderland and studying in Cambridge, she followed his triumphs and defeats avidly, participated vicariously in them, and repeatedly expressed her willingness to shoulder his burdens, which she tended to represent as greater than her own. They laughed together at the foibles of "the folks" (their parents), other relatives, and elders and, though she worried about him excessively, in her eyes he could do no wrong. Moreover, it was to Austin that she had, in 1851, sent the following verse which Richard Chase hastens to assure us did not have in that "innocent age" any undertone of sexual suggestiveness, although he also sees in it "the strange license of the perfectly innocent":[9]

> There is another sky,
> Ever serene and fair,
> And there is another sunshine,
> Though it be darkness there;

8. Two letters from Sue to Emily have been published. The first was written during the summer of 1861, shortly after the birth of Sue's first child. It appears in *The Letters of Emily Dickinson*, ed. Thomas H. Johnson, 3 vols. (Cambridge: Harvard University Press, 1958), 2: 379–80, and concerns "Safe in their Alabaster Chambers." See my chapter 8. The second letter, written in late October 1861, has been censored. What remains of it is printed in Richard B. Sewall, *The Life of Emily Dickinson*, 2 vols. (New York: Farrar, Straus and Giroux, 1974), 1: 203. This letter casts Sue as unsympathetic to Dickinson's feelings of having been neglected by her, despite her statement, "If you have suffered this past Summer, I am sorry." She alludes to a secret sorrow and says, in effect, if I can be brave and cheerful, why can't you. The original version of this letter might have qualified this impression of a hard-hearted Sue who is both a busy mother and somewhat priggish: "If a nightingale sings with her breast against a thorn, why not *we*?" Dickinson herself refers to Sue as hard-hearted in L85, though not in relationship to herself.

9. Richard Chase, *Emily Dickinson* (New York: William Sloane, 1951), p. 89.

Never mind faded forests, Austin,
Never mind silent fields—
Here is a little forest,
Whose leaf is ever green;
Here is a brighter garden,
Where not a frost has been;
In its unfading flowers
I hear the bright bee hum;
Prithee, my brother,
Into *my* garden come!   (2)

After his marriage, Austin's home provided Dickinson with some of the social resources of an extended family. Indeed, we catch some of our last glimpses of a gregarious Dickinson in his drawing room, though she referred to it as Sue's. In 1858 she wrote to the Bowleses, "I think Jerusalem must be like Sue's Drawing Room, when we are talking and laughing there, and you and Mrs. Bowles are by" (L189). And in 1859 she reported, "Austin and Sue went to Boston Saturday, which makes the Village very large. I find they are my crowd" (L212). And it was to be with them on the night in October 1883 when their youngest child died that she made her last conscious journey beyond her father's house and ground. She became violently ill after this arduous excursion to the house where, so a neighbor wrote, she had not set foot for fifteen years.[10]

Although Dickinson's affection for Austin before his marriage is apparent in her letters to him—he was the correspondent with whom she did the least "posing"—there was nevertheless some degree of sibling rivalry in her intense attachment to his fiancée. Furthermore, Dickinson's identification with Austin may have been a sublimation of her unconscious aggression toward him; she often appears *overconcerned* for his welfare, as was her mother. Austin himself was extremely high-strung, and there are fascinating similarities between his courtship letters to Sue and Emily's. Within this context, Mabel Loomis Todd's impression of Dickinson in later life is worth reiterating. She was, Mrs. Todd wrote, "the climax of all the family oddity."[11]

Dickinson's letters to both Austin and Sue during the mid-1850s

10. Marriette Thompson Jameson, as quoted in Leyda, *Years and Hours of Emily Dickinson*, 2: 406.
11. Mabel Loomis Todd, as quoted in Leyda, *Years and Hours of Emily Dickinson*, 2: 357.

record a heroic struggle to maintain her ideal self-image as a facilitator of family harmony. Her social circle was shrinking and this marriage might have strengthened both her relationship to her brother and to her friend, but her emotional demands on Sue were exorbitant, her desire to *be* Austin difficult to control. Austin was apparently unaware of the depth of his sister's attachment to his fiancée, preoccupied as he was with Sue's unpredictable behavior toward him. When she criticized him or failed to live up to his extravagant expectations of her, he was not infrequently driven to desperation, and some of his letters to Sue make Dickinson's descriptions of her loneliness sound well-balanced by comparison.[12] Sue was probably self-centered, but both Austin and Emily appear to have been attracted by her volatility. Superficially self-confident, she was scarred by the loss of her parents during her childhood and probably sought to defend herself against subsequent abandonment by initiating such rejections herself. In certain respects her later life was a tragic one; two of her children predeceased her and her husband ceased to love her.[13] The range of her enthusiasms, however, tended to compensate for their lack of depth. As Austin abandoned his plans to set up law practice in Chicago; as the marriage was postponed to await the completion of the elegant house Edward Dickinson offered the couple as a wedding gift and an inducement to remain in Amherst; as Mrs. Dickinson's depressive illness deepened; Emily Dickinson edged closer to a breakdown and to a voice of her own.

In July 1856 Austin and Sue were married at the home of her aunt in Geneva, New York. None of the Dickinsons attended the ceremony, although Professor Joseph Haven of Amherst College

12. There are numerous excerpts from Austin's letters to Sue in Cody, *After Great Pain*, pp. 187 ff.

13. For a full discussion of Austin's liaison with Mabel Loomis Todd, which ended with his death in 1895, see Sewall, *Life of Emily Dickinson*, 1: 170–96. The wife of David Peck Todd, professor of astronomy at Amherst College, and the mother of Millicent Todd (Bingham), the twenty-four-year-old Mrs. Todd moved to Amherst with her husband in 1881 and quickly ingratiated herself with both Austin and Sue. After an extended flirtation with their twenty-one-year-old son Ned, she and Austin became lovers in the fall of 1882. Lavinia abetted their relationship, and Emily probably knew about it, as did David Todd, who persisted in considering Austin his best friend. According to Mrs. Todd, Sue had a morbid fear of sexual intercourse, refused to consummate her marriage for many months after her wedding, and had a number of abortions because of her fear of childbirth. Although they were bitter enemies, Mrs. Todd continued to respect Sue's intelligence and viewed her as a woman of exceptional talents, though cruelly perverted.

made the trip and officiated. Originally the marriage was to have taken place in Amherst at the home of an older sister with whom Sue had lived for most of her adult life. On 19 May, Sue wrote the Reverend and Mrs. S. C. Bartlett in Manchester to explain the sudden change of venue, hinting at undisclosed family complications:

> You will be surprised doubtless to receive news of me with Geneva post-mark and I am half surprised myself to write from here about my wedding instead of from Amherst—It was in my heart to write from there, but the time was so filled up, I was obliged to defer notifications of my marriage till I arrived here—
> You will wonder why I am here—My dear Aunty, through the Winter has been besieging me to come to her house to be married asserting her claim to the high honor as a sort of foster-Mother of mine—After mature deliberation on my part—a balancing of the gains & losses &c &c I decided to come—The decision made great shaking among the old plans, and thawing of fancy's frost-works, but for reasons I cannot explain, both for prudence and prolixity, it was advisable, and almost an inevitable plan—No Mr Bartlett to marry me—or Mrs Bartlett for guest—strange hands to tie the silken knot, and some strange eyes to look on the tying—so I have said good-bye to some of the sweet old plans and pretend to believe the new ones are the best—[14]

Although these undisclosed "reasons" may have had nothing to do with the Dickinsons, it is surprising that they did not attend the ceremony. No explanation for their absence has been recorded. My own thought is that Mrs. Dickinson's illness precluded her from attending; that Emily's growing aversion to strangers, which would have been particularly intense on this occasion, would have made it difficult for her to attend; and that Vinnie and Edward Dickinson absented themselves to minimize the impression of the absence of the two Emilies. Furthermore, among the wealth of correspondence Emily exchanged with both Sue and Austin, there is no message of congratulations on their marriage, just the kind of letter they would have saved, as they saved so many others, had it been written.

We may infer something about Dickinson's state of mind at this time from a letter assigned provisionally to August 1856. It is a curious mixture of utopian enthusiasm for "that Paradise of which

14. Susan Gilbert Dickinson, as quoted in Leyda, *Years and Hours of Emily Dickinson*, 1: 341–42.

the good man writes" where parted friends shall be reunited and anxiety lest Mrs. Holland, whose health was excellent, should be snatched from her by a " 'reaper whose name is Death' ":

> Don't tell, dear Mrs. Holland, but wicked as I am, I read my Bible sometimes, and in it as I read today, I found a verse like this, where friends should 'go no more out'; and there were 'no tears,' and I wished as I sat down to-night that we were *there*—not *here*—and that wonderful world had commenced, which makes such promises, and rather than to write you, I were by your side, and the 'hundred and forty and four thousand' were chatting pleasantly, yet not disturbing us. And I'm half tempted to take my seat in that Paradise of which the good man writes, and begin forever and ever *now*, so wondrous does it seem. My only sketch, profile, of Heaven is a large, blue sky, bluer and larger than the *biggest* I have seen in June, and in it are my friends—all of them—every one of them—those who are with me now, and those who were 'parted' as we walked, and 'snatched up to Heaven'. . . .
>
> I'm so glad you are not a blossom, for those in my garden fade, and then a 'reaper whose name is Death' has come to get a few to help him make a bouquet for himself, so I'm glad you are not a rose—and I'm glad you are not a bee, for where they go when summer's done, only the thyme knows, and even were you a robin, when the west winds came, you would coolly wink at me, and away, some morning!
>
> As 'little Mrs. Holland,' then, I think I love you most, and trust that tiny lady will dwell below while we dwell, and when with many a wonder we seek the new Land, *her* wistful face, *with* ours, shall look the last upon the hills, and first upon—well, *Home!*
>
> Pardon my sanity, Mrs. Holland, in a world *in*sane, and love me if you will, for I had rather *be* loved than to be called a king in earth, or a lord in Heaven.   (L185)

Proud, wistful, defeated and yet hopeful, Dickinson pleads for Mrs. Holland's understanding "in a world *in*sane." After this letter, her voice is, for our purposes, temporarily silenced.

"'Tis a dangerous moment for any one," Dickinson later wrote in an undated prose fragment, "when the meaning goes out of things and Life stands straight—and punctual—and yet no content . . . come[s]. Yet such moments are. If we survive them they expand us, if we do not, but that is Death, whose if is everlasting" (PF49). Whether she ever experienced the complete breakdown in 1857 first suggested by Anna Mary Wells in an article bluntly entitled "Was Emily Dickinson Psychotic?" and subsequently argued more sympathetically by Cody will probably never be conclusively proved nor disproved by any objective documentation.[15] After carefully weighing the evidence, Theodora Ward concludes only that "it is perhaps fitting that at the close of Emily Dickinson's prolonged girlhood there should be a year of which she has left no record. . . . It is possible that during that year she had a serious illness." She goes on to characterize it as "a time of transition at the close of a phase of her life, and a preparation for the new and crucial period that was soon to begin."[16] 1857 is a virtual blank in our knowledge of the poet's life. There are no letters. This in itself is curious, since the record of her letters is continuous from the age of thirteen up to that point. She was appointed to a committee of the annual autumn Cattle Show to judge a bread-baking contest, but there is no proof that she ever served. Beyond that, she disappears from sight. Even the rumor mill of Amherst grinds to an unaccustomed halt. Nor do her letters, resumed in 1858, point unmistakably to a total or even partial collapse in 1857. A letter written to an uncle in the early summer alludes to depression and social isolation, but whether its concluding statement expresses a genuine concern with mental disorder there is no way of telling: "I hardly know what I have said—my words put all their feathers on—and fluttered here and there" (L190). The letter evokes an atmosphere of high emotional drama but the occasion is obscured, a stylistic propensity already apparent in her earlier letters but intensified here:

> Much has occurred, dear Uncle, since my writing you—so much— that I stagger as I write, in its sharp remembrance. Summers of bloom—and months of frost, and days of jingling bells, yet all the while this hand upon our fireside. Today has been so glad without, and yet so grieved within—so jolly, shone the sun—and now the moon comes stealing, and yet it makes none glad. I cannot always see the light—please tell me if it shines.

The first letter to the man she denominated "Master," dated about 1858, begins, "I am ill, but grieving more that you are ill, I make my stronger hand work long eno' to tell you" (L187). But the date is

15. Anna Mary Wells, "Was Emily Dickinson Psychotic?" *American Imago* 19 (Winter 1962): 309–21.
16. Theodora Ward, *The Capsule of the Mind: Chapters in the Life of Emily Dickinson* (Cambridge: Harvard University Press, 1961), p. 38.

provisional, the nature of the illness undisclosed. A letter to the Bowleses in about June 1858 explains, "I rode with Austin this morning. He showed me mountains that touched the sky, and brooks that sang like Bobolinks. Was he not very kind?" (L189), a comment that might or might not imply that as a convalescent she was receiving special attention. Similarly, rather heavily emphasized references in other letters to kindnesses she has received, as well as intensified fears for the welfare of others, may or may not reflect a heightened sensitivity to illness as a consequence of some prolonged trauma in 1857.

In part because Dickinson's letters of 1858 do point unmistakably to the excess of nervous tension that dominated Higginson's impression of the poet in their 1870 interview, in part because of her comments to him about the relationship between her muse and death, but most centrally because of her subsequent concern with bereavement disorders in her art, it seems likely that this problematic silence of 1857 signifies something more than an accident of historiography. Although she may have been alluding to her *mother's* breakdown in letter 190 with the phrase "this hand upon our fireside," the extended depression she describes, whatever its precise origin, obviously includes her state of mind as well. However, if Dickinson suffered a breakdown of any kind at this time, it is unlikely to have been of the magnitude Cody depicts. How likely is it, for example, that in a town such as Amherst where privacy was at a premium even for a courting couple, a serious illness lasting perhaps a year and a half could have escaped notice? And how likely is it that Dickinson, who was seldom reticent about dramas in her life, even when they barely existed, would never have mentioned an illness of this duration? It is, of course, true that we do not have all of Dickinson's letters and that some of the letters we do have were censored by such recipients as the Norcross cousins. Nevertheless, at the time of her puzzling and chronic eye disorder in 1864–65, she spoke of it repeatedly and to many correspondents. At the time of her breakdown in 1883–84, she stated simply, "The Physician says I have 'Nervous prostration.' Possibly I have—I do not know the Names of Sickness. The Crisis of the sorrow of so many years is all that tires me—" (L873).

In any event, she emerged from this apparently sterile interlude strengthened in her determination to create for herself a life in language independent of the network of unstable family alliances from which she was never wholly to extricate herself. "Her failures," Sewall asserts, "were with people."[17] If Dickinson's still powerful attachment to Sue precipitated a chronic depression in 1857, this would also explain why, in 1858, the year in which her art as we know it was born, she had also written her first letter to the "Master" whom she conceived as the alternative to her disappointed love for Susan Gilbert. His distant reality was, in the end, more amenable to her imaginative designs than the sharper presence of the sister who continued to live, for the rest of their lives, "a hedge away."

How accurate is it, then, to describe Dickinson as a suppressed lesbian? The materials for this thesis are unquestionably there. This thesis is in fact more compelling than the view that Dickinson was thwarted in her love for a particular man (other than her father) at a comparatively early age and that she never recovered from this disappointment. Recently, however, Catharine Stimpson has suggested, and properly I think, that a lesbian is not simply someone who prefers the company of other women. Rather, a lesbian "finds other women erotically attractive and gratifying. Of course a lesbian is more than her body, more than her flesh, but lesbianism partakes of the body, partakes of the flesh. That carnality distinguishes it from gestures of political sympathy with homosexuals and from affectionate friendships in which women enjoy each other, support each other, and commingle a sense of identity and well-being. Lesbianism represents a commitment of skin, blood, breast, and bone."[18] Within some letters and some poems, Dickinson probably views herself as a suppressed lesbian. "Carnality," however, was not the major focus of her relationship with Sue. Instead, as she herself suggested, it was her desire to "put them out," coupled with her desire to put herself in by identifying with Sue, who was a general favorite both within the Dickinson household and within Amherst society at large. Whom, then, was she intent on besting, and with whom did she wish to ingratiate herself?

The central letter in Dickinson's correspondence with Sue is the

17. Sewall, *Life of Emily Dickinson*, 2: 517.
18. Catharine Stimpson, "Zero Degree Deviancy: The Lesbian Novel in English," *Critical Inquiry* 8 (Winter 1981): 364. In *Surpassing the Love of Men*, p. 15, Faderman contends that "Emily's love letters to Sue were not simply an example of Victorian rhetoric, but neither was this a lesbian relationship as such relationships have been lived through much of our century." Her argument hinges, however, on the assumption that this relationship was free of guilt and anxiety and "the need to keep secrets from family and friends." In essence, she represents Dickinson as an asexual woman.

one in which she describes herself in church, mimicking hymn tunes, while substituting Sue's name for the name of "Our Heavenly Father." Dickinson's relationship with Sue was energized primarily by her attitudes toward her parents, whom she had come to view, during the mid-1850s, as repressive influences on her. This animosity was subsequently generalized toward the values they endorsed, which, however, she too endorsed insofar as she wished to be legitimized by them. To some extent unconsciously, Dickinson perceived herself as having been rejected by her parents. In particular, she perceived herself as having been most deeply rejected by her mother, the parent with whom she had the most extensive and most essential contact during her formative years. Like Jane Humphrey (her friend encourager, sincere counselor, rock, and strong assister), Sue fulfilled a multiplicity of psychological functions. She was a surrogate mother, a clever friend, a woman apparently in control of her life, and a buffer against heterosexual relationships which Dickinson perceived as fascinating yet threatening. Thus, to describe Dickinson as a suppressed lesbian is to oversimplify and to clarify her indeterminate stance. Lesbianism, for Dickinson, was one of the roads not taken, as was heterosexual promiscuity, as was monogamous marriage. Her deepest desire was, as she states in poem 661, to "ride indefinite / As doth the Meadow Bee." Had she been less intent on identifying herself with Sue as an exceptional yet unmistakably normal woman, she might or might not have found her "erotically attractive and gratifying." As late as 1864, she could write, "Where my Hands are cut, Her fingers will be found inside—" (L288). Haunted by Sue's identity (orphan, wife, and mother), she could describe mutilating herself to attain it. The word that needs to be stressed here is "orphan." When Dickinson told Higginson, "I never had a mother," she was also expressing her desire to repudiate the mother she had. Her relationship with Sue, at one time, appeared to hold out to her the possibility of effecting this repudiation costlessly. Instead, what she interpreted as a first betrayal was intensified by the second, and her sense of herself as "the slightest in the House" was correspondingly exacerbated.

Though I remain painfully aware of how much we do not know about Dickinson's relationships with other women, including Sue, I have attempted to demonstrate that the transformation of this relationship during the 1850s was one of the forces that exacerbated

Dickinson's sense of metaphysical homelessness, just as it served to obscure her psychological ambitions to herself. In so doing, it intensified her desire to clarify those ambitions in language. As late as 1884 she could explain, "I work to drive the awe away, yet awe impels the work" (L891). Dickinsonian awe is an emotion compounded of fear and wonder, activated by her perception of an untrammeled, unacculturated power. The psychological closure of her relationship with Susan Gilbert had blocked her access to one kind of power, the power of a secret sharer. It also kept the door ajar for visitations by an equally momentous figure, her muse:

> What fortitude the Soul contains,
> That it can so endure
> The accent of a coming Foot—
> The opening of a Door—   (1760)

The possibility exists, of course, that I am engaged in a usual Dickinsonian mistake: anticipating events which have not yet occurred. The possibility exists that Dickinson's problematic silence of 1857 signifies nothing more and nothing less than an accident in historiography and that it was not until the mid-1860s that Dickinson came to realize the extent to which her path and Sue's had diverged. Thus from Cambridge in 1864 she wrote, "Should I turn in my long night I should murmur 'Sue'—" (L294). And in about 1878:

> Susan—I dreamed of you, last night, and send a Carnation to indorse it—

> Sister of Ophir—
> Ah Peru—
> Subtle the Sum
> That purchase you—   (L585)

And in the penultimate year of her life, "The tie between us is very fine, but a Hair never dissolves" (L1024). In a plotless life, one looks for such strands, such single golden threads linking us to "Heaven." Whether or not the chronology of the events I have described is accurate, the emotional logic of these experiences is clear: "To say that she was 'in love' with Sue is to describe her emotional state accurately."[19] What is less clear is how Dickinson responded to disappointment in love during the year 1857. Beginning in about 1866, however, it is Dickinson who shuts the door when Sue searches her out. One function, then, among others, that her reclusion served was this: it enabled her to circumvent those human relationships within which, in nineteenth-century Amherst, unattached spinsters were apt to receive short shrift. The emotional logic of this scheme depended, however, on her ability to sustain herself independent of sharply focused relationships with either men or women. This was its fatal flaw.[20]

19. Faderman, "Emily Dickinson's Letters to Sue Gilbert," p. 209. Sewall, who at first relegates this theme to a dismissive footnote, subsequently reverses himself to affirm that "Emily was in love with Sue," although he does not pursue the consequences of this statement in any detail. See *Life of Emily Dickinson*, 1: 107n, 165. In "Emily Dickinson and 'Sister Sue,'" *Prairie Schooner* 52 (Spring 1977): 90–108, Jean McClure Mudge also concludes that this was "a homoerotic relationship . . . but also very much in the accepted mode of the day." She describes a romantic friendship whose influence on Dickinson's art "was tremendous." Her conclusion that Dickinson and Sue wrote poetry *together*, which she advances as a fact, is questionable. More cogently, Mudge rehabilitates Sue to imply that Dickinson may not have been a poor judge of character. Sue's biography remains to be written, though the materials for it may no longer exist.

20. Freud's explanation of repression is relevant here. In *Introductory Lectures on Psycho-Analysis*, he writes: "Repression corresponds to an attempt at flight by the ego from libido which is felt as a danger. A phobia may be compared to an entrenchment against an external danger which now represents the dreaded libido. The weakness of the defensive system in phobias lies, of course, in the fact that the fortress which has been so greatly strengthened towards the outside remains assailable from within." See "Anxiety," in *The Standard Edition of the Complete Psychological Works of Sigmund Freud*, trans. James Strachey, 24 vols. (London: Hogarth, 1975), 16: 410.

MASTER

The parameters of the debate about the identity of Dickinson's male lover, which began in Amherst during the poet's lifetime and quickly took on international proportions after the first posthumous publication of poems in 1890, may be summarized as follows. Was there a lover as distinguished from a figure of pure fantasy? What was the extent of Dickinson's knowledge—physical, emotional, and intellectual—of this person? Was the poet ultimately rejected by him or the other way around? Was Dickinson in love with several men simultaneously? If any of the above is true, what are the implications of this fact or set of facts for understanding her poems?

Of these possibilities, the least likely is that the lover was not one but two people whom Dickinson loved simultaneously with equal intensity, since this violates our fundamental intuition of human passion. The most harrowing is that the "Master" figure to whom Dickinson alludes in her letters of the early 1860s and to whom she drafted three extant letters (probably in 1858, 1861, and 1862) was a purely hallucinatory presence, invoked in a classically Freudian reaction-formation as a defense against the repressed homosexuality that was one of the components of her relationship with Susan Gilbert. If there was quite literally nobody, Dickinson either was posing in her letters by constructing a melodramatic history for herself, or she was unable to distinguish between the narrative she imagined and the events she recounted in her letters as having occurred. While it would be naive to assume that Dickinson's prose persona here is spontaneously artless, a random copy of a "real" self, it would be equally naive to ignore the unmistakable desperation of her self-revelations, particularly in the second and third "Master" letters which make extraordinarily painful reading even at the remove of a century and more. Evidently Dickinson was fully capable of constructing a fictive correspondence, had she wished to. That she would have constructed an *incoherent* fictive identity for herself seems improbable, nor is there any other known instance of her use of the prose letter for this solipsistic purpose alone. Elements of the identity she constructs—for example, her intermittent designation of herself as "Daisy"—are patently metaphorical. Nevertheless, I think we can dismiss out of hand the notion that these letters are self-addressed literary performances. Between the extremes, then, of delusional mania and literal happenings, a third possibility exists: that Dickinson's relationship with the man she denominated "Master," while focused on an actual person with whom she corresponded and had occasional meetings, was primarily a function of her own projective power; his inaccessibility was the necessary, although not sufficient, condition of his psycho-allegorical appeal. In my view, this third possibility has the most interpretative power for both her life and her art, and for that reason I shall explore it in some detail.

On 25 April 1862, Dickinson wrote to Higginson the famous "terror—since September—" letter, in which she explained, "When a little Girl, I had a friend, who taught me Immortality—but venturing too near, himself—he never returned—Soon after, my Tutor, died—and for several years, my Lexicon—was my only companion—Then I found one more—but he was not contented I be his scholar—so he left the Land" (L261). Whether the tutor is the same person who taught her immortality is unclear. What *is* clear is that Dickinson, without explicitly juxtaposing her "terror—since September" and the departure of the "one more" who because of dissatisfaction with her "left the Land," is encouraging any reasonably insightful reader to consider linking these two events as effect and cause, and thus to comprehend the departure of the "one more" as the inspiration for her art. It is, of course, impossible to say whether this is the meaning Dickinson intends, for her sequential sentence structure does not itself link these two events. Because Dickinson emphasizes that she has not confided her "terror" to any of the people around her, the reader may question whether she would have confessed herself, however obliquely, to Higginson, whom she had never met. Yet such confessions do occur, sometimes with greater ease than with one's habitual intimates. Whatever Dickinson's intention, this elliptical sequence has been properly perceived as an important self-revelation by a poet whose prose comments about her art are notoriously scant. Furthermore, although in all two or three of these relationships Dickinson characterizes herself as "scholar," it is apparent that her preceptors schooled her in the relationship between love and death, desire and rage, and that she considers her education unfinished.

Dickinson's confidence to Higginson is partially clarified by a letter she wrote on 13 January 1854, to another minister, Edward Everett Hale, also of Worcester, inquiring about the last days of Benjamin Franklin Newton, who had been her father's law student from 1847 to 1849 and who had died ten months earlier, in March 1853:

Rev Mr Hale—
Pardon the liberty Sir, which a stranger takes in addressing you, but I think you may be familiar with the last hours of a Friend, and I therefore transgress a courtesy, which in another circumstance, I should seek to observe. I think, Sir, you were the Pastor of Mr B. F. Newton, who died sometime since in Worcester, and I often have hoped to know if his last hours were cheerful, and if he was willing to die. Had I his wife's acquaintance, I w'd not trouble you Sir, but I have never met her, and do not know where she resides, nor have I a friend in Worcester who could satisfy my inquiries. You may think my desire strange, Sir, but the Dead was dear to me, and I would love to know that he sleeps peacefully.
Mr Newton was with my Father two years, before going to Worcester—in pursuing his studies, and was much in our family.
I was then but a child, yet I was old enough to admire the strength, and grace, of an intellect far surpassing my own, and it taught me many lessons, for which I thank it humbly, now that it is gone. Mr Newton became to me a gentle, yet grave Preceptor, teaching me what to read, what authors to admire, what was most grand or beautiful in nature, and that sublimer lesson, a faith in things unseen, and in a life again, nobler, and much more blessed—
Of all these things he spoke—he taught me of them all, earnestly, tenderly, and when he went from us, it was as an elder brother, loved indeed very much, and mourned, and remembered. During his life in Worcester, he often wrote to me, and I replied to his letters—I always asked for his health, and he answered so cheerfully, that

while I knew he was ill, his death indeed surprised me. He often talked of God, but I do not know certainly if he was his Father in Heaven—Please Sir, to tell me if he was willing to die, and if you think him at Home, I should love so much to know certainly, that he was today in Heaven. Once more, Sir, please forgive the audacities of a Stranger, and a few lines, Sir, from you, at a convenient hour, will be received with gratitude, most happy to requite you, sh'd it have opportunity. (L153)

Dickinson was eighteen when Newton, nine years her senior, left Amherst. They shared an affinity for modern literature and a distaste for conservative religion. Newton, a Unitarian, sent her "Ralph Emerson's Poems—a beautiful copy" (L30) in 1850, and admired her talent. She subsequently told Higginson, "My dying Tutor told me that he would like to live till I had been a poet, but Death was much of Mob as I could master—then—" (L265). However, when she reported Newton's death to Austin in March of 1853, the same month in which he became engaged to Sue, she wrote, "Oh Austin, Newton is dead. The first of my own friends. Pace" (L110), a comment that probably places the relationship in its proper contemporary perspective. Newton, already stricken with the tuberculosis that killed him at the age of thirty-two, had married a widow twelve years his senior in 1851, little more than a year after leaving Amherst. After writing to Hale in 1854 and again in 1856, since he had not answered her first letter, Dickinson does not mention him in any of her letters until 1862. The last stanzas of a poem written at about that time probably memorialize him, but they do so by counterpointing physical absence and symbolic presence:

> A Book I have—a friend gave—
> Whose Pencil—here and there—
> Had notched the place that pleased Him—
> At Rest—His fingers are—
>
> Now—when I read—I read not—
> For interrupting Tears—
> Obliterate the Etchings
> Too Costly for Repairs. (360)

If Dickinson consciously intended three people in her letter to Higginson, the original dead tutor was Leonard Humphrey, principal of Amherst Academy while Dickinson was there from 1846 to 1847. Shortly after Humphrey's death in 1850, Dickinson wrote a lengthy, self-dramatizing letter to Abiah Root that specifically uses the word "master" as an honorific for her dead teacher.[1] There are only two other references to Humphrey. In late autumn 1846 she wrote Abiah, "we have an excellent Principal in the person of Mr. Leonard Humphrey, who was the last valedictorian [of the senior class at Amherst College]" (L14). And in January 1848 from Mount Holyoke she told her, "Mr Humphrey brought Mary Warner over to see me the other day & we had a delightful time, you well know" (L20). Humphrey himself discusses a number of Amherst girls in letters to his close friend J. R. Brigham, but Dickinson is not one of them.[2] Therefore, a romantic attachment between Dickinson and Humphrey is even less likely than such an attachment between Dickinson and Newton. Newton, at least, was a bona fide literary companion. What we know, then, of Dickinson's relationships with men who were potential suitors before 1862 is that their deaths enlarged her memories of them and that, despite the presence of many eligible young men in the Dickinson home throughout her youth, she never exhibited any strong romantic interest in any of them. Thus we must be wary of attaching too much importance to Dickinson's elegiac comments about men who, as living presences, were relegated to the periphery of her vision. As she stated in her poetic tribute to Newton, "Death sets a Thing significant / The Eye had hurried by" (360).

Higginson was not the first person to whom Dickinson had confided, however cryptically, an erotic bereavement. In the summer of 1860 in a letter to Kate Scott—a schoolfriend of Sue's whom she had met during her visit of 1859—Dickinson remarked that she had been unaware that Kate was a widow. (Her husband had died after only two years of marriage and she had resumed her maiden name.) The reader may perhaps recall that, writing to Sue in 1852 in her "wife forgotten" marriage letter (L93), Dickinson had introduced her speculation by saying, "You and I have been strangely silent upon this subject." Eight years later she wrote to Kate,

> There is a subject dear—on which we never touch, Ignorance of its pageantries does not deter me—I, too went out to meet the "Dust" early in the morning, I, too in Daisy mounds possess hid treasure—therefore I guard you more—You did not tell me you had once been

1. The letter (39) was quoted and discussed on pp. 56–58.
2. Leonard Humphrey, as quoted in Jay Leyda, *The Years and Hours of Emily Dickinson*, 2 vols. (New Haven: Yale University Press, 1960), 1: 105–19, passim.

a "Millionaire." Did my sister think that opulence could be mistaken?—Some trinket will remain—some babbling plate or jewel! (L222)

Paraphrased, this letter says, "We have never discussed marriage, but don't think I am ignorant of its rituals. I too encountered death prematurely. I too have a lover buried in the grave. You didn't tell me you were once married. Did you think that erotic experience could be permanently concealed? Not so." This paraphrase, of course, does not adequately represent the strained sexual innuendo of phrases such as "I, too in Daisy mounds possess hid treasure" or the hyperbolic artifice of the extended "Millionaire" conceit.

In addition to these cryptic allusions to an ill-fated love affair to Higginson and Kate Scott, Dickinson sent the following spiritual marriage poem to Samuel Bowles early in 1862.[3] She appended the plea, "Here's—what I had to 'tell you'—You will tell no other? Honor—is it's own pawn—" (L250).

> Title divine—is mine!
> The Wife—without the Sign!
> Acute Degree—conferred on me—
> Empress of Calvary!
> Royal—all but the Crown!
> Betrothed—without the swoon
> God sends us Women—
> When you—hold—Garnet to Garnet—
> Gold—to Gold—
> Born—Bridalled—Shrouded—
> In a Day—
> "My Husband"—women say—
> Stroking the Melody—
> Is *this*—the way?   (1072)

Bowles was obviously astonished to receive this communication, the gist of which Dickinson had tried to tell him in person, and the nature of his response, now lost, can be inferred from her letter 251:

3. Bowles was the subject of a massive two-volume biography following his death. See George S. Merriam, *The Life and Times of Samuel Bowles* (New York: Century Company, 1885). Like Austin and Sue, Dickinson offered the letters he had sent her for inclusion in this work, but few, if any, were used and she is never mentioned by name.

Dear friend
    If you doubted my Snow—for a moment—you never will—
again—I know—
    Because I could not say it—I fixed it in the Verse—for you to
read—when your thought wavers, for such a foot as mine—

To confirm her snowy chastity, which Bowles's hasty reading of
"Title divine" might have overlooked (he might have responded,
"Emily, what in the world have you been up to?"), she enclosed a
statement of heroic martyrdom, sustained by faith in God, "the everlasting troth":

> Through the strait pass of suffering—
> The Martyrs—even—trod.
> Their feet—upon Temptation—
> Their faces—upon God—
>
> A stately—shriven—Company—
> Convulsion—playing round—
> Harmless—as streaks of Meteor—
> Upon a Planet's Bond—
>
> Their faith—the everlasting troth—
> Their Expectation—fair—
> The Needle—to the North Degree—
> Wades—so—thro' polar Air!   (792)

The poem clarifies the meaning of the word "foot" in her prose as a
synonym for sexual temptation. Although interpretations of the
precise meaning of her letter will differ, its tone seems inconsistent
with the notion either that Bowles interpreted her original communication as an expression of her relationship to him or that she was
concerned with this interpretation. What she is acknowledging, I
believe, is their mutual temptation, but in relation to other people.
    If one puts all these comments together, it is evident that the
substance is scant, even though her statement to Bowles ("Here's—
what I had to 'tell you'") makes an absolute identification between
herself and the speaker of her spiritual marriage poem. Were it not
for the presence of the "Master" letters to which we shall now turn,
one would be tempted to assume either that Dickinson's heterosexual erotic life never included anyone else at all and that the "one

more" who "left the Land" was a figment of her imagination or, somewhat less probably, that this person was Samuel Bowles, who sailed for Europe to recover his health on 9 April 1862, whatever his interest in her feet, phallic or metric. The burden of proof, then, converges on the "Master" letters, since Dickinson's correspondence with Bowles is thoroughly inconclusive and no one in her circle ever suggested a romance between them. There is no doubt that they were friends, that he was to some extent interested in her poetry, and that he had more insight than most people into the nature of her seclusion. He once wrote to Austin, "I have been in a savage, turbulent state for some time—indulging in a sort of [illegible word] disgust at everything and everybody—I guess a good deal as Emily feels."[4] Martha Dickinson Bianchi quoted his observation that Dickinson was "'part angel, part demon.'"[5] On at least one occasion, Bowles succeeded in getting her to emerge from the "fiery mist" in which, Higginson observed, she enshrouded herself. When in 1870 she refused to see him, Bowles is said to have hollered upstairs something to the effect of "Emily, you damned rascal, I've travelled all the way from Springfield to see you. Come down at once." And she did, apparently to their mutual delight.[6] But if any fact emerges from behind the veil of illusion in which Dickinson's human relationships are shrouded, it is that the "Master" letters cannot have been intended for Bowles, unless one assumes that her perceptions of reality were so fundamentally askew as to make her statements wholly unreliable guides to the simplest expressions of space and time. I see no reason to make that assumption.

On the basis of handwriting, the "Master" letters have been assigned to the years 1858, 1861, and 1862. The first two letters are in ink, the third in pencil, and all contain suggested emendations in parentheses. Letter 187, in the handwriting of 1858, begins

> Dear Master
>   I am ill, but grieving more that you are ill, I make my stronger hand work long eno' to tell you. I thought perhaps you were in Heaven, and when you spoke again, it seemed quite sweet, and wonderful, and surprised me so—I wish that you were well.

4. Samuel Bowles, as quoted in Leyda, *Years and Hours of Emily Dickinson*, 2: 77.
5. Bowles, as quoted in Martha Dickinson Bianchi, *The Life and Letters of Emily Dickinson* (Boston: Houghton Mifflin, 1924), p. 81.
6. The source of this anecdote is Gertrude M. Graves, "A Cousin's Memories of Emily Dickinson," *Boston Sunday Globe*, 12 January 1930.

Bowles, a close friend of Austin and Sue whose relationship with Dickinson deepened during the late 1850s and early 1860s, visited Amherst frequently and was a visible daily public presence in his capacity as editor of the *Springfield Republican*. Dickinson was unlikely to have wondered whether he was alive or dead. Furthermore, in the second "Master" letter (233), in the handwriting of 1861, she inquires,

> I want to see you more—Sir—than all I wish for in this world—
> and the wish—altered a little—will be my only one—for the skies.
> Could you come to New England—[this summer—could] would
> you come to Amherst—Would you like to come—Master?

Even though Bowles spent several months in New York in the winter of 1861–62 with his wife, who was there for medical treatment, he had lived in New England all of his life. Dickinson's language would be thoroughly inappropriate for a habitual resident of New England who was in and out of Amherst regularly on a casual basis. Although Bowles's departure for Europe may have intensified her sense of isolation and may have been a precipitating factor behind her decision to write to Higginson six days later, Samuel Bowles is not the person to whom the "Master" letters were addressed. This point is further clarified if one compares the letters Dickinson wrote to Bowles while he was in Europe, which refer to other people in Amherst who are missing him, to places he has known and loved, and which treat his absence, rather than his presence, as exceptional, with this statement. Even if one discounts the 1858 letter entirely and assumes that the 1861 letter either refers to Bowles's absence from late December 1861 to February 1862 or is somewhat misdated and refers to his absence in Europe, the letters Dickinson wrote to Bowles during his absence make it even more difficult to entertain the possibility that she had Bowles in mind when she wrote, "Could you come to New England—[this summer—could] would you come to Amherst—Would you like to come—Master?"

Even if one assumes that the "Master" letters were never sent and that Dickinson's correspondence with Bowles exists at two levels to account for the difference in tone between the letters she actually sent him and the letters he (supposedly) never received, she still would never have written to this man whose home was in New England and who had lived there all his life, "Could you come to New England—[this summer—could] would you come to Amherst—

Would you like to come—Master?" Whoever and whatever Master is, he is not Samuel Bowles, despite Sewall's conclusion that on the basis of proximity, he has a slight edge over the other men with whom Dickinson is known to have been corresponding. Proximity is exactly what Master does not have.

Although no one knows whether this series of three letters preserved in draft form among Dickinson's papers at the time of her death was sent unaltered, it is obvious that her letters respond to his, as in the first paragraph of number 187, cited above. Had Dickinson made substantial alterations before sending these letters, it is likely that she would have preserved the other drafts. Thus we may assume that what we encounter in Dickinson's drafts is essentially what her correspondent received and that the letters were sent, although this is a much more questionable assumption for the 1862 penciled letter, the most chaotic and least finished of the three.

These letters are a code within a code, and parts of them would have been enigmatic to Master himself. As with many of the other letters we have examined, the impulse toward confession is undercut by the impulse to preserve the emotion that confession would deny. Similarly, the impulse to exteriorize emotion within some action is undercut by the impulse to isolate desire from behavior. The one piece of information Master would have possessed is whether, impulsively, Emily Dickinson at some point in their relationship actualized her desire for sexual experience by seducing him. When, for example, she writes, "I heard of a thing called 'Redemption'—which rested men and women. You remember I asked you for it—you gave me something else," Master might not have known exactly what she meant. He would, however, have known what she could not have meant. His knowledge is not ours. Similarly, when she compares herself to "the little mother—with the big child," remarking, "Thomas' faith in Anatomy, was stronger than his faith in faith," he would have known whether she was or was not attempting to blackmail him by hinting that she might be pregnant: "I did'nt tell you for a long time, but I knew you had altered me—" (L233). Though this seduction scene is unlikely to have occurred, I raise the possibility because, "To a discerning Eye," Dickinson herself implies it. Within this scenario, the experience of sex itself appears to have been pleasurable. What came after was not. She would have liked to perpetuate this liaison and was willing to let Master dictate the terms of their relationship. Either because she had displeased him sexually (her "odd Backwoodsman ways"), or because of his fear of scandal, or because of his guilty conscience, or because of other pressures in his life (or any of the above in any rational combination), he chose after a decent interval to sever their relationship. Improbable? Yes and no. Certainly this is one of the stories her letters imply. Presumably Master is the only person who could attest to its truth or untruth. Hence the zeal of her biographers to discover his identity. Hence Dickinson's zeal to discover her own identity through him, so as to distinguish between an impulse toward heterosexual promiscuity and an impulse toward disaster. Let me now turn to what is more likely to have occurred.

If we know that Master did not live in New England, we also know that they had at least one face-to-face interview:

Oh, did I offend it—[Did'nt it want me to tell it the truth] Daisy—Daisy—offend it—who bends her smaller life to his (it's) meeker (lower) every day—who only asks—a task—[who] something to do for love of it—some little way she cannot guess to make that master glad—

A love so big it scares her, rushing among her small heart—pushing aside the blood and leaving her faint (all) and white in the gust's arm—

Daisy—who never flinched thro' that awful parting, but held her life so tight he should not see the wound—who would have sheltered him in her childish bosom (Heart)—only it was'nt big eno' for a Guest so large—*this* Daisy—grieve her Lord—and yet it (she) often blundered—Perhaps she grieved (grazed) his taste—perhaps her odd—Backwoodsman [life] ways [troubled] teased his finer nature (sense). Daisy [fea] knows all that—but must she go unpardoned—teach her, preceptor grace—teach her majesty—Slow (Dull) at patrician things—Even the wren upon her nest learns (knows) more than Daisy dares—

Low at the knee that bore her once unto [royal] wordless rest [now] Daisy [stoops a] kneels a culprit—tell her her [offence] fault—Master—if it is [not so] small eno' to cancel with her life, [Daisy] she is satisfied—but punish [do not] dont banish her—shut her in prison, Sir—only pledge that you will forgive—sometime—before the grave, and Daisy will not mind—She will awake in [his] your likeness.

Wonder stings me more than the Bee—who did never sting me—but made gay music with his might wherever I [may] [should] did go—Wonder wastes my pound, you said I had no size to spare—

(L248)

We know that he was probably married and that the poet expressed the desire to come to live near him, while also acknowledging that this was not "God's will":

> If it had been God's will that I might breathe where you breathed—and find the place—myself—at night—if I (can) never forget that I am not with you—and that sorrow and frost are nearer than I—if I wish with a might I cannot repress—that mine were the Queen's place—the love of the Plantagenet is my only apology—To come nearer than presbyteries—and nearer than the new Coat—that the Tailor made—the prank of the Heart at play on the Heart—in holy Holiday—is forbidden me—   (L233)

We know that he may have had religious authority:

> Master.
> If you saw a bullet hit a Bird—and he told you he was'nt shot—you might weep at his courtesy, but you would certainly doubt his word.
> One drop more from the gash that stains your Daisy's bosom—then would you *believe*? Thomas' faith in Anatomy, was stronger than his faith in faith. God made me—[Sir] Master—I did'nt be—myself. I dont know how it was done. He built the heart in me—Bye and bye it outgrew me—and like the little mother—with the big child—I got tired holding him. I heard of a thing called "Redemption"—which rested men and women. You remember I asked you for it—you gave me something else. I forgot the Redemption [in the Redeemed—I did'nt tell you for a long time, but I knew you had altered me—I] and was tired—no more—   (L233)

And we know that in a more general sense he was baffled by her:

> You make me say it over—I fear you laugh—when I do not see—[but] "Chillon" is not funny. Have you the Heart in your breast—Sir—is it set like mine—a little to the left—has it the misgiving—if it wake in the night—perchance—itself to it—a timbrel is it—itself to it a tune?
> These things are [reverent] holy, Sir, I touch the [reverently] hallowed, but persons who pray—dare remark [our] "Father"! You say I do not tell you all—Daisy confessed—and denied not.
> Vesuvius dont talk—Etna—dont—[Thy] one of them—said a syllable—a thousand years ago, and Pompeii heard it, and hid forever—She could'nt look the world in the face, afterward—I suppose—Bashfull Pompeii! "Tell you of the want"—you know what a leech is, dont you—and [remember that] Daisy's arm is small—and you have felt the horizon hav'nt you—and did the sea—never come so close as to make you dance?   (L233)

Beyond this, we know that Dickinson sent him some of her poems, or "flowers," and that he had difficulty understanding them:

I wish that I were great, like Mr. Michael Angelo, and could paint for you. You ask me what my flowers said—then they were disobedient—I gave them messages. They said what the lips in the West, say, when the sun goes down, and so says the Dawn.

Listen again, Master. I did not tell you that today had been the Sabbath Day.

Each Sabbath on the Sea, makes me count the Sabbaths, till we meet on shore—and (will the) whether the hills will look as blue as the sailors say. I cannot talk any more (stay any longer) tonight (now), for this pain denies me.

How strong when weak to recollect, and easy, quite, to love. Will you tell me, please to tell me, soon as you are well. (L187)

We know that he had a beard:

I dont know what you can do for it—thank you—Master—but if I had the Beard on my cheek—like you—and you—had Daisy's petals—and you cared so for me—what would become of you? (L233)

We know, in short, that although Master has some of the attributes of an actual person, he exists primarily as a function of Dickinson's need for an eroticized father figure. Fulfilling this need imperfectly, he alleviated even as he intensified her suffering:

Oh how the sailor strains, when his boat is filling—Oh how the dying tug, till the angel comes. Master—open your life wide, and take me in forever, I will never be tired—I will never be noisy when you want to be still. I will be [glad] [as the] your best little girl—nobody else will see me, but you—but that is enough—I shall not want any more—and all that Heaven only will disappoint me—will be because it's not so dear (L248)

Of the men with whom Dickinson is known to have corresponded, the Reverend Charles Wadsworth, pastor of the Arch Street Presbyterian Church in Philadelphia, is the most likely recipient of the "Master" letters. He visited her in Amherst in 1860 and again in 1880. She may have heard him preach in Philadelphia in 1855 on her way home from a visit to Washington, where her father was a one-term congressman. Writing to Sue from Washington on 28 February 1855, she explained, "I have not been well since I came here, and that has excused me from some gaieties, tho' at that, I'm gayer than I was before" (L178). Writing to Mrs. Holland from Philadelphia, she seems mainly concerned lest her friends forget her. As might be expected, there is no mention of Wadsworth:

> Dear Mrs. Holland and Minnie, and Dr. Holland too—I have stolen away from company to write a note to you; and to say that I love you still.
>
> I am not at home—I have been away just five weeks today, and shall not go quite yet back to Massachusetts. Vinnie is with me here, and we have wandered together into many new ways.
>
> We were three weeks in Washington, while father was there, and have been two in Philadelphia. We have had many pleasant times, and seen much that is fair, and heard much that is wonderful—many sweet ladies and noble gentlemen have taken us by the hand and smiled upon us pleasantly—and the sun shines brighter for our way thus far.

After an extended description of a visit to Washington's tomb she remarks:

> I wonder if you have all forgotten us, we have stayed away so long. I hope you haven't—I tried to write so hard before I went from home, but the moments were so busy, and then they *flew* so. I was sure when days *did* come in which I was less busy, I should seek your forgiveness, and it did not occur to me that you might not forgive me. Am I too late today? Even if you are angry, I shall keep praying you, till from very weariness, you will take me in. It seems to me many a day since we were in Springfield, and Minnie and the *dumb-bells* seem as vague—as vague; and sometimes I wonder if I ever dreamed—then if I'm dreaming now, then if I *always* dreamed, and there is not a world, and not these darling friends, for whom I would not count my life too great a sacrifice. Thank God there is a world, and that the friends we love dwell forever and ever in a house above. I fear I grow incongruous, but to meet my friends does delight me so that I quite forget time and sense and so forth. (L179)

Although Dickinson's letters barely mention Wadsworth before his death on 1 April 1882 (the pattern of postmortem revelations is a consistent one), shortly thereafter she wrote Higginson, "My closest earthly friend died in April" (L765). Her romance, following the death of her father, in the late 1870s and early 1880s with Judge Otis Lord, a man seventeen years her senior, had in no way obscured Wadsworth's memory, despite the fact that Lord appears to have made a rejected proposal of marriage. (Although Dickinson's relationship with Lord can be much more conclusively documented than her relationship with Wadsworth because her letters to him survive, it had little direct impact on her art. Most of her love poetry was written before 1867.) To Elizabeth Holland she exclaimed, "the

Death of the Loved is all moments—*now*—Love has but one Date—
'The first of April' 'Today, Yesterday, and Forever'—" (L801). But it
was in correspondence initiated through a gift of his sermons by
Wadsworth's longtime intimate, James D. Clark of Northampton,
that Dickinson provided the most detailed account of their friendship. Calling Wadsworth her "dearest earthly friend," she identified
him as "my Shepherd from 'Little Girl'hood" and referred to an
"intimacy of many years with the beloved Clergyman" (L766). After
James Clark's death in 1883, she continued this correspondence
with his brother Charles. In all, she sent the Clark brothers twenty-
one letters, many of them tributes to Wadsworth.[7] She also invited
both Clark brothers to come to Amherst to speak with her, when
such gregariousness toward strangers was unprecedented for her.
Her letters make it clear that she knew rather little of his personal
life, and never mention his wife at all:

> In an intimacy of many years with the beloved Clergyman, I have
> never before spoken with one [met one] who knew him, and his Life
> was so shy and his tastes so unknown, that grief for him seems almost
> unshared.
> He was my Shepherd from 'Little Girl'hood and I cannot conjec-
> ture a world without him, so noble was he always—so fathomless—so
> gentle.
> I saw him two years since for the last time, though how unsus-
> pected!
> He rang one summer evening to my glad surprise—"Why did you
> not tell me you were coming, so I could have it to hope for," I said—
> "Because I did not know it myself. I stepped from my Pulpit to the
> Train," was his quiet reply. He once remarked in talking "I am liable
> at any time to die," but I thought it no omen. He spoke on a previous
> visit of calling upon you, or perhaps remaining a brief time at your
> Home in Northampton.
> I hope you may tell me all you feel able of that last interview, for
> he spoke with warmth of you as his friend, and please believe that
> your kindness is cherished. (L766)

7. In "After Calvary: The Last Years of Emily Dickinson's 'Dearest Earthly
Friend,'" *Dickinson Studies* 34 (December 1978): 13–18, I examine the factual basis for
her sense of him as a "Man of sorrow." After his return from San Francisco in 1869,
where he was pastor of the Calvary Church, Wadsworth suffered from the ill health
that Ann Douglas, in *The Feminization of American Culture* (New York: Alfred A.
Knopf, 1977), describes as an occupational hazard. In particular, he suffered from a
vocal impediment to which Dickinson refers, obliquely, in her eulogy for him, "The
Spirit lasts—but in what mode—" (1576).

Perhaps Affection has always one question more which it forgot to ask.

I thought it possible you might tell me if our lost one had Brother or Sister.

I knew he once had a Mother, for when he first came to see me, there was Black with his Hat. "Someone has died" I said. "Yes"—he said, "his Mother."

"Did you love her," I asked. He replied with his deep "Yes." I felt too that perhaps you, or the one you confidingly call "Our Charlie," might know if his Children were near him at last, or if they grieved to lose that most sacred Life. Do you know do they resemble him? I hoped that "Willie" might, to whom he clung so tenderly. How irreparable should there be no perpetuation of a nature so treasured! Please forgive the requests which I hope have not wearied you, except as bereavement always wearies.

The sharing a sorrow never lessens, but when a Balm departs, the Plants that nearest grew have a grieved significance and you cherished my friend.   (L773)

It is almost an apparitional joy to hear him cherished now, for I never knew one who knew him.

The Griefs of which you speak were unknown to me, though I knew him a "Man of sorrow," and once when he seemed almost overpowered by a spasm of gloom, I said "You are troubled." Shivering as he spoke, "My Life is full of dark secrets," he said. He never spoke of himself, and encroachment I know would have slain him. He never spoke of his Home, but of a Child—"Willie," whom, forgive me the arrogance, he told me was like me—though I, not knowing "Willie," was benighted still. I am glad you loved him and please to thank your Brother for prizing him so much. He was a Dusk Gem, born of troubled Waters, astray in any Crest below. Heaven might give him Peace, it could not give him Grandeur, for that he carried with himself to whatever scene—

> Obtaining but his own extent
> In whatsoever Realm—
> 'Twas Christ's own personal Expanse
> That bore him from the Tomb.

Thank you for the Face [a photograph of Wadsworth]—which I fear it fatigued you too much to seek—and for the monition, tho' to disclose a grief of his I could not surmise—   (L776)

Although I have argued elsewhere that these ex-post revelations are suspect, these letters have the ring of truth, in part because they acknowledge the narrow boundaries of their verbal intimacy, in part because of the density of their contextual detail. Wadsworth was fifteen years her senior, a married man, a dynamic preacher whose life was never touched with scandal, a man whom the poet is known to have seen privately only twice, since there is no record of a meeting between them in 1855, although such a meeting would not have been unlikely. The Coleman family with whom she was staying were members of his church. If he was the "one more" who "left the Land," and if her "terror—since September" was related to this event, she was either anticipating his departure on 1 May 1862 for the Calvary Church in San Francisco, where he remained until returning to Philadelphia in 1869, or conflating his probable interference, via the mails, in her dream-life with his physical absence.

Only one letter from Wadsworth to Dickinson, its date unknown, her name misspelled, his signature omitted, has survived. He writes as a pastor "distressed beyond measure" by her note describing an affliction whose magnitude he has comprehended but whose specific etiology is to him unknown:

> My Dear Miss Dickenson
>   I am distressed beyond measure at your note, received this moment,—I can only imagine the affliction which has befallen, or is now befalling you.
>   Believe me, be what it may, you have all my sympathy, and my constant, earnest prayers.
>   I am very, very anxious to learn more definitely of your trial—and though I have no right to intrude upon your sorrow yet I beg you to write me, though it be but a word.
>   In great haste
>   Sincerely and most
>   Affectionately *Yours*—   (L248a)

On what then does the case against Wadsworth rest? Extant photographs of him, none dated 1862, show him without a beard. Letter 773 to Clark describes a discussion during Wadsworth's 1860 visit about his mother's death. Yet the second "Master" letter observes, "you did'nt come to me 'in white,' nor ever told me why," a remark which, if it refers to Wadsworth's mourning, is undercut by her recollection of their conversation several decades later. However, unless "Master" is a complete unknown, a dubious possibility given Dickinson's habit of tantalizingly incomplete self-revelation, the pattern of her relationships with other men, including Lord, confirms my belief that if Wadsworth was not the "one more" who "left the

Land," someone very much like him was. Unless future biographical research produces new evidence, we may conclude on the basis of our present knowledge that Wadsworth and "Master" were synonymous but that Dickinson's statement that his departure for California was motivated by his desire to leave her behind is a purely subjective fiction. David Higgins's assertion that Wadsworth cannot have been the muse of her love poems because "There came a Day at Summer's full" (322) describes a summer meeting, whereas Wadsworth's 1860 visit occurred in the early spring, is not to the point.[8] We know that Sue married on 1 July yet "Ourselves were wed one summer—dear—" refers to a June marriage. Data of this sort are trivially uninteresting, for they deny the poet her freedom of invention and are wholly unreliable as a guide to biographical knowledge. What *is* relevant is the pattern of separation and deferred reunion in many of the love poems, together with their religious terminology. Any correspondence or lack of correspondence between the known facts of Dickinson's interaction with Wadsworth in regard to time or place and the temporal or spatial parameters of the poems is not the level of discourse at which we can perceive the psychic unity of Dickinson's self-portraits in prose and in verse.

Let us return now to the questions I posed at the start of this chapter. Was there a lover as distinguished from a figure of pure fantasy? What was the extent of Dickinson's knowledge—physical, emotional, and intellectual—of this person? Was the poet ultimately rejected by him or the other way around, and why? Was Dickinson in love with several men simultaneously? What are the implications of this psychobiographical context for understanding the poems?

Dickinson's love for the Reverend Charles Wadsworth was based on her ideal image of his sexual and religious redemptive powers and was predicated on the unalterable distance between them. There was never any chance that he would divorce his wife to marry her, had such a thing been possible, nor was their contact sufficiently extensive as to make this even a remote possibility. Although she may once have heard him preach and had read some of his published sermons, she knew very little of his personal life. It was not until after the marriage of Austin and Sue and her putative breakdown of 1857 that he took on any special importance to her. When

8. David Higgins, *Portrait of Emily Dickinson: The Poet and Her Prose* (New Brunswick, N.J.: Rutgers University Press, 1967), p. 81.

he began to comprehend the construction she was placing on his solicitous interest in her, his response was to withdraw. He probably embraced her during his 1860 Amherst visit, although her phrase "the knee that bore her once unto [royal] wordless rest" certainly admits another construction. They continued to correspond, perhaps with a significant hiatus beginning in 1862 when he moved to California, until his death twenty years later. If she sent him the third "Master" letter, the hiatus may have been very long indeed. A tradition in the Holland family affirms that they forwarded letters for Dickinson to Philadelphia, but her letters do not refer to this practice until 1876. He made an unannounced call on her in 1880 while he was in New England; although whether his journey was motivated primarily by a desire to see her, again no one knows. He said that she reminded him of his son Willie, his favorite child. Although her complicated inner life and verbal genius must have intrigued him, as it did many of the men with whom she had contact, Wadsworth never reciprocated the passion Dickinson lives out in her art, nor would she have respected him or herself if he had. What she needed was a male figure of unimpeachable personal integrity she could adore from afar, whose physical reality would not encroach on the solitude she had elected to perpetuate the spiritual boldness of her strongest self, while controlling the masculine sexual identification close friendships with women activated. Her friendship with Samuel Bowles was too immediate to be subordinated to her own designs: he was too close to her in age, he was too much a part of New England daily life, his relationships with women were too comradely. Although Dickinson tested out this relationship, sending him love poems and letters he might easily misconstrue and that have been misconstrued by subsequent biographers, she identified with his restless personal life too much to see him as the psychological savior she sought. In 1862 he was himself on the verge of nervous collapse, brought on by compulsive overwork and the complications of his difficult marriage. Wadsworth, with very little doing on his part, fulfilled Dickinson's need for a father figure who was also a forbidden source of erotic experience. His inaccessibility as a lover was the cornerstone of her psychological design, since as "Empress of Calvary" she compensated through her suffering for her solitary pride.

The lover of the poems, then, while in all probability not a figure of pure fantasy, is best understood as an idealized masculine alter ego, a composite of Dickinson's experience of self and world who expresses and distances her ambivalence toward her own femininity. Wadsworth's friendship, which she converted in her art into an unconsummated marriage, enabled her to view "the Girl's life" as a rite of passage into the upper world of redeemed heterosexuality. Whoever "Master" was, this was his primary function.

PART II

The Poems

4

THE BIRTH OF CONSCIOUSNESS:
THE CONSCIOUSNESS OF
EXCLUSION

In the ominous stillness of her recoil from the circumstances within which her muted sexual drama had transpired, Dickinson had begun to transcend nature, or things as they are, through her conception of an all-powerful, yet faithless Master. Another suitor lay in waiting for her when this grandiose conception was insufficiently reinforced by the extravagant fluctuation of her moods. Her vehement desire not to be what George Eliot calls "the world's wife" concealed an arduous truth. At the level of deep structure, marriage was Dickinson's only metaphor for effective union with her world. To resist this trope was to resist the affirmative closure of her own quest for identity and to discover that "supple Suitor," Death, who "wins at last—" (1445). Thus, though her poetry may be, as Richard Howard believes, "the most relentless epic of identity in our literature," David Porter's formulation of this problem is equally astute: "It is the most powerful reflection of dispossession and failed identity in our literature."[1] These two propositions are not, however, mutually exclusive, and this chapter explores some of their intersections. Specifically, it examines some of the ways in which the ambitions of Dickinson's persona are frustrated, together with her response to this frustration. Some of these setting-out texts delineate

1. Richard Howard, "A Consideration of the Writings of Emily Dickinson," *Prose* 6 (Spring 1973): 95–96; David Porter, *Dickinson: The Modern Idiom* (Cambridge: Harvard University Press, 1981), p. 242.

a sexual struggle directly. Others do not. Instead, they develop an attitude toward frustration that exists to some extent independent of social context, an attitude within which this context continues to function, however obliquely, as Dickinson, the "only Prince cast out—" (959), oscillates between her desire to distance herself from an emphatically patriarchal social system and her desire to be legitimized by it. And this too is Dickinson's generative obsession: that which she values in herself is her uniqueness; that which she despises in herself is also her singularity. Consequently, hers is a style within which the force of personality overwhelms the experience of it.

That is, gender as an aspect of Dickinson's style exists most comprehensively within a point of view toward her own ambitions, a point of view within which she has not only failed to gratify her wants, but failed to identify for herself the finite nature of them. This freedom from finite designation coexists, within Dickinson's style, with a remarkable vocabulary of physical and mental limitation.[2] The tension between these two styles suggests that she perceives her immediate environment as an insufficient or actively menacing place, but that she also perceives it as the only comprehensible source of personal gratification. I propose, then, to delineate a Dickinson who rejects her world in order to endorse it, but who also fails to transcend, for any significant duration, her experience of having been rejected by it.

Dickinson's quest for sexual identity was also a quest to free herself from the fact of it. To this end, she developed a poetics in which the goals she sets for herself are often abstractions of her desire for identity rather than representations of the incremental and reciprocal relationships that confer it. These goals represent the resolution to the speaker's experience of privation, homelessness, bereavement, childishness, impotence, and the like. They objectify enabling experiences the speaker is capable of imagining, up to a point. This point is exactly what defines the finity of her vision:

> I've seen a Dying Eye
> Run round and round a Room—
> In search of Something—as it seemed—
> Then Cloudier become—
> And then—obscure with Fog—

2. For a technical study of Dickinson's diction, see William Howard, "Emily Dickinson's Poetic Vocabulary," *PMLA* 72 (March 1957): 225–48.

And then—be soldered down
Without disclosing what it be
'Twere blessed to have seen— (547)

It is perhaps unnecessary to observe that were the world a less threatening place for Dickinson, she would have been less inclined to focus on escaping from it, on dying into eternity, as a radical liberation from her propensity to disease in the root meaning of that word: restlessness, agitation, perpetual motion. Radical dilemmas, however, demand radical solutions. Dickinson's dilemma, as I understand it, was the following. Her ambivalence toward the specific relational opportunities her immediate environment afforded was so thoroughgoing as to have been generalized into an ambivalence toward relationships as such. Withdrawing from the world in order to master both it and herself, "The Battle fought between the Soul / And No Man" was, she discovered, incapable of termination because its origins in that "not familiar Peninsula" (PF2), the unconscious, precluded an adequate definition of the issues over which it was fought. Her theory, derived in part from Emerson, holds that "The Outer—from the Inner / Derives its Magnitude—" (451). Her practice suggests that the converse of this proposition is truer. What Dickinson demonstrates most convincingly is her conclusion that alterations in consciousness depend on some mode of access to altered circumstances. To observe reality, "the Disease / Not even God—can heal—" (744), is to be insufficiently liberated from it.

All poets deeply committed to their craft, one assumes, encounter this difficulty: the need for experience, the need for its suspension in order to contemplate the significance of it. Dickinson encountered this difficulty in a particularly exaggerated form. At some fundamental level of her sensibility, she was convinced that encounters with her world would impede rather than enhance her capacity for growth. Her desire to escape from such bruising encounters forced her into a life in which language sustained her, but it was a sustenance, "a dry Wine," that never appeased her hunger for something beyond it. "The flow of deprived sensation on the quick"[3] was also the flow of her life's blood, that flow in which, she intoned venomously, fastidiously, the impulses to murder and to create threatened to converge:

3. R. P. Blackmur, "Emily Dickinson's Notation," *Kenyon Review* 18 (1956); reprinted in *Emily Dickinson: A Collection of Critical Essays*, ed. Richard B. Sewall (Englewood Cliffs, N.J.: Prentice-Hall, 1963), p. 81.

Sang from the Heart, Sire,
Dipped my Beak in it,
If the Tune drip too much
Have a tint too Red

Pardon the Cochineal—
Suffer the Vermillion—
Death is the Wealth
Of the Poorest Bird.

Bear with the Ballad—
Awkward—faltering—
Death twists the strings—
'Twas'nt my blame—

Pause in your Liturgies—
Wait your Chorals—
While I repeat your
Hallowed name—   (1059)

It would be reassuring to know whether this poem, attributed to the year 1865, was in fact composed in that year when so much of Dickinson's creative energy had already been expended. It would be equally reassuring to know something about the circumstances surrounding its composition: why she felt it necessary at that time to defend both herself and one of her styles, a style of "personal confession, blasphemous and, in its self-revelation, its honesty, almost obscene."[4] This circumstantial ballast is denied us as, in some basic sense, it was denied her. Thus "the vexed question of access to experience, the worst limitation, it is always assumed, that society has imposed upon the woman writer," is vexed continuously in the work of this writer who discovered her poetic identity in her consciousness of exclusion.[5]

Because she is, most profoundly, a hunger-artist, Dickinson's style is most consistently organized by a brilliantly simple, endlessly expandable "I want" formula.[6] In many poems, the speaker argues convincingly that she knows what she wants and cannot get it. These tend to be poems of love and friendship in which her ideal alter ego

4. Allen Tate, "Emily Dickinson," *Collected Essays* (1932); reprinted in *Emily Dickinson*, ed. Sewall, p. 27.

5. Ellen Moers, *Literary Women* (Garden City, N.Y.: Doubleday, 1976), p. 82.

6. Barbara Clarke Mossberg develops this motif in "Reconstruction in the House of Art: Emily Dickinson's 'I Never Had a Mother,'" in *The Lost Tradition: Mothers and Daughters in Literature*, ed. Cathy N. Davidson and E. M. Broner (New York: Ungar, 1980), pp. 128–38.

has withdrawn beyond "Circumference": beyond a measurable time-space which is also a measurable psychological demarcation. In still other poems, Dickinson's dying "I," a self threatened with extinction from without and from within, either acknowledges the terminal obscurity of her vision or seeks to bring her loss to consciousness. In still others, she claims more for herself in the way of perceptual clarity than her texts demonstrate. In its largest dimensions, however, her art depicts a life imperfectly apprehended even by its principal. All of her best poems acknowledge the radical loss of connection to pleasure and the attendant distortions of self-intimacy with which her art begins. Her weakest poems revenge themselves on the reader by hinting that she has a pleasurable secret she will not share. Her spectacular and painterly images of natural beauty notwithstanding, Dickinson has very little of interest to say about a self at home in the world. But if she participates, however obliquely, in the common estrangement of the post-Christian sensibility from a coherent text of natural or social signs, the extremity of her exile from that complex of stable associations she designated "home" inscribes itself throughout her art as an individual doom. Her experience had suggested that essential lessons are transferable, up to a point. This point also defines the superb historicity of her vision: a vision suspicious of lives deprived of the ethical satisfactions of religion, but equally suspicious of the presumptuous formulas fashioned by an intellectual tradition in which woman is other:

> The Grieved—are many—I am told—
> There is the various Cause—
> Death—is but one—and comes but once—
> And only nails the eyes—
>
> There's Grief of Want—and Grief of Cold—
> A sort they call "Despair"—
> There's Banishment from native Eyes—
> In sight of Native Air—
>
> And though I may not guess the kind—
> Correctly—yet to me
> A piercing Comfort it affords
> In passing Calvary—
>
> To note the fashions—of the Cross—
> And how they're mostly worn—
> Still fascinated to presume
> That Some—are like My Own— (561)

What always rings true in Dickinson is her diagnosis of disease: her delineation of emotions that are incoherent and uncontrollable. What sometimes rings less true is her prescription for control.

If Gethsemane is a province "in the Being's Centre," so too is Eden. These two places are not equally explored in Dickinson's poetry. Pleasure is no less real but it is rarer than grief. The anguished balance she establishes between pleasure and pain is bitterly asymmetric. Because of Dickinson's fascination with pain, even her staunchest admirers have difficulty in freeing themselves from the suspicion that hers is a morbid art. Archibald MacLeish, for example, praises her mastery of tone while commenting, "To write constantly of death, of grief, of despair, of agony, of fear is almost to insure the failure of art, for these emotions overwhelm the mind, and art must surmount experience to master it. A morbid art is an imperfect art."[7] Without suggesting, as MacLeish seems to, that Dickinson's is a perfect art, I do wish to suggest that no character can be as obsessed with suffering as the Dickinsonian "I" without getting something out of it. The poem cited below provides a clue as to what:

> For each extatic instant
> We must an anguish pay
> In keen and quivering ratio
> To the extasy.
>
> For each beloved hour
> Sharp pittances of years—
> Bitter contested farthings—
> And Coffers heaped with Tears!   (125)

The cost of pleasure Dickinson conceives is exorbitant. Why is it necessary to pay so much for pleasure? Against whom or what is she competing? In many poems, of course, Dickinson is competing against herself. In still others, she is competing against time and nature. More fundamentally, however, Dickinson is competing against a world that she insistently defines as a male-dominated sphere. Though this world often appears to her ungoverned or governed only by that "dainty Democrat," death, who violates the hopeful aspirations of women and of men with sublime indifference

7. Archibald MacLeish, "The Private World: Poems of Emily Dickinson," *Poetry and Experience* (1961); reprinted in *Emily Dickinson,* ed. Sewall, p. 157.

to a politics of temporality, this world is also governed by a Father-God whose stinginess is equaled only by her determination to outwit him by withholding her assent from the world which He has created. The price of pleasure Dickinson both consciously and unconsciously refuses to pay involves a capitulation to this character who, when he is not an actively menacing presence, is a trivial one:

> I know that He exists.   (338)
>
> I asked no other thing—   (621)

There are a number of ways in which the persona can be reunited with this character. One of them would be to request something inconsequential. This she never does, since her tactics are designed, in part, to test his resoluteness. As a good capitalist, she believes that conflict is energizing. Moreover, she is not interested in a shared hegemony of power. She wants to topple her "Mighty Merchant" from his throne, the world. One of the difficulties she encounters, however, is that he seems oblivious to her presence except in her hours of greatest need which also coincide, of course, with her desire to effect a truce with him:

> Of Course—I prayed—
> And did God Care?
> He cared as much as on the Air
> A Bird—had stamped her foot—
> And cried "Give Me"   (376)

Still another difficulty she encounters is that this character seems to have singled her out for exceptional misfortune:

> God gave a Loaf to every Bird—
> But just a Crumb—to Me—   (791)

There is, however, one way, and a very effective way at that, in which Dickinson can circumvent the authority of her Father-God, and that is to withdraw from his sphere, the world, into hers, an interior world which, though it appears ungoverned and erratic, is in fact governed by her internalization and neutralization of his power. Observing her exclusion from a politics of temporality, Dickinson also records her indifference to it:

I'm Nobody! Who are you?   (288)

Still another way in which Dickinson's persona can neutralize his power is to die. Since the dead are incapable of being disappointed or defeated, this temptation is a very powerful one in Dickinson's poetry, particularly in poems that work close to the edge of her sense of biographical, rather than metaphysical homelessness. This struggle is further intensified by the fact that "No Great Mother archetype underlies Dickinson's poetic vision."[8] Suffering—conflict with her world—both links Dickinson to this advocate of the strenuous life and enables her to perpetuate her own will-to-power. What this scheme does not permit is the expression of this aggression within finite historical relationships, since such relationships will necessarily diffuse her antagonism toward him, an antagonism that is the obverse of love. Though Dickinson's is a multifaceted sensibility and no single conflict can include the totality of her experience, some such struggle with her archetype of male governance constitutes the basic obsession of her psyche and of her art: an art without an ending because it is rooted in an inconsistent set of psychological attitudes toward a precursor-text which is always fragmented, occasionally ignored, and often suppressed.

I have suggested that Dickinson perceives the expression of pleasure as a capitulation to the Father. To suffer injustice is her métier. To inflict it through attention or inattention is his. In certain moods, Dickinson wishes to resolve this warfare. In others, she does not. Both to resolve this conflict and to defer its resolution, her persona tends to set herself consistently inaccessible goals, which can at best be realized only sporadically, spasmodically, imperfectly. Probably no other aspect of her sensibility is more difficult to comprehend. Probably no other aspect of her sensibility caused her more difficulty in living.

Gender as an aspect of style also manifests itself in Dickinson's determination to isolate the workings of a composite mind from the specific manifestations of personality. And so, with some justification, Jonathan Morse calls her "the poet of the contentless an-

8. Nina Baym, "God, Father, and Lover in Emily Dickinson's Poetry," in *Puritan Influences in American Literature*, ed. Emory Elliott (Urbana: University of Illinois Press, 1979), p. 198. She observes that "in Dickinson's poetry the mother does not have the nurturing function; the father does."

guish."[9] She might with equal justification be called the poet of the contentless pleasure:

> Come slowly—Eden!—
> Lips unused to Thee—
> Bashful—sip they Jessamines—
> As the fainting Bee—
>
> Reaching late his flower,
> Round her chamber hums—
> Counts his nectars—
> Enters—and is lost in Balms. (211)

Both of these statements are, however, overstatements, since even Dickinson's "impersonal" poems imply a prior context of first-person experience. Rereading this poem within that context, we observe that "Eden" signifies the intense pleasure released by an unaccustomed visitation. Depicting this visitation, Dickinson sexualizes it; sexualizing it, she depicts a loss of self-confidence which is beautifully controlled by the flower-bee analogy. This analogy simultaneously screens her from her sexual anxiety and perpetuates it within a paradoxical attitude toward resolutions that are both desired and feared: feared because they are unknown, unknown because they are feared. Building on her anxiety of gender, Dickinson achieves an insight into the relationship between the quality of an experience and the duration of it. This sexualized imagination of alteration, an imagination of excess activated by her experience of want, remains a continuous problem for her, though not for us as readers of this text.

Evidently Dickinson's experience of human relationships had engendered in her a lack of clarity about the historical uses of her own will-to-power. What she made of this lack of clarity was a poetry that both analyzes her ambivalence toward power and, when it fails, reflects it. To this extent, then, Dickinson is, as Clark Griffith implies, a sexist writer.[10] Caricaturing physical power as a male prerogative, Dickinson resists it. Resisting physical power, she also resists her

9. Jonathan Morse, "Memory, Desire, and the Need for Biography: The Case of Emily Dickinson," *Georgia Review* 35 (Summer 1981): 259.
10. Clark Griffith, *The Long Shadow: Emily Dickinson's Tragic Poetry* (Princeton: Princeton University Press, 1964).

imagination of the historical relationships in which physical power, allied with spirit and directed toward a specific end, manifests itself. Thus she could state, in 1870, "I find ecstasy in living—the mere sense of living is joy enough" (L342a). Thus she could write, in about 1863,

> To be alive—is Power—
> Existence—in itself—
> Without a further function—
> Omnipotence—Enough—
>
> To be alive—and Will!
> 'Tis able as a God—
> The Maker—of Ourselves—be what—
> Such being Finitude!   (677)

In an alternate version, the word "Maker" reads "Further." The extension of ourselves, its further development, is infinite. But so too is life "Without a further function," without the need for action. Dickinson catches the self in the process of escaping from this need. "Consistent in her concerns but inconsistent in her attitudes," she concerns herself consistently with this state in which the self is both freed from the need for experience and incapable of it.[11] She also concerns herself with a prior time, as in this poem where a naive speaker sets out to explore her opportunities for adventure:

> I started Early—Took my Dog—
> And visited the Sea—
> The Mermaids in the Basement
> Came out to look at me—
>
> And Frigates—in the Upper Floor
> Extended Hempen Hands—
> Presuming Me to be a Mouse—
> Aground—upon the Sands—
>
> But no Man moved Me—till the' Tide
> Went past my simple Shoe—
> And past my Apron—and my Belt
> And past my Boddice—too—
>
> And made as He would eat me up—

11. Richard Wilbur, "'Sumptuous Destitution,'" *Emily Dickinson: Three Views* (1960); reprinted in *Emily Dickinson*, ed. Sewall, p. 128.

As wholly as a Dew
Upon a Dandelion's Sleeve—
And then—I started—too—

And He—He followed—close behind—
I felt His Silver Heel
Upon my Ancle—Then my Shoes
Would overflow with Pearl—

Until We met the Solid Town—
No One He seemed to know—
And bowing—with a Mighty look—
At me—The Sea withdrew—   (520)

This text recapitulates one of Dickinson's basic plots. An inexperienced heroine ventures confidently into the world, only to discover that the world is a man and that "His Requirement[s]" include the negation of her power over him. Unwilling to submit to his disguised yet callous demands, she withdraws from his presence. This resolution of her status anxieties depends on the suppression of her sexual appetites, so that her victory remains a partial one.

In this deceptively straightforward tale a young girl of indeterminate age, accompanied by her dog, visits the sea. She is encouraged by a magical audience of mermaids and partially personified frigates, but does not pause to examine her response to their presence. Her self-consciousness is thus attributed to them; they are intelligent and empathetic. Feeling and intellection are parceled out to them, suggesting, on a second reading, that it may be useful to understand the audience as the bearers of her withheld response. The central action involves an encounter between the blank-faced speaker and the sea personified, beginning with the third stanza, as a man. The water moves progressively past her shoe, her apron, her belt, and her bodice, until she almost drowns. During her retreat to the shore, she feels the receding water on her ankle and in her shoe. Finally, having been bested by her, the sea withdraws with a deferential bow toward a worthy antagonist.

Although her flight clearly dramatizes her fear of drowning, the speaker does not comment on her dalliance with danger once the action is completed. Like Alice in Wonderland, Dickinson's speaker encounters the extraordinary without herself appearing to be psychologically altered by it. Her quasiallegorical seascape permits innocence to be tested and to emerge intact. What sort of innocence the speaker has salvaged for herself warrants closer examination and turns primarily on the meaning one gives to the sea.

Four major systems of symbolism have been suggested, all of them appropriate to the action, none of them excluding the others: death, nature, sex, the unconscious.[12] Since nature is represented as death and the unconscious portrayed through its erotic desires and inhibitions, we can reduce this system of four to two. The sea represents both sex and death, eroticized thanatos and thanatized eros. Thus this opportunity for sexual development also forecloses the possibility of it.

If one limits the sea's meaning to death alone, then the speaker makes a life-affirming choice in refusing to be devoured by it. If one limits the sea's meaning to male sexuality, then the speaker resists that contact with a foreign nature which might initiate her into its mysteries. Because the sea represents both positive and negative values, the poem has the moral ambiguity of a dream. A secondary level of symbolism equating the sea with a house, Dickinson's habitual emblem of the self, suggests that the comparison with Alice's dream vision of her inner world is again relevant here. Each of the strange creatures Dickinson's speaker observes implicates her in a discovery of identity she cannot accept as her own. Specifically, this speaker wishes not to discover her eroticism, which implicates her in the discovery of her mortality. For reasons both comprehensible and mysterious, Dickinson often conflates these two discoveries.

Projecting her sexuality onto a lascivious male stranger apparently intent on violating her, the perception she attributes to the frigates, that she is "a Mouse / Aground—upon the Sands," is an expression of the grotesque indeterminacy of her stunted eroticism. Neither out far nor in deep, on the sands, she makes the extraordinary statement, "But no Man moved Me," as though a hidden voice had suggested the lure of the male siren song which she initially encour-

---

12. In "Emily Dickinson and the Limits of Judgment," in *In Defense of Reason* (1938), Yvor Winters writes, "The sea is here the traditional symbol of death; that is, of all the forces and qualities in nature and in human nature which tend toward the dissolution of human character and consciousness." Reprinted in *Emily Dickinson*, ed. Sewall, p. 30. In *Long Shadow*, pp. 18–24, Griffith equates the sea with male sexuality, itself symbolic of the savage and terrifying in nature. In *After Great Pain: The Inner Life of Emily Dickinson* (Cambridge: Harvard University Press, 1971), pp. 306–07, John Cody, pursuing the Freudian implications of Griffith's commentary, identifies the sea as the unconscious, a suggestion implicit in Winters's reference to "qualities in . . . human nature which tend toward the dissolution of human character and consciousness."

ages and then resists. This utterance, "But no Man moved Me," is contextually unmotivated. It also explains the motive behind her journey. The poem dramatizes the ambivalence of a self divided between the desire for sexual experience and the determination to resist its ego-annihilating potential. Although the speaker reaffirms her allegiance to the "Solid Town," this reaffirmation occurs only after she cunningly expresses her instinctive erotic aggression. The language of the penultimate stanza ("I felt His Silver Heel / Upon my Ancle—Then my Shoes / Would overflow with Pearl—") with its especially tricky conditional verb, preceded by the word "Then," causes us to think of an orgasm which may or may not have occurred but which is accessible to consciousness only as a symbolically disguised event. If her orgasm has occurred, the pleasure associated with it is repressed as soon as it is experienced. If it is about to occur, she succeeds in turning off the sensations that are about to erupt into consciousness. While the poet unconsciously identifies herself with all the characters, including the mermaids who may represent the mysteriousness of female fantasy—a strikingly withheld aspect of the speaker's character—the child persona is intent on sustaining a remarkable detachment toward her own responses. And so she tells her story without seeming to grasp its meaning.

Like the rest of us, Dickinson's character operates on the basis of imperfect knowledge and finds herself compelled to make choices for which her experience has left her inadequately prepared. Nevertheless, at the heart of the poem's insight into the relationship between risk and maturation lies a thanatized vision of love and an eroticized vision of death, a blinding vision of powerful mystery which she cannot simultaneously experience and tell. In the end, whether the sea represents the persona's repressed sexual aggression projected onto a lascivious male universe or whether the sea is genuinely shaped as male otherness matters little. What is important here is that the *probable* outcome of this aborted struggle is refracted through the lens of the speaker-poet's history, of the life she has known, and of the finite outcomes she has observed. Encountering the "man of noon," the sun god in his watery habitat, Dickinson shapes a contest her childlike persona has no chance of winning in frontal combat. Given this shrewdly politicized sensibility of unequal sexual and natural odds, what she represents here is necessarily a victory of caution over daring. "The shore is safer . . . but I love to buffet the sea" (L39), Dickinson had written to a friend in her nineteenth year. But by 1862, when she composed her seascape, she had been further schooled in the need for renunciation, that "piercing Virtue," lest the "Wild Nights" of which she dreamed drown her voice in pearly silence.

Because Dickinson tends to project her socially conditioned sexual anxieties into her imagination of nature, her access to socially un-conditioned natural relationships usually turns out to be no access at all. Despite her well-known saying, "nature is a stranger yet" (1400), one seldom has the sense in Dickinson that any nature other than her own is a mystery to her. "The fairer—for the farness— / And for the foreignhood" (719), nature's strangeness depends on her ability to withdraw herself from it, either physically or psychologically:

> To pity those that know her not
> Is helped by the regret
> That those who know her, know her less
> The nearer her they get.   (1400)

Close-up, nature's mystery vanishes, as its uniquely potent sexual threat is fatally inscribed. Thus her problem, her lack of access to empowering social or natural relationships, is perpetuated by its solution. The sexual attitudes that cause Dickinson to isolate herself also cause her to view herself as having been deserted. There are some splendid moments when she is able to turn this desertion to her advantage. "Because in going is a Drama / Staying cannot confer," she would "rather recollect a setting / Than own a rising sun" (1349). There are other times when she accuses herself of cowardice, as she withdraws from emblematic male powers who, like her sea, are subtle devourers of naive women; but this accusation is easier to bear than a resounding defeat at the hands of someone else.

In nature and in society, men and women are unequal. Once physical and psychological barriers are erected between the self and its world, human nature—the only nature Dickinson is genuinely interested in—becomes less predictable. If its natural social ambitions are thwarted, the female psyche may be enriched by its fantasies of power and by its liberation from a man's inauthentic or overwhelming "Requirement[s]." It may also become the prey of a stranger within: "One need not be a Chamber—to be Haunted—" (670).

In many poems, however, Dickinson claims to have shed her social

identity, together with its attendant sexual anxieties. These claims
are believable, up to a point. Again, this point defines the superb
historicity of her vision:

> I'm ceded—I've stopped being Their's—
> The name They dropped upon my face
> With water, in the country church
> Is finished using, now,
> And They can put it with my Dolls,
> My childhood, and the string of spools,
> I've finished threading—too—
>
> Baptized, before, without the choice,
> But this time, consciously, of Grace—
> Unto supremest name—
> Called to my Full—The Crescent dropped—
> Existence's whole Arc, filled up,
> With one small Diadem.
>
> My second Rank—too small the first—
> Crowned—Crowing—on my Father's breast—
> A half unconscious Queen—
> But this time—Adequate—Erect,
> With Will to choose, or to reject,
> And I choose, just a Crown—   (508)

Casting a cold eye on the infantilizing social forces that made
"perpetual childhood" one of the "careers open to women" in the
nineteenth century, or so Richard Chase would have it, the speaker
declares that she has "ceded" her childlike social self, that she has
yielded it up or, alternatively, that she has "seceded" from the small
rural society she evokes so economically through the countrified
imagery of baptism.[13] The poem is most obviously structured
around a comparison between a mature and an immature self and
expressed through the conceits of a double baptism. The speaker
says she has renounced her former self and acquired a new sense of
who she is and what she is about and I believe her, for you do not
renounce an old life this firmly without having acquired a new one.
Or do you, if you are Emily Dickinson? Most discussions of this
poem have attempted to expand the central symbol of newfound
selfhood, the diadem or crown the regal speaker confers upon her-

---

13. Richard Chase, *Emily Dickinson* (New York: William Sloane, 1951), pp. 93–94.

self, so that it refers to some enabling rite of passage the poem recapitulates.[14] Religious conversion, marriage, or artistic creation seem to me to exhaust the possibilities, and I shall examine each of them shortly. The poem presents no other significant problems of interpretation and is indeed a model of clarity in describing the false and incomplete self the speaker rejects. Leaving behind her childhood as emphatically as she abandons her dolls and the repetitive tasks of her girlhood, she also abandons the name, emblematic of an inherited identity, imposed upon her when her status and her comfort depended on her relationship to her father and the larger society he represents. The contrast between the baptism conferred upon her and the baptism she confers upon herself, between her biological birth and her birth into consciousness, rings with the confidence of unconflicted self-definition. The essential difference Dickinson posits between childhood and maturity is an awareness of competing systems of value and an ability to choose decisively between them. Beyond God the Father, beyond the human father, beyond the patriarchal society from which she boasts of her secession, there lies a fully feminine nature represented by a series of circles: the toy spools of childhood, the crescent or partial moon of girlhood, and finally the completed arc, the diadem or crown of womanhood. What, then, is the crown? To what experience does it allude? And why is it "*just* a Crown—" (italics mine)? Why is there some suggestion, however distant, of anticlimax in the concluding phrase?

One's first impulse on coming up against this kind of precise imprecision with which Dickinson's poetry abounds is to assume that "Crown" is a private symbol and to examine other poems for its associations.[15] Crowns and other royal tropes are easy to find, less easy to restrict within a context of either secular history or sacred antihistory, since many of her poems work to reconcile this antagonism, as does "I'm ceded." The association of baptism and coronation, coronation and salvation was endemic to the neo-Calvinist religious culture on which Dickinson drew so extensively for her

14. For a summary of this extensive commentary, see Joseph Duchac's useful bibliographical tool, *The Poems of Emily Dickinson: An Annotated Guide to Commentary Published in English, 1890–1977* (Boston: G. K. Hall, 1979), pp. 275–77.

15. For an elegant analysis of Dickinsonian metonymy, a relationship of contiguity rather than metaphorical equivalence in which "the specific referent can not be found in the text," see Roland Hagenbüchle, "Precision and Indeterminacy in the Poetry of Emily Dickinson," *ESQ: A Journal of the American Renaissance* 20 (First Quarter 1974): 33–56.

vocabulary of personal power, but the absence of either a God or a bridegroom figure makes it difficult to read this poem as depicting a marriage between a female self and a male other. Thus, although Dickinson rarely employs this royal imagery to identify herself as an artist, there is some merit in considering the possibility that her "Crown" represents her art. The poet-heroine of Elizabeth Barrett Browning's *Aurora Leigh*, for example, crowns herself with an ivy wreath on her twentieth birthday, and this scene may be embedded in Dickinson's poem. Unlike Aurora, however, who is secretly observed by her cousin Romney as she contends that " 'The worthiest poets have remained uncrowned / Till death has bleached their foreheads to the bone' " (2:28–29), Dickinson has no audience beyond herself.[16] Her sensibility need not manifest itself in tangible forms such as poems and remains suspended above the demonstrable feats it might perform. Why not say, then, that we have here a Dickinsonian version of Emersonian self-reliance ("Nothing is at last sacred but the integrity of your own mind") with an important proviso:

> What I must do is all that concerns me, not what the people think. This rule, equally arduous in actual and in intellectual life, may serve for the whole distinction between greatness and meanness. It is the harder because you will always find those who think they know what is your duty better than you know it. It is easy in the world to live after the world's opinion; it is easy in solitude to live after our own; but the great man is he who in the midst of the crowd keeps with perfect sweetness the independence of solitude.[17]

Within Dickinson's poem, preserving one's independence "in the midst of the crowd" is impossible. The tone is not one of "perfect sweetness" but of controlled anger toward those others against whose strength she measures her own. For the great woman, strategic withdrawal is essential.

The difficulty with this line of interpretation, which has considerable appeal, is the crown symbolism itself, together with the associated concept of "Rank." Is Dickinson denying the validity of hierarchical orderings even as she lays claim to their organizing properties? Is she

16. See Elizabeth Barrett Browning, *The Poetical Works of Elizabeth Barrett Browning* (Boston: Houghton Mifflin, 1974), p. 241.

17. "Self-Reliance," in *The Complete Works of Ralph Waldo Emerson*, ed. Edward Waldo Emerson, 12 vols. (Boston: Houghton Mifflin, 1903–04), 2: 53–54.

endorsing an egalitarian ethic of self-reliance within her neo-Calvinist vocabulary of spiritual aristocracy and, if so, to what end? If we expand this crown symbolism so that it reenters a religious, social, or literary context, we misconstrue its contextual abstraction. Nevertheless, crowns come from somewhere; they are handed down and passed on; they are artifacts, not socially unconditioned natural signs.

This totemistic object either partially veils the experience signified or points to nothing beyond itself. Let us consider this latter possibility first, that we are being asked to consider the exclusive function of the symbol within the poem. In that case, the poem itself is the enabling experience. The speaker's transformation is being demonstrated in the saying. The poem is its own cause. A word can both free itself from its traditional associations and gather to itself that which has been renounced. A word can preserve the aura, the atmosphere, the style of the associated life while simultaneously excluding its conformist pressures. The difficulty with this reading is that it suggests that Dickinson is engaged in a kind of word magic. Intelligible language has some referential function. Poems both create experiences and allude to them. Thus, while this possibility cannot be wholly renounced (that the speaker is discovering who she is in the process of saying the poem), neither can it be wholly endorsed.

Moreover, this language-centered explanation is too abstruse to capture the full flavor of the poem's tonal range. It emphasizes what has already happened; it is downright and blunt; the abrupt rhythms do not reflect a mood of unbounded reverie but suggest a consciousness of some sharply bounded choice. Although the final choice ("And I choose, just a Crown—") is cast in the present tense, it would be overingenious to suggest that this choice is made as the poem unfolds. What is being described is a present past, a choice that has been made and that is as alive as it was at its inception: "Called to my Full—The Crescent dropped— / Existence's whole Arc, filled up, / With one small Diadem." This call may have been emitted by the speaker's self-reliant muse, but Dickinson's phrase arouses our curiosity about the source of her calling. Insofar as a source is named, the prepositional phrase "of Grace" in stanza two identifies it; however, the preposition "of" rather than "by" loosens this connection between the speaker's calling and the name, "Grace," that designates its origin. If the poem is specifically about religious grace or a *hieros gamos,* a holy marriage, it is underdetermined. If it is about a human marriage, it is unconvincing.

Many of Dickinson's poems allude to equally mystifying achievements. Some readers will therefore continue to expect her biographers to elucidate them. Nevertheless, there are two questions at issue: what experience enabled Dickinson to write such a poem and what experience prevented her from completing it. The visionary consciousness she celebrates claims more for itself than it can demonstrate. Her crown symbol remains somewhat obscure because her experience has provided no models of the marriage she wishes to effect between masculinity and femininity without sacrificing the competing claims of either party. The experience to which this poem builds is thus inconceivable; her desire for this experience is wonderfully palpable. Her "Full[fillment]" maximizes the positive aspect of her relationship to patriarchal tradition while expunging its negative component. Consequently, it is even more tempting to link this poem to the experience that often enabled Dickinson to control her social anxieties, the experience of language.

This temptation is worth resisting. Dickinson's achievement as an autobiographical poet privileges her experience as an exceptional woman, rather than her status as a poet working within an established tradition. Nor is it primarily as a poet that Dickinson wishes to be understood, either within this poem or within her work as a whole. Instead, she wishes to be understood as a woman in quest of a vocation: a woman unable to translate her vocation—"ecstasy"—into a more limited experience of it. The poem has fully satisfied many readers, however, because its stylistic incompletion arouses our curiosity about the presumably denser context of the poet's life. "To disappear enhances—" (1209).

From the beginning, then, an unresolved tension informs the Dickinsonian sensibility. The world is both the place from which she escapes in order to preserve her hopeful style and the place she wishes to reenter in order to gratify her thirst for experience. This tension is only partially resolved by her insistence that insight and experience can never be compelled to coalesce. Progress is also loss:

> Eden is that old-fashioned House
> We dwell in every day
> Without suspecting our abode
> Until we drive away   (1657)

While this theory of perception has a certain logical coherence, the felt life on which her poetry thrives has been driven from it.

As an idealist, Dickinson is a cynic in disguise. Her critique of patriarchal history depends on her ability to distance herself from it. Though this distance enables her to affirm the integrity of her ego in a universe in which fathers rather than mothers negotiate between their daughters and the world, this defensive posture also prevents her from fulfilling her quest for a self. As a realist, however, Dickinson wished to discover the art of the possible. One possibility she discovered was a psychodynamics of desire in which pleasure is enhanced by a prior context of frustration. If she could believe in this internal system of inhibition and release, she might, under some circumstances, be able to call her privation good:

> Tho' I get home how late—how late—
> So I get home—'twill compensate—
> Better will be the Extasy
> That they have done expecting me—
> When Night—descending—dumb—and dark—
> They hear my unexpected knock—
> Transporting must the moment be—
> Brewed from decades of Agony!
>
> To think just how the fire will burn—
> Just how long-cheated eyes will turn—
> To wonder what myself will say,
> And what itself, will say to me—
> Beguiles the Centuries of way! (207)

Dickinson is interested in this sequence both as it manifests itself in her own life and as a law of human nature. To the extent that she has a world view, it consists in the proposition that pleasure is enhanced by a previous experience of pain. Pain, she wishes to believe, has an ethical function. Order emerges out of disorder, ecstasy out of agony. Conflict is energizing. In many poems, the proposition that "Defeat—whets Victory—" is presented as a Christian-derived cultural cliché unconfirmed by her prior experience. Nevertheless, her immediate experience is organized by her attempt to understand it:

> Defeat—whets Victory—they say—
> The Reefs—in old Gethsemane—
> Endear the Coast—beyond!
> 'Tis Beggars—Banquets—can define—
> 'Tis Parching—vitalizes Wine—
> "Faith" bleats—to understand! (313)

Similarly, in the perfect poem "Success," Dickinson initially endorses this compensatory justification of historical powerlessness before she permits the fury of her indignation to be heard:

> Success is counted sweetest
> By those who ne'er succeed.
> To comprehend a nectar
> Requires sorest need.
>
> Not one of all the purple Host
> Who took the Flag today
> Can tell the definition
> So clear of Victory
>
> As he defeated—dying—
> On whose forbidden ear
> The distant strains of triumph
> Burst agonized and clear! (67)

Dickinson saw that this formula for pleasure could be perverted into a formula for despair. Yet what "they say" was also what she had been telling herself for years and what, in one form or another, she continued intermittently to tell herself to the very end. The Dickinson canon is rife with poems asserting that the have-nots know how to value better than the haves, that those deprived of experiential pleasure compensate through an imagination of gratified desire for experience which, if accessible, might, would, or should prove disappointing. The vehemence with which she pursued this proposition that privation has an ethical function, the vehemence with which she exploded it, derives in part from her sense that, in a hostile universe, emphatically qualified pleasure is better than no pleasure at all. Moreover, Dickinson feared that her unwillingness to compromise with her world was not a sign of strength but of weakness. Her unwillingness to compromise was, she feared, an inability to do so, or to compromise the competing attitudes she perceived within herself toward religious faith, for example, toward a literary career, and toward sexual experience. As Gilbert and Gubar have shown, other women poets of the nineteenth century endorsed an esthetic of renunciation "as necessity's highest and noblest virtue."[18] As Dickinson shows, this esthetic is precariously poised between self-affirmation and self-destruction.

18. Sandra M. Gilbert and Susan Gubar, "The Aesthetics of Renunciation," *The Madwoman in the Attic: The Woman Writer and the Nineteenth-Century Literary Imagination* (New Haven: Yale University Press, 1979), p. 564.

If we observe that rarely in her poems does she describe a vital externalized relationship, since what activates her is not correspondingly activated by her, Dickinson remarks on this fact as well. Repelling her world, she is also repelled by it. Nevertheless, she is too self-aware not to realize that she may be the dupe of her desire for desire. Asserting that " 'Heaven'—is what I cannot reach! / The Apple on the Tree— / Provided it do hopeless—hang— / That— 'Heaven' is—to Me!" (239), Dickinson conducts a running debate with herself throughout her poetry about her need to reject the possible by coveting the unattainable. Thus she asserts

> Undue Significance a starving man attaches
> To Food—
> Far off—He sighs—and therefore—Hopeless—
> And therefore—Good—
>
> Partaken—it relieves—indeed—
> But proves us
> That Spices fly
> In the Receipt—It was the Distance—
> Was Savory—   (439)

Within most poems, however, this experience of partaking is denied her. As a consequence, the reality principle invoked above is inhibited, and consciousness is correspondingly distorted. When Dickinson insists that fantasy is the only fulfillment, decadence threatens to invade her world. Typically, she wards off this implied loss of life-hunger by insisting on the pleasures, sometimes the universalized pleasures, of the antithetical imagination:

> Who never wanted—maddest Joy
> Remains to him unknown—
> The Banquet of Abstemiousness
> Defaces that of Wine—
>
> Within it's reach, though yet ungrasped
> Desire's perfect Goal—
> No nearer—lest the Actual—
> Should disenthrall thy soul—   (1430)

The setting is formal: a banquet for one. "Abstemiousness" serves as food and drink and is superior in its ability to confer pleasure to Wine, which represents any tangible physical substance. The chastened abstraction "Abstemiousness," following a sequence that prepares for the introduction of some actual food or drink, startles the reader into attending closely to what follows. The image itself brings the banquet tantalizingly near, then whisks it away. The imagery in the second stanza where Desire, another abstraction, grasps like a hand, again brings the material world up close, yet distances it. The second stanza indicates that life's banquet is to remain untouched, except by the imagination. This notion that anticipated gratification is always superior to the achievement of it is the most limited aspect of Dickinson's ethic of "sumptuous Destitution" and one that her poetry as a whole, in its concern for preserving and gratifying the urgent thirsts and hungers of the social self, refuses to accept.[19] Having established a psychological law in this representative poem, which in effect posits an absolute cleavage between experience and the imagination of it, Dickinson predictably violates the tenets of this rigid dualism when she explores the internal consequences of privation with greater particularity, as we have already observed. Though her "Banquet of Abstemiousness" praises the power to take while cautioning against the act of taking, the pressure of that which has been renounced pushes against the text. Renouncing boredom, Dickinson's speaker also renounces any meaningful conception of progress. What she praises is the power of the exceptional beginning.

Dickinson's analysis of involuntary self-denial is even more persuasive than her analysis of deliberate abstinence, and some of her most brilliant poems describe the transformation of rational responses into phobias. For example, in "I had been hungry, all the Years—" (579) prolonged starvation at first enhances her appetite.

19. Although virtually all book-length studies of Dickinson's poetry have explored this theme, Wilbur's 1960 essay, cited earlier, has stood the test of time particularly well. He writes that "the creature of appetite . . . pursues satisfaction, and strives to possess the object in itself; it cannot imagine the vaster economy of desire, in which the pain of abstinence is justified by moments of infinite joy, and the object is spiritually possessed, not merely for itself, but more truly as an index of the All" (p. 133). Wilbur has, however, more faith than most critics, including myself, in the extent to which Dickinson's election of an "economy of desire" enabled her to call her "privation good." For some of my earlier speculations on the interrupted cycle of privation, self-privation, and attempted self-reliance her poetry incorporates as influenced by the sexual politics of her age, see "Thirst and Starvation in Emily Dickinson's Poetry," *American Literature* 51 (March 1979): 33–49, where I suggest that the ethic of abstinence Dickinson came to employ grew out of the cultural tensions she shared with the women of her generation.

Eventually, however, she discovers that her malnourishment has generated powerful internal inhibitions. The nominal object of her desire, "food," can no longer compete with her imagination of it. As her metaphor suggests, her situation is untenable; no one can live without eating. Dickinson dines on the discovery of her anorexia and sustains herself on her witty self-diagnosis:

> I had been hungry, all the Years—
> My Noon had Come—to dine—
> I trembling drew the Table near—
> And touched the Curious Wine—
>
> 'Twas this on Tables I had seen—
> When turning, hungry, Home
> I looked in Windows, for the Wealth
> I could not hope—for Mine—
>
> I did not know the ample Bread—
> 'Twas so unlike the Crumb
> The Birds and I, had often shared
> In Nature's—Dining Room—
>
> The Plenty hurt me—'twas so new—
> Myself felt ill—and odd—
> As Berry—of a Mountain Bush—
> Transplanted—to the Road—
>
> Nor was I hungry—so I found
> That Hunger—was a way
> Of Persons outside Windows—
> The Entering—takes away—

After years of unsatisfied hunger, the speaker's "Noon" has come "to dine." Either because of her diligence or because of a miracle— the syntax obscures whether she has come to it or it has come to her—the moment she has been enlarging is before her. She had imagined this opportunity often enough as she stared into opulent houses where people were apparently feasting and now believes that she has purchased the privilege of consumption through her social ostracization. Trembling with eagerness, she approaches the table and merely touches its strange wine. Having anticipated some ultimate communion, her reaction startles her: she feels awkward, over-burdened, maimed. Comparing herself to a berry transplanted from a secluded mountain bush to a public highway, she implies that such dislocations can be fatal. Having been exiled from human society and reduced to the company of birds, she has grown accustomed to crumbs; "ample Bread" overwhelms her. The self has been so completely defined by its starvation that food threatens to destroy it. Thus she suppresses her compulsion to eat in order to survive, restraining herself after a parsimonious world has ceased to do so. Ironically, however, Dickinson concludes that external barriers perpetuate the appetites they inhibit. When such barriers vanish, phobias that enable the self to order its experience may be viewed as life-enhancing.

Taking an even closer look at the adjustment she has made to a life in which the possibility of disappointment barely exists, since her ambitions almost coincide with the shrunken parameters of her world, Dickinson demonstrates the stages by which "A Prison gets to be a friend." At first she contends that memory still has the power to liberate her from "this Phantasm Steel," or at least that memory functions to remind her of what liberty was. But by the end of the poem, which is structured around a single extended analogy between external and internal inhibition, she is avoiding any pleasurable recall of the past, because she has transferred her allegiance from joy to despair. The concluding lines, with their swift escape into the future, expand and then contract the residual hopefulness of her self-conception:

> A Prison gets to be a friend—
> Between it's Ponderous face
> And Our's—a Kinsmanship express—
> And in it's narrow Eyes—
>
> We come to look with gratitude
> For the appointed Beam
> It deal us—stated as our food—
> And hungered for—the same—
>
> We learn to know the Planks—
> That answer to Our feet—
> So miserable a sound—at first—
> Nor even now—so sweet—
>
> As plashing in the Pools—
> When Memory was a Boy—
> But a Demurer Circuit—
> A Geometric Joy—

The Posture of the Key
That interrupt the Day
To Our Endeavor—Not so real
The Cheek of Liberty—

As this Phantasm Steel—
Whose features—Day and Night—
Are present to us—as Our Own—
And as escapeless—quite—

The narrow Round—the Stint—
The slow exchange of Hope—
For something passiver—Content
Too steep for looking up—

The Liberty we knew
Avoided—like a Dream—
Too wide for any Night but Heaven—
If That—indeed—redeem—   (652)

Within this hermetic scene she finds what she calls "A Geometric Joy" in its absolute predictability. Perhaps because she is personifying the prison as her keeper, when she introduces the "Key" image in stanza five there is a momentary lapse in the coherence of her statement. If "The Posture of the Key / That interrupt the Day / To Our Endeavor" is a further illustration of "A Geometric Joy," the syntax is overly elliptical. More probably, "The Posture of the Key" is a separate example, the third in the series of illustrations of the pleasures prison affords, and what is missing is an adjectival evaluation of "The Posture." Interestingly, this minor flaw in an otherwise tightly constructed poem occurs at the point where she introduces an image that suggests the possibility of an escape. A key implies a door. But since she is herself prison, prisoner, and keeper, whether her "Endeavor" shall be to plot her escape or to prevent it she no longer knows. Just as light is dealt out by the prison and not an invasion of this terrible sanctuary by nature, so too the only genuine exit she imagines depends on her death. But even this escape into "Heaven" is too easy, and the poem concludes with a sardonic qualification, "If That—indeed—redeem." Diminished by a diminishing environment, the speaker forces us to consider this grotesque friendship as she does: as a violation of her desire for freedom so extreme that any escape, even death, may be preferable to the status quo. The speaker who insists that "I never hear the word 'escape' /

Without a quicker blood, / A sudden expectation, / A flying attitude!" confesses repeatedly that she finds no exit: "I never hear of prisons broad / By soldiers battered down, / But I tug childish at my bars / Only to fail again!" (77).

Under such circumstances, small wonder that she sometimes attempts, with mock despair, despairing of mockery, to kill off her hungers. In the following poem, which is structured around a single extended analogy between a powerless "living Child" and an artful gnat, she tries to shrink herself into nothingness, only to discover that no matter how rigidly unseducible her environment, her nature is equally intransigent:

> It would have starved a Gnat—
> To live so small as I—
> And yet I was a living Child—
> With Food's necessity
>
> Upon me—like a Claw—
> I could no more remove
> Than I could coax a Leech away—
> Or make a Dragon—move—
>
> Nor like the Gnat—had I—
> The privilege to fly
> And seek a Dinner for myself—
> How mightier He—than I—
>
> Nor like Himself—the Art
> Upon the Window Pane
> To gad my little Being out—
> And not begin—again—   (612)

The (male) gnat can be forthrightly aggressive and acquisitive; she can only wait, dependent as she is on mysterious forces beyond her control to supply her wants, reduced now to the elemental urge to eat. The gnat can kill himself on the imprisoning windowpane, ensuring the cessation of all consciousness. As a (female) human being she recognizes that, even after contriving her own death, she might have to "begin—again." In context, this suggestion of life after death is not comforting. The life that would begin again, she infers, would be a life so small, so constricted by want, that she would continue to envy gnats.

However far-reaching the ramifications of Dickinson's belief that frustration enhances desire, her experience had instructed her in an even harsher reality: that persons deprived of experiential pleasure come to participate in their own self-destruction. To choose oneself is to choose death. To choose unity is to renounce diversity. And it was, finally, on diversity that Dickinson took her stand. "Renunciation," the "piercing Virtue" she practices within individual poems, was precisely the sacrificial art she refused to master. Had she mastered this art, her voice—a voice protesting against the circumstances of its generation—would have been silenced. Her poems are thus not in quest of a subject (her subject is herself) but in quest of an object. This object is a relationship other than her relationship to language that will maximize her sense of personal freedom. This relationship cannot, strictly speaking, be said to exist in Dickinson's poetry, since her imagination is activated by those relational losses against which she protests most vehemently. For this reason, social powerlessness is Dickinson's most thoroughly explored, consistently interesting, and intransigently feminist theme.

SISTERHOOD

Dickinson's innate feminism also informs those texts that memorialize another woman who has the power to confer identity on her. Ideally, these romantic friendships enhance Dickinson's self-confidence, defend her against the threat of patriarchal power, and compensate her for her lack of a magically potent mother: someone, for example, like the bewitching Elizabeth Barrett Browning, who seemed to transform a "sombre Girl" into an Amazonian beauty (593). Nevertheless, Dickinson's self-sufficient sisterhood is subtly impregnated by sexual rage, and the major theme, "never quite disclosed / And never quite concealed" (1173), is her suppression of a complex homosexual identity. Like Shakespeare, Dickinson writes love poems to men, to women, and to figures whose gender is unknown. Relatively few of Dickinson's love poems are unmistakably inspired by a woman, but once the presence of even a small body of such poems is noted, we also note how many of her poems are addressed to a sexually indeterminate "Thee," as in the celebrated "Wild Nights," with its perfect and perfectly ambiguous concluding stanza, "Rowing in Eden—/ Ah, the Sea! / Might I but moor— Tonight— / In Thee!" (249).[1] When Higginson was preparing the second posthumous edition of poems in 1891, he wrote to his coeditor, Mabel Loomis Todd, "One poem only I dread a little to print—

---

1. See my discussion of this poem on p. 185.

that wonderful 'Wild Nights,'—lest the malignant read into it more than that virgin recluse ever dreamed of putting there."[2] Presumably Higginson was troubled by the poem's heightened eroticism, whereas some modern readers have faulted the concluding image for its supposed biological role reversal.[3]

If her lover's gender is sometimes problematic, the psychic identification Dickinson makes with "the Man within" (746) is unmistakable. She associates the recovery of her prelapsarian past "When Memory was a Boy—" (652) with this latent power; adopts male personae, child or adult, even in the love poems; and describes positive elevations in status by an ineffectual female as the transformation into maleness, as in the following example, addressed to someone—probably a woman who has slighted her—she calls "Sweet":

> No matter—now—Sweet—
> But when I'm Earl—
> Wont you wish you'd spoken
> To that dull Girl?
>
> Trivial a Word—just—
> Trivial—a Smile—
> But wont you wish you'd spared one
> When I'm Earl?
>
> I shant need it—then—
> Crests—will do—
> Eagles on my Buckles—
> On my Belt—too—
>
> Ermine—my familiar Gown—
> Say—Sweet—then
> Wont you wish you'd smiled—just—
> Me upon?   (704)

2. Thomas Wentworth Higginson, as quoted in Millicent Todd Bingham, *Ancestors' Brocades: The Literary Discovery of Emily Dickinson: The Editing and Publication of her Letters and Poems* (New York: Dover, 1945), p. 127.

3. Albert Gelpi, in *The Tenth Muse: The Psyche of the American Poet* (Cambridge: Harvard University Press, 1975), pp. 242–43, observes that "the poem is perhaps the most unabashedly passionate poem that Dickinson wrote," that it "indicates something of the difficulties of Dickinson's emotional life," and that "the sexual roles are blurred," in order to conclude, "Something more subtle than an inversion of sexual roles is at work here, and the point is not that Emily Dickinson was homosexual, as Rebecca Patterson and John Cody have argued." Gelpi does not, however, explain this subtlety.

Dickinson's self-transformations are checked both by the reality of her situation and by her fear of the stranger within, as we see in the following instance. Though sent to Samuel Bowles in 1859, the poem was apparently intended for his wife Mary:

> Her breast is fit for pearls,
> But I was not a "Diver"—
> Her brow is fit for thrones
> But I have not a crest.
>
> Her heart is fit for *home*—
> I—a Sparrow—build there
> Sweet of twigs and twine
> My perennial nest. (84)

The tone here is undeniably regressive. Symbolically castrating herself, Dickinson inhibits the boldness she associates with male identity and is drawn back into a nest which is also, uncomfortably, a womb. Silencing the voice of the "'Diver'" leads to a declension in poetic power; imperious demands are retracted by a diminished alter ego—the Sparrow—who functions to sweeten nature, rather than to explore it.

Generalizations about the ninety or so poems in which other female figures appear must necessarily be qualified by the inherent ambiguity of Dickinson's imagery, but in fact the range of relationships depicted is rather narrowly circumscribed. Virtually all the poems of Dickinson's sisterhood group are concerned with some form of loss or renunciation, as in the example just cited. Most of them describe a relationship that has never been actualized or that has already disintegrated. Typically, these friendships matter more to the speaker than they do to her friend; in some crucial dimension, her love is unrequited.[4] When this is not the case, there is a curious doubling effect, as though Dickinson were projecting the narcissism of a divided self into a barely credible social situation. In most poems Dickinson's subject, by which I mean the subject she consciously shapes, is her response to the inaccessibility of a female other. Consequently, the vitality of these relationships must be inferred from her attitudes toward their demise:

4. In "Emily Dickinson's Homoerotic Poetry," *Higginson Journal* 18 (1978): 19–27, Lillian Faderman observes that these poems depict love "that has been frustrated in one way or another" and that none of them "celebrates fulfillment."

I meant to find Her when I came—
Death—had the same design—
But the Success—was His—it seems—
And the Surrender—Mine—

I meant to tell Her how I longed
For just this single time—
But Death had told Her so the first—
And she had past, with Him—

To wander—now—is my Repose—
To rest—To rest would be
A privilege of Hurricane
To Memory—and Me.   (718)

Dickinson has transformed her specific loss of an actual woman into the symbolic loss of any lover. This point can be clarified if we change the word "Her" to "Him" and "she" to "he." We have some precedent for this kind of metamorphosis in Dickinson's own practice, since there are a number of poems in which alternate versions change the genders of pronouns.[5] Arguably, something is lost when the triangle is an unindividuated "I," "He," and "Death." The last line of stanza two becomes cramped (And he had past, with Him); the seductiveness of death, especially in stanza two, is robbed of its force. But stanza one remains almost intact, and stanza three is identical. The possibility of this gender inversion suggests that Dickinson has created a psychological allegory which subordinates female friendship to her more pervasive interest in death, the betrayer of human connections.

Yet this is not one of the double-gender poems. The poem Dickinson actually wrote begins with her intention to locate another woman for some unspecified purpose. Its development describes the invasion of this embryonic female community by an alien male who destroys it. Its conclusion, at once urgent and meditative, describes the speaker's disorientation because of this affectional loss. Wandering has become repose; rest, hurricane. To distance this bereavement, the speaker wishes to annihilate her past, but to annihilate her past is to annihilate her identity. Wiping out memorial detail with hurricane force, death is both the speaker's competitor and her imperfectly repressed double. Dickinson created this third character

5. See, for example, poems 41, 446, 494, 1249, and 1562.

to dissociate herself from rage, jealousy, and sexual passion—demeaning emotions that disrupted some of her relationships with other women. Her personification of death suppresses key elements of her experience as a daughter, a sister, and a friend. The poem reenacts a partially repressed drama, reproducing the original triangle (a female figure, an "I" of undefined gender, and a deathly male) in a less threatening form. Given this symbolic displacement, the reader must look to other poems and to Dickinson's life for a fuller presentation of the germinal occasion.

Like other Dickinsonian narratives, "I meant to find Her when I came—" begins with a hopeful occasion and concludes with an empirically justified moral—a definition that negotiates between the speaker's intention (to find a woman she loves) and her achievement (a stoical grief). In many of the poems of Dickinson's sisterhood group, the speaker's original aspirations are either disrupted or clarified by some form of death. Because this paradigmatic plot informs many of her heterosexual love poems, there are striking similarities between the narrative occasions of both groups of poems.[6] There is the same "Day at Summer's full" ("Ourselves were wed one summer—dear—"); comparable episodes in which the speaker rededicates herself to someone who ignores her ("Precious to Me—She still shall be— / Though She forget the name I bear— / The fashion of the Gown I wear— / The very Color of My Hair—"); the same unregulated "awful leisure" the death or desertion of the other leaves behind ("The last Night that She lived / It was a Common Night / Except the Dying—this to Us / Made Nature different").[7] But whereas Dickinson anticipates a heavenly reunion with her male lover in a significant cluster of poems, she never anticipates a postmortem resurrection of her devastated sorority. As a consequence, when her relationship to another woman is deadlocked, Dickinson's need to preserve her friendship is exceeded only by her desire to destroy it. To this end, she often introduces a symbolic male figure who relieves her of the burden of repudiating either her homosexual or her heterosexual identities. This closure corresponds both to her inner necessity and to the historical conclusion of her relationship with Susan Gilbert Dickinson during the 1850s.

Until sisterhood is drawn into the vortex of Dickinson's quarrel

---

6. Absent clear indications to the contrary, when Dickinson associates her lover with the sun or the deity, she is describing a heterosexual relationship.

7. The quotations are from poems 322, 631, 727, and 1100.

with death and reformulated as an ideal created through the loss of an actual relationship, her poems of female friendship are peripheral to her achievement as an artist. Nevertheless, even those poems that clearly depict active social relationships expose some of the psychological associations that enabled Dickinson to exclude limiting biographical facts from her art. For example, the following poems were addressed to Susan Gilbert Dickinson and reflect the quest of a childlike persona for a surrogate mother:

> One Sister have I in our house,
> And one, a hedge away.
> There's only one recorded,
> But both belong to me.
>
> One came the road that I came—
> And wore my last year's gown—
> The other, as a bird her nest,
> Builded our hearts among.
>
> She did not sing as we did—
> It was a different tune—
> Herself to her a music
> As Bumble bee of June.
>
> Today is far from Childhood—
> But up and down the hills
> I held her hand the tighter—
> Which shortened all the miles—
>
> And still her hum
> The years among,
> Deceives the Butterfly;
> Still in her Eye
> The Violets lie
> Mouldered this many May.
>
> I spilt the dew—
> But took the morn—
> I chose this single star
> From out the wide night's numbers—
> Sue—forevermore!   (14)

> ---
>
> You love me—you are sure—
> I shall not fear mistake—
> I shall not *cheated* wake—
> Some grinning morn—
> To find the Sunrise left—

And Orchards—unbereft—
And Dollie—gone!

I need not start—you're sure—
That night will never be—
When frightened—home to Thee I run—
To find the window dark—
And no more Dollie—mark—
Quite none?

Be sure you're sure—you know—
I'll bear it better now—
If you'll just tell me so—
Than when—a little dull Balm grown—
Over this pain of mine—
You sting—again!   (156)

At first glance these poems appear to be relatively uncomplicated accounts of an increasingly troubled friendship. The first, written in 1858, begins by comparing the sister in the house (Vinnie) and the sister "a hedge away," next door in the Evergreens, the house Sue shared with her husband. Stanza two builds on the contrast between the sisters with some devaluation of Vinnie, the younger sister who wore the poet's "last year's gown" and traveled the same road of family experience, always a pace behind. Stanza three suggests that Sue was happier and less influenced by public opinion than the Dickinsons. Lines three and four shift the analogy between Sue and a singing bird to an analogy between Sue and a bumble bee. In other poems, Dickinson's bumble bee is often a phallic symbol, but this association is not obviously present here. Stanza four begins by contrasting the present with childhood and describes a journey, presumably into womanhood, that is controlled by Sue's reassuring hand. Stanza five introduces the radically new motif of deception. Sue's beelike hum "Deceives" an unidentified butterfly. Thus, when the motif of deception is introduced, Dickinson's language becomes significantly more cryptic. Lines three through six say both that Sue's eyes are exempt from the mortality May violets suffer and also that her eyes "lie." The pun on "lie" may be intentional or inadvertent; the word choice may have been determined by the rhyme. The concluding stanza reemphasizes Sue's uniqueness and introduces other emblems of her spiritual innocence. The phrase "I spilt the dew" with Sue as flower is enigmatic if one asks what spilling the dew involves in terms of human experience. The word "spilt" may suggest either that the speaker made a mistake or that she deliberately renounced something physical and inconsequential for something more permanent and comprehensive.

The second poem, written two years later, reintroduces the deception motif and develops it further. It incorporates the bee figure and again alludes to Dollie's (a pet name for Sue) capacity to calm the speaker's fears. The poem upbraids Sue for neglecting her and sounds as if it were a response to Sue's assurance of continued love. The surrealistic phrase "Some grinning morn" is superior to anything in the previous poem, drawing as it does on Dickinson's superlative vocabulary of misplaced emotions and displaced actions. A number of poems written to Sue beginning at about this time (1860) when she was pregnant with her first child allude to rebuffs that cause Dickinson (one wants to say "Emily" here) to feel cheated. Again, the poem's significance is primarily biographical.

Moving beyond these poems and others like them ("Is it true, dear Sue? / Are there *two?*" [218]; "Could I—then—shut the door— / Lest *my* beseeching face—at last— / Rejected—be—of *Her?*" [220]) that are too closely tied to the external frame of events, one finds a poem such as the following:

> Dying! Dying in the night!
> Wont somebody bring the light
> So I can see which way to go
> Into the everlasting snow?
>
> And 'Jesus'! Where is *Jesus* gone?
> They said that Jesus—always came—
> Perhaps he does'nt know the House—
> This way, Jesus, Let him pass!
>
> Somebody run to the great gate
> And see if Dollie's coming! Wait!
> I hear her feet upon the stair!
> Death wont hurt—now Dollie's here!   (158)

The persona makes no attempt to explain why she is "Dying! Dying in the night!" and this abrupt beginning opens up a more psychologically suggestive situation. The urgency of her situation is conveyed by a series of repetitions, by vocative ejaculations, and by strategically placed sentence fragments. The sequence Jesus-Dollie suggests that the speaker is more likely to be rescued by her friend than by the proverbial "Savior" who "does'nt know the House." The cause of her desperation may be her friend's absence. The line "I hear her feet upon the stair!" anticipates an image that is thoroughly developed in the second stanza of one of Dickinson's most erotic heavenly-marriage poems, "A Wife—at Daybreak I shall be—" (461):

> Midnight—Good Night! I hear them call,
> The Angels bustle in the Hall—
> Softly my Future climbs the Stair,
> I fumble at my Childhood's prayer
> So soon to be a Child no more—
> Eternity, I'm coming—Sir,
> Savior—I've seen the face—before!

These poems, "One Sister have I in our house," "You love me— you are sure," and "Dying! Dying in the night!" depict Sue as a maternal guide and as a faithless or faithful friend. These themes reappear throughout Dickinson's poetry of female friendship, both in poems addressed to Sue and in poems that were probably inspired by other women.

A poem written in 1862 introduces an explicit marriage motif. "Ourselves were wed one summer—dear—" neither mentions Sue by name nor, apparently, was it sent to her, although Dickinson shared more of her poems with Sue than with any other person. Given the biographical context of Dickinson's letters, together with the evidence of poems that either mention Sue or that Dickinson sent her as tributes to their friendship, I am convinced that "dear" and Sue are synonymous:

> Ourselves were wed one summer—dear—
> Your Vision—was in June—
> And when Your little Lifetime failed,
> I wearied—too—of mine—
>
> And overtaken in the Dark—
> Where You had put me down—
> By Some one carrying a Light—
> I—too—received the Sign.
>
> 'Tis true—Our Futures different lay—
> Your Cottage—faced the sun—
> While Oceans—and the North must be—
> On every side of mine

> 'Tis true, Your Garden led the Bloom,
> For mine—in Frosts—was sown—
> And yet, one Summer, we were Queens—
> But You—were crowned in June—   (631)

The symbolism is complicated but not impenetrable. Sue's "Vision" of her future has morbid consequences for the speaker. In other poems, Dickinson describes marriage as a ritual that obliterates the freedom she associates with girlhood, and this meaning is present in stanza one. When Sue's "little Lifetime" fails, the speaker loses interest in her own. Stanza two recalls the "Dark" of "Dying! Dying in the night!" and implies that Sue had carried her as a mother carries her child, before abandoning her. A third figure, a light-bearer, then rescued Dickinson from despair by bestowing a "Sign" upon her. The first two stanzas suggest that the "Sign" Dickinson received must be some emblem of love, but in stanzas three and four she continues to compare herself to Sue, rather than to describe her vision of her more recent lover. Sue's "Cottage" faces the sun; Dickinson's is surrounded by sunless "Oceans—and the North." Sue's "Garden" symbolizes the richness of her sexual nature and of her domestic experience; Dickinson's symbolizes a lesser triumph over sterility, because she never effectively renounced her love for Sue, transferred her affection to anyone else, or recovered from Sue's betrayal of her. The poem stops short of an unequivocal assertion that she and Sue were originally wed to each other, but Dickinson's reaction to Sue's marriage can be explained only if we assume that she felt displaced by Sue's husband. Together, she and Sue were "Queens" or powerful women and Sue's marriage is compared, in the poem's concluding line, to a coronation. Dickinson, however, was dethroned by it.

Even in 1862, six years after Sue's marriage, this narrative in its painful particularity was still profoundly unacceptable to Dickinson. Although she had effectively excluded some of the biographical facts that she wished to ignore, the symbolism is cryptic because she was not yet in command of her story. As late as 1872, Sue still had the power to wound her deeply and Dickinson continued to feel betrayed by her. The following poem, for example, opens strongly by contrasting physical presence and emotional remoteness, surely a metaphor for Sue's relationship to Dickinson at that time. Beginning with the fourth line of the concluding stanza, however, Dickinson retreats from storytelling and hastens to resolve a dilemma that has been inadequately explored. Unable to explain "Love's transmigration" to herself, she attempts to achieve a broader perspective on any worthless sacrifice:

> Now I knew I lost her—
> Not that she was gone—
> But Remoteness travelled
> On her Face and Tongue.
>
> Alien, though adjoining
> As a Foreign Race—
> Traversed she though pausing
> Latitudeless Place.
>
> Elements Unaltered—
> Universe the same
> But Love's transmigration—
> Somehow this had come—
>
> Henceforth to remember
> Nature took the Day
> I had paid so much for—
> His is Penury
> Not who toils for Freedom
> Or for Family
> But the Restitution
> Of Idolatry.   (1219)

Poems such as these in which her self-analysis is deflected by her analysis of someone else's neglect of her tend to be cluttered and underdeveloped. Furthermore, these poems arouse our suspicion that Dickinson was an overdemanding friend, though she portrays herself as a constant woman in an inconstant world. Both esthetic and psychological necessity converged to demand some further excision of her friend from her texts, but, as we have seen, the extent to which Dickinson could renounce or wished to renounce her dependence on Sue was precisely the issue she was struggling to resolve. One solution to this problem, which she had already begun to explore even in "One Sister have I in our house," was to compress a social narrative into a nature allegory. Depicting Sue as a bird, a bee, the morn, or a star, Dickinson simultaneously dehumanized and immortalized her. Still another solution, as we have also seen, was to introduce a male third who stabilizes Dickinson's sororities by destroying them and who also deflects the homoeroticism toward which these relationships tended. How is it, then, that when Dickinson reimagines the crisis of passionate renunciation of "Ourselves were wed one summer—dear," which had been imperfectly worked out in that poem, makes death the defining characteristic of a living relationship, and introduces no male third, she writes a drama of haunting and unforgettable intensity? Perhaps no one could fully answer this question except some ideal version of Dickinson as critic. Nevertheless, one important difference between "Ourselves were wed one summer—dear—" and "Like Eyes that looked on Wastes—" is that, in the latter poem, also written in about 1862, both figures are equally implicated in deadlocked struggle. The other "Queen" no longer has a separate "Vision" as she had in the inferior poem. Uniting these characters apparently freed Dickinson to concentrate on the despair of imperfectly achieved renunciation. Having gratified her desire to make the other an agent of the self, she also makes the duality of the self the poem's focus:[8]

> Like Eyes that looked on Wastes—
> Incredulous of Ought
> But Blank—and steady Wilderness—
> Diversified by Night—
>
> Just Infinites of Nought—
> As far as it could see—
> So looked the face I looked upon—
> So looked itself—on Me—
>
> I offered it no Help—
> Because the Cause was Mine—
> The Misery a Compact
> As hopeless—as divine—
>
> Neither—would be absolved—
> Neither would be a Queen

8. Roy Harvey Pearce's insight in *The Continuity of American Poetry* (Princeton: Princeton University Press, 1961), p. 179, also helps to explain this procedure: "In these poems the natural images exist only that they may contribute to the definition of a moral experience; they are not in any sense there for their own sakes, scenically; the language in which they are cast has no meaning except as it is focused on the moral experience involved. . . . The qualities . . . imputed to the natural scene are human qualities, but their humanness explicitly derives from the situation of the poet-protagonist—as though the objective reality of nature were irrelevant, whereas the felt quality were everything."

Without the Other—Therefore—
We perish—tho' We reign— (458)

The poem opens with an extended analogy implying that language is inadequate to represent emotional truth, that we are being offered an approximation of an essentially incommunicable suffering. Completing the analogy ("So looked the face I looked upon— / So looked itself—on Me—") redoubles the tension between the deliberately ambiguous perspective (who is seeing what?) and the absolute "Nought" of the landscape. The repetition with its rhythmic and thematic emphasis on "looked" causes us to examine whether the speaker is describing the way the wasted face of the mirroring other looks to her and vice versa or the mutual sight their eyes jointly perceive. That is, the connection between the eyes and the face or faces is severed, so that "Eyes" is no longer a synecdoche for "face" or "it." Stanzas one and two lack an independent subject-verb construction, nor are they grammatically associated with the self-contained complete sentence of stanza three, line one. The syntax, then, reflects the radical dissociation from any familiar order which is the effect of a compact "As hopeless—as divine." These eyes have seen too far into the "Night" where unconscious and conscious merge, where spiritual brideship is equated with sexual embrace, where self and double are no longer distinguishable. The word "absolved" suggests what we must already know. Although some feminist critics have suggested that homoerotic female friendships in nineteenth-century America were easily reconciled with heterosexual commitments and untainted by guilt, for Dickinson the bonds of womanhood are more confining.

The paradoxical logic of the concluding stanza sets up an ironic tension between the speaker's desire to extricate herself from this relationship and her desire to perpetuate it. If her "Compact" is nullified, both she and her lover will be absolved from guilt, but this absolution will eradicate their mutual erotic pleasure. Divided as they are against themselves, neither woman can aid the other and each is condemned to be Waste Land's Queen. Thus, in a rare poem in which Dickinson implicates both women equally in this proud homosexual terror, freedom and impotence meet. The climactic epithet "Infinites of Nought" brilliantly compounds the psychological duplicity of this symbiotic relationship—or indeed of any losing battle against obsession.

Since most poems totally exclude sisterhood as an immediate presence from the poetic structure, concentrating instead on the isolated
speaker-survivor's adjustment to bereavement, it is with some interest that one turns to a poem that enables us to observe how and
when the sororal bond is ruptured:

> We talked as Girls do—
> Fond, and late—
> We speculated fair, on every subject, but the Grave—
> Of our's none affair—
>
> We handled Destinies, as cool—
> As we—Disposers—be—
> And God, a Quiet Party
> To our Authority—
>
> But fondest, dwelt upon Ourself
> As we eventual—be—
> When Girls to Women, softly raised
> We—occupy—Degree—
>
> We parted with a contract
> To cherish, and to write
> But Heaven made both, impossible
> Before another night.   (586)

This lucid narrative, colloquial and lofty, concludes with an apparently unmotivated punishment, yet its outcome is thoroughly conditioned by the sexual politics of the relationship depicted. Dickinson's
sorority provides her with an authentic social structure that subordinates "God" or masculine authority to the role of "Quiet Party." Her
friendship reaches an impasse when the subject of marriage is
broached, albeit euphemistically. The poem moves into a semipri-
vate symbolism as the speaker begins to expatiate on the content of
those romantic aspirations which, she gives us to understand,
formed the sentimental nucleus of their confidences. Stanza three
employs another recurrent Dickinsonian figure for marriage: the
transition from girlhood (at any age) to womanhood is an elevation
in status, or "Degree." Linguistic coherence begins to break down
when social forms are themselves inadequate to contain the loosely
formulated dreams for the future that have already undermined the
duration of this relationship. Similarly, the passive construction
"softly raised" stands in sharp contrast to the active verbs previously
employed. The concluding stanza severs their intellectually audacious yet sexually innocent union as "God" asserts his authority to

destroy the bonds of sisterhood by making the grave, the only subject never broached by these friends, very much their affair. Heaven's intervention freezes this union as a perfect memory; "Heaven" destroys Dickinson's female community before one of the parties to this ambitious affectional "contract" can desert the other by marrying. The "Grave" is a social and psychological reality that was never comprehended by the women themselves. It symbolizes both the death of their relationship and the destruction of their community from within. We can look back now on the lines "We handled Destinies, as cool— / As we—Disposers—be—" and observe the ruthlessness of these female overreachers, which is subsequently chastened by a violent death. If maleness and aggression are fully identified in this remarkable drama, so too are hubris and punishment. The poem knows more than it says.

Despite differences in the sexual component of their political imaginations, writers such as Hawthorne, Melville, Whitman, and Twain explicitly link male bonding to contemporary economic and political issues. As the basis for a more democratic society, male bonding is dignified in such works as *The Blithedale Romance, Moby Dick, Leaves of Grass,* and *Huckleberry Finn,* even though the relationships that are described fall short of their potential. Dickinson, however, describes socially subversive relationships that may alter individuals but that never have the potential to transform society, even metaphorically. In this extreme isolation from public history, her female communities participate in a normative nineteenth-century tradition of female separatism. One critic, Nina Auerbach, observes that "initiation into a band of brothers is a traditional privilege symbolized by uniforms, rituals, and fiercely shared loyalties; but sisterhood . . . looks often like a blank exclusion. A community of women may suggest less the honor of fellowship than an antisociety, an austere banishment from both social power and biological rewards."[9] Lacking official social or biological function, Dickinson's communities introject the cultural, psychological, and metaphysical tensions they are ideally designed to exclude. Death's antagonists, they become death-ridden. Queenly enclaves, they threaten her with a diminished, dysfunctional male identity and with the subsequent loss of heterosexual experience. After they have ceased to exist they may, like perfect works of art, symbolize an unattainable ideal. For Dickinson, this "sumptuous Destitution" (1382) "edible to longing, /

9. Nina Auerbach, *Communities of Women: An Idea in Fiction* (Cambridge: Harvard University Press, 1978), p. 3.

But ablative to show" (1744) is sometimes enough. "Dear Sue," she writes in 1862, "You see I remember," enclosing the following poem:

> Your—Riches—taught me—poverty!
> Myself, a "Millionaire"
> In little—wealths—as Girls can boast—
> Till broad as "Buenos Ayre"
> You drifted your Dominions—
> A Different—Peru—
> And I esteemed—all—poverty—
> For Life's Estate—with you!
>
> Of "Mines"—I little know—myself—
> But just the *names*—of *Gems*—
> The *Colors*—of the *Commonest*—
> And scarce of Diadems—
> So much—that did I meet *the Queen*—
> Her glory—I should know—
> But *this*—must be a *different Wealth*—
> To miss it—beggars—so!
>
> I'm sure 'tis *"India"*—all day—
> To those who look on you—
> Without a stint—without a blame—
> Might I—but be the Jew!
> I know it is "Golconda"—
> Beyond my power to dream—
> To have a smile—for mine—each day—
> How *better*—than a *Gem!*
>
> At least—it solaces—to know—
> That there *exists*—a *Gold*—
> Altho' I prove it, just in time—
> It's distance—to behold!
> It's far—far—Treasure—to surmise—
> And estimate—the Pearl—
> That slipped—my simple fingers—thro'
> While yet a Girl—at School!   (299)

But if Dickinson here finds solace in the shapeliness of poverty, when she zooms in for a close-up, gem-encrusted idolatry yields to a more searching poem and a more limited conclusion:

> Her sweet Weight on my Heart a Night
> Had scarcely deigned to lie—

When, stirring, for Belief's delight,
My Bride has slipped away—

If 'Twas a Dream—made solid—just
The Heaven to confirm—
Or if Myself were dreamed of Her—
The power to presume—

With Him remain—who unto Me—
Gave—even as to All—
A Fiction superseding Faith—
By so much—as 'twas real—   (518)

With its dreamlike nocturnal setting, this poem admits an image
of physical intimacy rarely found in Dickinson's poetry of womanly
love. The ambiguous phrasal modifier ("When, stirring, for Belief's
delight") at first refers back to the speaker, roused with pleasure,
and then forward to her lost bride. This slippery syntax fuses the
identities of the speaker and her lover; the boundary between them
has been temporarily eliminated. Such a fusion arouses the speaker's
apprehensiveness, arrests the development of her delight, and accounts for her bride's disappearance. Realizing this fantasy (whether
it happened or not) raises moral issues Dickinson deflects by appeal-
ing to a third party, "Him" or God. Was this solid dream intended to
confirm her faith in heaven? Did her bride reciprocate her affection,
or was her "sweet Weight" a lie? The power to resolve these mysteries is attributed to a God whose authority is undercut by the word
"presume"; even He has no final power, since Dickinson prefers
hallucinatory fictions to an even more hallucinatory faith. The fiction, that is, corresponds to some deeper imperative to usurp "The
power to presume" and to recapture her bride.

"Another elegy on Mrs. Browning," asserts John Evangelist
Walsh.[10] There is no basis for this speculation. Throughout her
sisterhood group, Dickinson's relationship to her animus—to the
psychic reservoir of male-identified behavior and emotion which, or
so Jung has posited, all women possess—is activated when she com-
petes with male figures for possession of a female other.[11] As I have

10. John Evangelist Walsh, *The Hidden Life of Emily Dickinson* (New York: Simon
and Schuster, 1971), p. 255.
11. But see Martin Bickman's "Kora in Heaven" in *The Unsounded Centre: Jungian
Studies in American Romanticism* (Chapel Hill: University of North Carolina Press,
1980). He argues that the concept of "animus" is of "little use to us in analyzing
Dickinson's male figures."

already suggested, this anima-animus conflict is typically objectified through three separate characters: a weak female, herself, and a powerful male often personified as death or God. Thus Dickinson's social powerlessness takes on a psychological fatality within a pattern of fortuitous occurrences for which she bears no responsibility and from which the poetic structure specifically absolves her. Yet because metaphors of loss and death and emotional remoteness are so fully functional for Dickinson's art—in freeing her from the threat of sex they tend to universalize her status anxieties—critics have usually ignored the suppressed homoeroticism that defines one pole of Dickinson's sexual imagination. As Leslie Fiedler has shown, writers who are engaged in a flight from adult heterosexuality are often attracted by "innocent homosexuality."[12] What remains to be emphasized is that Dickinson's style can transform innocent homosexuality into self-loathing.

Although most of the poems we have been examining cast the speaker-poet in the (female) victim tradition, in the touchstone text "My Life had stood—a Loaded Gun—" (754) pain's underside, rage, is more fully explored. Instead of competing with Death or God, the speaker cooperates with a demonic male who appears to invest her with authentic social power. Preserving her paradigmatic oedipal triangle, Dickinson moves beyond the accidental victimization of her "I" into an implied critique of the autotherapeutic value of her language. In comparing her self-expression to the outbursts of a rifle or the eruptions of a volcano, Dickinson both expresses her rage and attempts to control it. The object of her fury is another woman, a composite sister-lover-mother whom she represents through two static animal figures that rob her nemesis of any independent volition in the drama. As the speaker and her Master prey on other women, as they "hunt the Doe," she becomes overdependent on him. The speaker recognizes this overdependency in the poem's difficult concluding stanza but is unable to view him as a permanent ally. Having exorcized the seductive feminine element from her universe, Dickinson has committed herself to a dehumanizing relationship and therefore fantasizes the perpetuity of her affectional impotence.

How one reads the poem depends, of course, on what one thinks

---

12. Leslie A. Fiedler, *Love and Death in the American Novel* (New York: Stein and Day, 1966), p. 12.

these characters, the Life-Gun and her Owner, are up to. Does the action objectify "the psychological dilemma facing the intelligent and aware woman, and particularly the woman artist, in patriarchal America,"[13] or does the poem reflect that dilemma? May her relationship to her Owner be viewed as a loving one, her aggression as an effective defense of it? We can begin to make sense of the text's significant ellipses by observing that Dickinson's extended analogy speaks for itself. Her gun kills:

> My Life had stood—a Loaded Gun—
> In Corners—till a Day
> The Owner passed—identified—
> And carried Me away—
>
> And now We roam in Sovreign Woods—
> And now We hunt the Doe—
> And every time I speak for Him—
> The Mountains straight reply—
>
> And do I smile, such cordial light
> Upon the Valley glow—
> It is as a Vesuvian face
> Had let it's pleasure through—
>
> And when at Night—Our good Day done—
> I guard My Master's Head—
> 'Tis better than the Eider-Duck's
> Deep Pillow—to have shared—
>
> To foe of His—I'm deadly foe—
> None stir the second time—
> On whom I lay a Yellow Eye—
> Or an emphatic Thumb—
>
> Though I than He—may longer live
> He longer must—than I—
> For I have but the power to kill,
> Without—the power to die—

Inert, loaded, cornered, the speaker is identified by her Owner, the male personification of her aggression, and transported into emotional terrain hitherto denied her. The poem does not encour-

13. Albert Gelpi, "Emily Dickinson and the Deerslayer: The Dilemma of the Woman Poet in America," *San Jose Studies* 3 (1977); reprinted in *Shakespeare's Sisters: Feminist Essays on Women Poets*, ed. Sandra M. Gilbert and Susan Gubar (Bloomington: Indiana University Press, 1979), p. 122.

age us to identify further this animus type, but, rather, to define him as the speaker does, solely by his dramatic function in her psychic economy. The initial consequence of her contact with him is a rejuvenated relationship with nature. As she projects the sovereignty she feels onto the woods where they together roam, as she "speak[s]" for Him, she revels in her magical power to obliterate an alien environment. The mountains echo her assumed omnipotence back at her; her smiles radiate explosive, Vesuvian light onto the glowing valleys; her fiery "Yellow Eye" and triggering "emphatic Thumb" command the power of life and death. In all these orgiastic figures, eroticized death and thanatized love have been perfectly commingled: gun and "I" are indistinguishable, as are the ambitions of the speaker and her Master. Boasting of her selfless fidelity, she wards off his foes, and again the poem does not encourage us to inquire who these foes might be, since Dickinson's orgiastic self-expression is dissociated from its moral context. Lulled into mute acquiescence by the rollicking rhythms and simple coordinate sentence structure, we find ourselves responding as the Life-Gun does, by obliterating other points of view. Drawn into this all-encompassing present, we focus only on the miraculous transformation of a useless into an aimed life. How this transformation has occurred and what its long-range consequences are likely to be concern us no more than they do the speaker, throughout the first five stanzas.

The only alternative to these episodes of joyous carnage is rejected by the Life-Gun in stanza four, when she compares her nocturnal vigilance to a softer, drowsier ending: "And when at Night—Our good Day done— / I guard My Master's Head— / 'Tis better than the Eider-Duck's / Deep Pillow—to have shared." A proverbial symbol of maternal devotion, the Eider-Duck lines her nest with feathers plucked from her breast.[14] This comparison is slipped in so easily and rejected so firmly that its significance seems negligible, but within the context of the poems we have been examining it takes on greater clarity. The defeminized or neutered self, the male Owner, and the maternal female reproduce the oedipal configuration we

---

14. This regressive symbolism would have been somewhat more accessible to Dickinson's contemporaries than it is to us. The *Springfield Republican*, for example, published an essay in 1860 entitled "When Should We Write" employing this eider-duck figure and warning against the perils of what it saw as the characteristic female genre, "the literature of misery." As quoted in Richard B. Sewall, *The Life of Emily Dickinson*, 2 vols. (New York: Farrar, Straus and Giroux, 1974), 2: 489–90. Poem 1059, "Sang from the Heart, Sire," may be a response to the *Republican* essay.

have observed in other poems. Dickinson's rejection of this alternative source of female identity suggests that the poem will develop in the direction of even greater destruction, as it does.[15] After this comparison, the syntactical parallels ("And now," "And do," "And when") are halted by a construction that moves the consequences of this euphoric killing into the foreground of the speaker's consciousness: "To foe of His—I'm deadly foe." The lines "None stir the second time— / On whom I lay a Yellow Eye— / Or an emphatic Thumb—" acknowledge the slaughter more directly than any of the previous declarations of power, as they extend the gun analogy and allow the speaker to overwhelm her Master. Thus her fantasy of phallic womanhood bursts the bonds of her subservience to him; having completely subordinated herself to his purposes, she achieves the maximum illusion of personal autonomy.

The concluding stanza, by examining what would happen were the Life-Gun to outlive her Master, directs our attention to the speaker's automatic behavior, to the absence of moral context in which the fantasy has been played out, and to the internal incoherence of her emotions. Although we might expect the resolution to turn on the opposition between killing and loving, instead the poem turns on the opposition between "the power to kill" and "the power to die," which separates the Life-Gun from her Owner by positing alternative conclusions for them. The Owner, or the liberating mania he represents, can die; his miraculous appearance at the poem's beginning has already implied the possibility of an equally sudden disappearance. The Life-Gun cannot in a trivial sense (never having been human, a gun does not have the "Capacity to Terminate"). Nor can a gun "live ever—or else swoon to death." A gun is incapable of dying in the Shakespearean or Keatsian sense of the word, of achieving human sexual climaxes. At night the Life-Gun has guarded rather than shared her (its?) Owner's bed. More crucially, rage split off from its origins is unable to comprehend its generation and thus can achieve no final catharsis or death. Were

15. As Janet Todd remarks in her valuable study of female friendship in the novel, the attitudes of women toward other members of their sex are informed by a constellation of interdependent social relationships. One of these is "the first female tie," the tie between mother and daughter which, in Dickinson's poetry, is extremely weak. Todd extends her argument to suggest that, in seeking to recapture "the mother who failed her," a literary heroine may wish to revenge herself on other women "for the first female hurt." See *Women's Friendship in Literature* (New York: Columbia University Press, 1980).

the Owner to predecease the Life-Gun, the speaker would return to the psychological stasis of the opening lines. Although "the power to kill" is no longer enough, unless the speaker can integrate the Owner into her self, no further neutralization of her aggression or of her death instinct can be achieved. The poem's resolution, however, separates the Life-Gun and her Owner more firmly than ever before.[16]

Throughout "My Life had stood—a Loaded Gun," rage has triggered language. In the summation, where style and tone shift to an epigrammatic moral, the speaker wishes to deny that rage has been her muse. Thus the moral emphasizes her Owner's mortality, together with her fear of being abandoned by him. He is mortal, she is immortal. She can imagine his death, but she cannot imagine her own. As a gun, however, there is a sense in which she is already dead: her rage is, quite literally, inhuman. Because rage activates her voice, her language does not express the power to love. That the moral does not quite fit is, in essence, the poem's point. The predatory or regressive relationships with other women Dickinson has depicted impede the integration of the masculine and feminine components of her personality. When "I" is also "It" rather than "She," the Life-Gun is engaged in a parody of creative resolution. To restrain her rage, Dickinson collapses her analogy, but the poem concludes with an imperfect death, ˗ partial renunciation. The alternatives posited (life as a loaded gun, used or unused) make adequate commentary impossible. If the power to die implies the power to be reborn, the Life-Gun does not have this power. Although the poem is predicated on the assumption that repression is deathly, it is to qualified repression that the poem resorts for its sense of an ending. No other Dickinson poem testifies more urgently to the rage engendered by her suspicion of the feminine principle in her universe, seeks more urgently to expel it, or fails more absolutely in the attempt. This conclusion is not a pretty one, but this is the poet who likes "a look of Agony" because she knows "it's true—" (241).

Despite its allusion to "a Vesuvian face," "My Life had stood—a Loaded Gun—" may be the most "American" poem Dickinson ever wrote. Its frontier psychology participates in a recognizable native

---

16. Poem 358 repeats the phrase "the power to kill," poem 1651 "the power to die." To the best of my knowledge these are unique instances of a pivotal word group repeated among poems.

tradition which dwells lovingly on physical conflict and on savage emotion. Some of Dickinson's most striking metaphors for herself are, however, unmistakably European, and these compensatory images are often most pronounced when her anger is thoroughly blocked. Whether as Queen or Earl, Emily Dickinson attempts to uproot herself from a culture that impedes female bonding. Although she herself stated in 1856 that home "is where the *house* is, and the adjacent buildings" (L182), she later modified this conclusion. In her poetry, national identity is a state of mind.

Adopting an aristocratic, European male persona, Dickinson returns once again to the paradigmatic situation recounted in "Ourselves were wed one summer—dear—" and develops still another allegory of competition with a male figure:[17]

> The Malay—took the Pearl—
> Not—I—the Earl—
> I—feared the Sea—too much
> Unsanctified—to touch—
>
> Praying that I might be
> Worthy—the Destiny—
> The Swarthy fellow swam—
> And bore my Jewel—Home—
>
> Home to the Hut! What lot
> Had I—the Jewel—got—
> Borne on a Dusky Breast—
> I had not deemed a Vest
> Of Amber—fitt—
>
> The Negro never knew
> I—wooed it—too
> To gain, or be undone—
> Alike to Him—One—   (452)

This searching parable of insufficient courage distances its origins in Dickinson's life so effectively that Robert Weisbuch has argued that the poem does not refer to any subject, that it carries on "the moral recommendation of certain attitudes, the 'teaching' function of traditional allegories, without referring to extrapoetic codes of

---

17. Poem 270, "*One Life* of so much Consequence!" employs the same pearl-diver figure and is perhaps a transitional poem between "Her breast is fit for pearls," previously quoted, and "The Malay—took the Pearl."

conduct. The poem gracefully transforms material to spiritual gain to illustrate a forceful moral: that nothing will come to the man who waits in selfish fear—not wealth in any real sense of the word, not paradise, not beauty, not a realization of the meaning of things, not any of the potential values contained in Dickinson's pearl. Yet this recommendation of risk does not derive from any particular moral system and it does not apply to any particular sphere of action."[18] In one sense, of course, Weisbuch is right. The pearl need not be Sue, the Malay need not be Austin, and the Earl need not be Emily. Yet however generalizable the situation depicted, the poem is informed by the sexual temptations of Dickinson's experience. Rather than wooing her pearl of great price, she merely covets it, both because she feels polluted and because she views "the Sea" that is the pearl's element as frightening. Although "the Sea" is the poem's most powerful emblem, it is the least fully explored, and I have seen no discussion of this poem that adequately explains it. Perhaps the Sea represents the speaker's unconscious or female sexuality or an alien environment or nature or death. Probably the Sea represents the unknown. As such, it can never be comprehended either by Dickinson or her readers.

In calling herself the "Earl," Dickinson wishes to legitimize a threatening male identity. Because this status-transformation is psychologically incomplete, she is forced to witness the triumph of raw physical acquisitiveness over her Puritanical self-restraint. The poem's most poignant moment turns on her inability to explain her inhibition to herself: "I—feared the Sea—too much / Unsanctified— to touch." The disintegrated syntax obscures her history and her reasoning; sexual anxiety almost unhinges her thought. Finally, the poem's three figures represent the internal divisions of a single nature. The unattainable ideal self (the Pearl), the paralyzing conscience (the Earl), and the admired and despised id (the Malay-Negro) are locked together by incestuous doublings of sound that emphasize the ironic contiguity and dispersion of the characters. Dickinson satirizes the primitivism of male dominance, fears the sea-change of homosexual conquest, and laments an unlived life.

18. Robert Weisbuch, *Emily Dickinson's Poetry* (Chicago: University of Chicago Press, 1975), p. 58.

THE WIFE—
WITHOUT THE SIGN

Informed by our reading of Dickinson's sisterhood poems, let us now turn to the much larger group of poems to and about male figures. Of these are hundreds. Among these hundreds, perhaps forty, in whole or in part, are concerned with wedlock, figurative or actual. This latter cluster suggests that Dickinson was engaged neither in a continuous critique of the frustrations of marriage nor in a continuous affirmation of its pleasures. Instead, her poetry accommodates both attitudes, attitudes prefigured by her 1852 letter to Sue (93), which is centrally concerned with the risks of this venture. Just as this letter does not describe the risks of marriage to a particular man, so too Dickinson's marriage group reflects sexual anxieties that predetermine her responses to any lover. Thus, the fantasy-husband whom Dickinson imagines herself addressing in several poems is a faceless personage who represents the idea of home as fireside, as garden, and as "Celestial Sea." Such abstract images enable Dickinson to describe departures from this secure yet various place, the patterns of a safe return, and a mutual ministry "to poorer lives." Though this home does not include children, it includes childhood as a sheltered state of mind. Though this home includes mutual work, both partners also fulfill their separate tasks. His, some "Problem—of the Brain—"; hers, "some foolisher effect— / A Ruffle—or a Tune—":

> This seems a Home—
> And Home is not—
> But what that Place could be—
> Afflicts me—as a Setting Sun—
> Where Dawn—knows how to be—   (944)

Such domestic idylls are, however, atypical of this autobiographical poet who, in describing herself as "The Wife—without the Sign!" underscored a set of biographically verifiable absences: her lack of a husband, her lack of marital sexual experience, and her lack of the social status she associated, rather consistently, with a wife's clearly demarcated official position. Such absences may have afforded Dickinson a freedom of opportunity that was incompatible with a particular marriage to a particular man, but the facts of Dickinson's life were, in some respects, unpalatable to her, and the psychologically ambiguous fictions she constructed continue to reflect this background of self-distrust. Since most of these poems describe a marriage that in some crucial dimension has not yet been transacted, the ideal of marriage rather than the experience of it emerges as a major focus of interest. These poems also suggest that the feelings Dickinson associated with unsuccessful marriages, within which a beloved bride becomes "the *wife forgotten*" (L93), were not exorcized by her biographical evasion of the risks of being rejected by a particular husband or even, it appears, by a particular lover.

This situation is a highly suggestive one. To avoid dependency on or rejection by a particular man, Dickinson distanced herself from men. The same emotions that inspired this avoidance were, however, perpetuated by the strategy she employed to countermand them. Dickinson's morbid image of herself as a weak and unlovable woman was offset by her vital image of herself as a strong and loving one. Paradoxically, she transformed her social isolation into a test of strength, as if to say, "See how long I can wait!" Though this transformation was not always fully achieved, Dickinson's experience as an outsider accounts for the astonishing tonal range of her love poetry, for the diversity of her response to a historically indeterminate male other within it, and for her exaggeration of the closural power of marriage, closure that she likens to death. In general, then, Dickinson's poems seek to accommodate both her fear that nature's heterosexual text inevitably reinforces the dependency of women on men and her fear that the suspension of such relationships inevitably reinforces the alienation of women from nature, from society, and from each other.

To transcend her fear of nature's heterosexual text, Dickinson resorted to a cult of self-immolation and, occasionally, of corpses, as in the poem beginning, "If I may have it, when it's dead, / I'll be contented—so," which concludes

> Forgive me, if the Grave come slow—
> For Coveting to look at Thee—
> Forgive me, if to stroke thy frost
> Outvisions Paradise! (577)

To transcend her fear of the void, Dickinson developed her art, within which male corpses are more commonly perceived as disembodied lovers. The process of purification she conceives is twofold. First, her lover departs or dies. In either case, her lover is sexually inaccessible. Then, her lover is reborn:

> Think of it Lover! I and Thee
> Permitted—face to face to be—
> After a Life—a Death—We'll say—
> For Death was That—
> And this—is Thee— (577)

After life, Dickinson may permit herself to rejoin him. This concern with lapsed prohibitions is often projected onto another such as God whom Dickinson conceives as punitive, in that He mandates her lover's absence. Within her most problematic texts, Dickinson seems unaware of her use of Christian iconography to justify her self-inhibition. This iconography, however, leads to an antithetical vision of secular and sacred love that apparently masked, to Dickinson's satisfaction, some of the social origins of her erotic frustrations. Ironically, this imagery also expresses Dickinson's social frustrations; in savaging God, she revenges herself on His believers. Those poems within which she herself appears least lovelorn reconcile this antithesis between too much and too little control of her own sexual nature.

The nature of women, as perceived by Dickinson, makes them vulnerable to men, whom she tends to perceive either as excessively conventional or as amoral. In a favorite metaphor, she compares women to flowers who depend on the sun's phallic potency. Though woman's nature cannot thrive without some exposure to the sun's heat and light, constant exposure to it entails the fact or the threat of death. The structure of society, as perceived by Dickinson, is based on this biological metaphor. That is, society is based on a hierarchy of sexual status, and women's accomplishments ("A Ruffle—or a Tune—") are correspondingly devalued. She herself, as I have shown, devalues the accomplishments of motherhood and describes herself as a motherless child. Women's affectional relationships with each other are also influenced by their natural history of sexual vulnerability. As I suggested in the last chapter, heterosexual relationships rend the bonds of sisterhood; however, as I suggested in my analysis of Dickinson's early letters, romantic relationships with men can provide women with a common basis of association, an insight that is sustained by the poems of Dickinson's marriage group. Thus a woman who has neither husband nor lover is exiled from "Home," though such a woman may, of course, have a father or a religion of Him. If it should happen, as it apparently did in the case of Dickinson, that a woman's "natural" fears of male dominance should be further complicated by her tendency to associate lovers and fathers, this association would reinforce her ambivalence toward men as sexual partners.

To recapitulate. Dickinson is engaged neither in a continuous flight from heterosexual experience nor in a continous quest for it. Instead, her poetry expresses both attitudes, though the former is the more heavily disguised. Often, this disguise takes the form of idolatry. Joanne Feit Diehl explains,

> The masculine erotic "other" in Dickinson serves a generative function as source and occasion for her poems; a figure of astounding authority, it is he to whom she owes her existence. She lives as if he listens; the internal adversary becomes her sole audience:

> All that I do
> Is in review
> To his enamored mind
> I know his eye
> Where e'er I ply
> Is pushing close behind

> Not any Port
> Nor any flight
> But he doth there preside

What omnipresence lies in wait
For her to be a Bride   (1496)

The ominous echo of approaching death merges with the omnipre-
sent image of the lover, a fusion that betrays an anxiety that has its
sources in the fear of mortality.[1]

Dickinson's association of sex and death also has its sources in the
fact that her potential lover (Master, God, or Internal Adversary) is
psychologically invested with the authority of an actual father. This
investiture causes her to avoid heterosexual relationships, alienates
her from other women, and intensifies her relationship to her biological progenitor. Under these circumstances, Dickinson's family
romance becomes a nightmare of conflicted loyalties—to herself, to
others, to various aspects of herself—and it is now time to consider
more directly how Dickinson to some extent transcended her anxieties of gender.

She rose to His Requirement—dropt
The Playthings of Her Life
To take the honorable Work
Of Woman, and of Wife—

If ought She missed in Her new day,
Of Amplitude, or Awe—
Or first Prospective—Or the Gold
In using, wear away,

It lay unmentioned—as the Sea
Develope Pearl, and Weed,
But only to Himself—be known
The Fathoms they abide—   (732)

Seeking to preserve the psychological freedom she associates with
play, with childhood, and with the unconscious, Dickinson discovers
her work in balancing this vision of marriage as a rise in social status
against her equally compelling vision of marriage as entrapment.
This is a trap into which Dickinson's honored woman has, it appears,
propelled herself, and for good reason; to evade this snare would be

---

1. Joanne Feit Diehl, *Dickinson and the Romantic Imagination* (Princeton: Princeton
University Press, 1981), p. 77.

to define herself as a socially irrelevant being, a "Nobody."[2] With characteristic vehemence, Dickinson exaggerates this point, perhaps recalling Byron's epigram, "Man's love is of man's life a thing apart, / 'Tis woman's whole existence."[3] With characteristic resourcefulness, Dickinson anticipates the words of a later poet, written in the last week of her thirty-year-old life,

> The woman is perfected.
> Her dead
>
> Body wears the smile of accomplishment,
> The illusion of a Greek necessity
>
> Flows in the scrolls of her toga,
> Her bare
>
> Feet seem to be saying:
> We have come so far, it is over.[4]

Dickinson too describes a woman who can go no further, but unlike Sylvia Plath, she suggests that terminal accomplishments breed new necessities—here the necessity of regressing from achieved heterosexuality into a prior and more fluid androgyny. Having discovered the unmentionable—that in rising to *his* requirements, she has scanted her own—Dickinson's typic woman liberates herself from the power of social convention by reappropriating the powers of imperfection, of introspection, and of silence.

The news that the institution of marriage may impede the development of selfhood comes to us who have read the antiinstitutional texts of that transcendental moment, the 1850s, as no surprise. What

2. Nina Baym has shown that virtually all of the domestic novels written by and for American women between 1820 and 1870 linked female social identity to marital status. She also shows that the normative heroine's quest for identity is usually precipitated by her deprivation "of the supports she had rightly or wrongly depended on to sustain her throughout life" (p. 11). Such supports often meant the support of a male parent who, having made his way in the world, did not force the heroine to face "the necessity of winning her own way" in it. See *Woman's Fiction: A Guide to Novels by and about Women in America, 1820–1870* (Ithaca: Cornell University Press, 1978).

3. George Gordon, Lord Byron, *Don Juan*, 1. 194. Edward Dickinson owned Byron's complete works. In *Emily Dickinson's Reading: 1836–1886* (Cambridge: Harvard University Press, 1966), Jack L. Capps observes that "from the roll of major Romantic poets only the names of Byron and Keats appear in Emily Dickinson's letters" (p. 79). As he suggests, several of Dickinson's poems contain Byronic echoes. For an analysis of references to other texts in Dickinson's poetry, see my article "Emily Dickinson's Literary Allusions," *Essays in Literature* 1 (Spring 1974): 54–68.

4. Sylvia Plath, "Edge," *Ariel* (New York: Harper & Row, 1966), p. 84.

is interesting here is that this news surprises Dickinson's typic woman. Within this poem, social status initially implies a rise in self-esteem as a consequence of the work with which it is associated. This work is surprisingly complex. Though Dickinson may view marriage as a fall into antiself-consciousness, she also views marriage as an opportunity for moral altruism and for social responsibility. Such values are not ordinarily associated with Dickinson, whose earnestness was frequently offset, as it is here, by her penchant for play. Nevertheless, it is tempting to conclude that Dickinson's playfulness was primarily a reaction against an excessively burdened conscience. Thus she begins by staking out a conservative and, so to speak, antitranscendental position. Certainly what she emphasizes in the end is that institutionalized marriages epitomize an inauthentic, antiprogressive, and antinatural state. The route by which Dickinson reaches this conclusion is a fascinating one. She leaps backward in order to leap forward. Her forward leap is, however, psychologically conservative, since she shows that certain psychological regressions are necessitated by certain psychological progressions. Thus one theme that reappears throughout many of Dickinson's love poems is that the "first Prospective" of marriage, its anticipated or actual being, is superior to the extended experience of it. As we have already seen in chapters 4 and 5, this belief informs her imagination of other relationships as well. Dickinson's typic woman cannot, however, afford to integrate this knowledge into her consciousness; to do so would rob the "first Prospective" of its mysterious qualities of "Amplitude" and "Awe." She progresses toward this demystifying conclusion in order to retreat from it. The power of regression is also the power to repress insights which, in illuminating "Weed[s]," obscure "Pearl[s]."

When a dependent female consecrates herself to an all-powerful male, what she accrues in solemnity and in enriched self-worth is often counterbalanced by a diminution in her capacity for play:

> The World—stands—solemner—to me—
> Since I was wed—to Him—
> A modesty befits the soul
> That bears another's—name—
> A doubt—if it be fair—indeed—
> To wear that perfect—pearl—
> The Man—upon the Woman—binds—
> To clasp her soul—for all—

A prayer, that it more angel—prove—
A whiter Gift—within—
To that munificence, that chose—
So unadorned—a Queen—
A Gratitude—that such be true—
It had esteemed the Dream—
Too beautiful—for Shape to prove—
Or posture—to redeem!   (493)

Idolizing a masculine erotic other, Dickinson imagines herself as the recipient of comparable adoration. Suggesting that marriage represents an antiprogressive state, Dickinson acknowledges the appeal of stasis. Again, though modesty and gratitude are not qualities usually associated with Dickinson, here she associates such qualities with herself. We note, however, that the opening lines lead us to expect a different text—one that focuses on an altered world rather than on an altered self. Other features of the poem are puzzling: Dickinson's emphasis on the awesome responsibility of bearing "another's name—"; her description of "that perfect—pearl—" (whatever it symbolizes) as something exterior to her; her prayer for a more "angel" soul and for "A whiter Gift—within—"; her characterization of her former self as an unadorned "Queen"; and her more comprehensive vision of a relationship without reciprocity. In receiving the munificent gifts of her lover, she bestows none on him. This is the text's most troubling element. It suggests that, because she does not perceive herself as loved, she does not perceive herself as capable of loving. He transforms her; she has no effect on him. If Dickinson is here married to someone rather like God, this god derives no pleasure from the adoration of his creatures. Her doubts "if it be fair" are well-founded and for several reasons. First, as I have already suggested, Dickinson perceives her loving as either inauthentic or superfluous. Second, because she perceives herself as sexually undesirable or "unadorned," but also because of her romantic vision of her lover's perfection, she views herself as unworthy of him. Finally, because this relationship depends on the suppression of skepticism, it impedes her freedom of thought. To some extent, Dickinson wishes to free herself from the burden of this freedom. She remains, however, fundamentally unconvinced that such a self-surrender is fair, either to herself or to her lover. In divesting herself of the burden of selfhood, she causes him to become her keeper. Because this marriage is predicated on the inequality of its partners, her doubts "if it be fair—indeed—" dominate the text. Her lover has placed her on a pedestal from whose height the shapes and postures of reality are barely discernible; within the concluding three lines, however, a transfigured skepticism triumphs.

Dickinson's need to divest herself of the burdens of selfhood while preserving the privileges of it resulted in one of the most extraordinary compromises in the history of American letters. Styling herself "The Wife—without the Sign," she describes a marriage that is and is not, that has been and is not now, that will be and is not yet, a marriage thwarted by nature, God, and social convention, validated by faith alone. A compromise of this sort between self-surrender and self-control is obviously delicately balanced and susceptible to deconstruction into its component parts. On the one hand, Dickinson preserves her autonomy by distancing her lover from herself or by distancing herself from him. On the other hand, her anxieties are intensified by this distance, because she also wishes to divest herself of—among other burdens—the burden of sexual frustration. Wishing to be dominated by her lover, Dickinson also wishes to dominate him. Consequently, she arouses our interest in precisely this question: how much has she expended, how much has she reserved of what Kate Chopin's awakened heroine Edna Pontellier was to call, some forty years later, her real self? And for a poet, where does reality end and illusion begin?

The center of Dickinson's love story is a marriage that may or may not have been—once—consummated physically but that for reasons either unspecified, specified summarily, or specified inadequately (I am conflating for the moment the point of view of reader and speaker) is thwarted in the temporal world. It is thus an interior marriage, a marriage of the spirit divorced from social circumstances, which imposes on her the pleasures and the burdens of a double life. She sometimes looks forward to the reunification of her public and private selves in an eternity filled with angels, cherubim, and seraphim, described in the language of nineteenth-century Christian evangelism, language suffused with the tone of the Book of Revelation and Watts's hymnal. This stylistic atmosphere of eros redeemed through "Calvaries of Love," through a lifetime of heroic martyrdom, will strike many readers as a perfectly charming if somewhat dated form of Victorian science fiction, a New World fiction that derives its strength from Dickinson's economical evocation of a world better forgotten. For example, consider this stanza:

> Was Bridal—e'er like This?
> A Paradise—the Host—
> And Cherubim—and Seraphim—
> The unobtrusive Guest—   (625)

The question is evidently a rhetorical one, the answer no. The word "unobtrusive," which conjures up its opposite (the busybody who spoils any social occasion) grounds this fantasy in a world we know and gives it its vulnerable, defended, privatistic Dickinsonian slant.

It takes a good deal of work to recover this story, for reasons both accidental and fundamental to Dickinson's "lyric" sensibility. First, standard modern reading editions do not isolate the poems thematically, so there is the initial problem of recovering the appropriate group of texts. This is, however, a problem of no mean proportions, and the history of Dickinson criticism has demonstrated that no two readers would be likely to retrieve an identical set. Ignoring for the moment the problem of poems at the margin, let us assume that we have identified the basic episodes of the plot. Second, the story is seldom, if ever, presented in its entirety in a single poem; aspects of the plot that dominate the structure of particular poems are suppressed entirely elsewhere so that other facets of the unfolding drama may be revealed. The feeling order of the kernel story we retrieve may be summarized as follows: the privation of love, a moment of fulfillment, a moment of sharp sudden loss or renunciation, a lifetime of mingled regret and awe for which the poet imagines either no conclusion or an affirmative conclusion after death. Along the way, either before or after this moment of fulfillment, there are pleas for acceptance, temporary rebuffs, fears that her behavior has been either inappropriate or misinterpreted, and confessions that

> If *He dissolve*—then—there is *nothing*—*more*—
> *Eclipse*—at *Midnight*—
> It was *dark*—*before*—
>
> *Sunset*—at *Easter*—
> *Blindness*—on the *Dawn*—
> *Faint* Star of Bethlehem—
> *Gone down!*   (236)

The mode is alternately desperate and ecstatic and sometimes both. Since our interest is consistently directed either toward the speaker's anticipated or recollected pleasures or toward her losses and renunciations, our curiosity about her lover, though indirectly aroused, is never fully gratified. Hence the least stable element of the plot is who abandoned whom, particularly since many poems assume that her lover's absence or death was unwilled by either party.

Were I compelled to choose a single poem that best represents the nucleus tale, it would be the following:

> There came a Day at Summer's full,
> Entirely for me—
> I thought that such were for the Saints,
> Where Resurrections—be—
>
> The Sun, as common, went abroad,
> The flowers, accustomed, blew,
> As if no soul the solstice passed
> That maketh all things new—
>
> The time was scarce profaned, by speech—
> The symbol of a word
> Was needless, as at Sacrament,
> The Wardrobe—of our Lord—
>
> Each was to each The Sealed Church,
> Permitted to commune this—time—
> Lest we too awkward show
> At Supper of the Lamb.
>
> The Hours slid fast—as Hours will,
> Clutched tight, by greedy hands—
> So faces on two Decks, look back,
> Bound to opposing lands—
>
> And so when all the time had leaked,
> Without external sound
> Each bound the Other's Crucifix—
> We gave no other Bond—
>
> Sufficient troth, that we shall rise—
> Deposed—at length, the Grave—
> To that new Marriage,
> Justified—through Calvaries of Love—   (322)

The only significant element missing here is the presence of or quest for a scapegoat. Unless that scapegoat be the old, awkward, leaky, profane, unjustifiable imperfection of the slippery, falling, fallen human condition itself.

There also exists a pretext, a prior context of experience, that presses against the discontinuous narrative line of these poems. Behind the acknowledged guilts, the acknowledged shames, the acknowledged obstacles to the fulfillment of desire, lurks an unacknowledged need to court martyrdom and to elicit punishment, so as to extinguish a demonic self masquerading as a compliant victim. This demonic self undermines the saintliness of Dickinson's woman in white or her "little girl" equivalent, expresses the sadistic component of Dickinson's sado-masochistic sexual imagination, and will not be silenced.

The interrupting or subordinated pretext depends on Dickinson's preoccupation with hierarchies of sexual status. Associating masculinity with power, she associates male sexual power with violence. Associating femininity with powerlessness, she associates female sexuality with masochism. Thus this pretext incorporates Dickinson's envy of her lover's power, her fear of it—he can cause her to cringe, to cower—and her fear of her own sexual rage. Projecting her aggression onto her lover, she is victimized by him.[5] Repressing the unwomanly power of blackness, she celebrates the power of whiteness. Within Dickinson's democratic heavenly utopia, this hierarchical pretext will have been extinguished.

Within her undemocratic earthly dystopia, however, Dickinson occasionally suggests that a brutal Master is better than none at all. Such brutality numbs her into insensibility toward a peripheral range of equally disturbing relationships. In subordinating herself to her Master, she liberates herself from other forms of subordination. Acquiescing in his power, she participates decisively in it, as the syntactical ambiguity of the following poem suggests. His gestures, within lines three through six of the first stanza, are also hers:

> He put the Belt around my life—
> I heard the Buckle snap—
> And turned away, imperial,
> My Lifetime folding up—
> Deliberate, as a Duke would do
> A Kingdom's Title Deed—
> Henceforth, a Dedicated sort—
> A Member of the Cloud.

5. In "The Poetics of Emily Dickinson," *ELH* 38 (March 1971), Eleanor Wilner describes Dickinson's ego as threatened by an internal "unintegrated force" which she projected onto her Master (p. 128).

Yet not too far to come at call—
And do the little Toils
That make the Circuit of the Rest—
And deal occasional smiles
To lives that stoop to notice mine—
And kindly ask it in—
Whose invitation, know you not
For Whom I must decline? (273)

Whether Muse or Master, God or Internal Adversary, Dickinson's "He" confers identity upon someone who is still perceived by others and who formerly perceived herself as an "it." As "A Member of the Cloud," she looks down on those who look down on her.

Whether located in this world or in the next, Dickinson's marriage fiction is more successful in conveying the urgency of her quest for psychic integration than in persuading the reader that the union she describes is, ever will be, or ever has been fully accomplished. We know and value the other through her response to him; he activates more pain than joy. This imbalance subjects her marriage fiction to pressures that place extraordinary demands on her poetic intelligence. If we as readers find it difficult to determine whether Dickinson's pain is caused by her lover's absence, by her imagination of his presence, or by her experience of actual men, this is because Dickinson herself is finally unable to make this determination. Similarly, if we as readers find it difficult to distinguish between the facts and the fictions of Dickinson's erotic experience, she herself appears to have been caught up in a comparable confusion. Hence her habit of dressing all in white, dating from about 1862 when her passion for the recipient of the "Master" letters had, in all probability, been checked by his refusal to submit to deification.[6] Dickinson's biographical and poetic identities may also have coincided in another way. The most enduring feature of her religion of love, which ideally insulates her from the pressures of other human relationships, is its inability to do so for any extended duration. This is at once its strength and its weakness.

Consider, for instance, the following speech, in which her ecstatic

6. For other interpretations of Dickinson's costume, see Sandra M. Gilbert and Susan Gubar, *The Madwoman in the Attic: The Woman Writer and the Nineteenth-Century Literary Imagination* (New Haven: Yale University Press, 1979), pp. 613–22.

image of mystic bridal has degenerated into a desperate experience of secret suffering:

> Rearrange a "Wife's" affection!
> When they dislocate my Brain!
> Amputate my freckled Bosom!
> Make me bearded like a man!
>
> Blush, my spirit, in thy Fastness—
> Blush, my unacknowledged clay—
> Seven years of troth have taught thee
> More than Wifehood ever may!
>
> Love that never leaped its socket—
> Trust entrenched in narrow pain—
> Constancy thro' fire—awarded—
> Anguish—bare of anodyne!
>
> Burden—borne so far triumphant—
> None suspect me of the crown,
> For I wear the "Thorns" till *Sunset*—
> Then—my Diadem put on.
>
> Big my Secret but it's *bandaged*—
> It will never get away
> Till the Day its Weary Keeper
> Leads it through the Grave to thee.   (1737)

Her version of the story runs something like this. Some voice has counseled that she give up her dangerous fantasy of secret wifehood, which is at once the avatar of her normal womanhood and the obstacle to its fulfillment. The quotation marks around "Wife" stress that she is not actually married, but that she experiences herself as wed to the "thee" who makes a sudden appearance in the poem's last word. To repudiate this dangerous counsel, she responds by turning what she perceives as the violent assault of this suggestion upon herself. Until "they" mutilate her physically or transform her into a grotesque man, events that she does not expect to occur, her allegiance to her lover cannot be altered. There is, however, something embarrassing about this situation. Before concluding that seven years of betrothal have taught her more about love's perpetuity than any actual marriage ever could, she urges her spirit and her body, her "unacknowledged clay," to blush for their steadfastness. Judged from an external perspective, her anguish has been unrewarded. Judged from an internal perspective, she has been strengthened by it. Stanza four, however, permits us to see that she has been arguing all along not with someone else but with herself. No one *suspects* her of this burden, which amounts to a kind of hidden pregnancy. The phrase "till *Sunset*" suggests that, after death, she will replace the martyr's crown with the bride's diadem. It may also suggest that at night the speaker rewards herself, perhaps through sexual fantasies or through masturbation. Although the ending of the poem is fatigued, a postmortem reunion of "I" and "thee," imagined more energetically elsewhere, is posited.

Why isn't the speaker's version of her triumphant anguish adequate? Is it because she is drawing on a context of religious associations no longer equally available to us? I think not. We can read *Paradise Lost* without encountering this difficulty, although our reading can be enriched by extratextual aids. Moreover, in his article "Paradise Deferred: The Image of Heaven in the Work of Emily Dickinson and Emily Stuart Phelps," Barton Levi St. Armand has reconstructed the popular appeal of this fantasy of a heavenly reunion of lovers or families separated on earth. He points out that the image of "Heaven Our Home" was a sentimental reaction against the orthodox stereotype of a God-centered, impersonal afterlife. This reaction peaked during the 1860s and extended back at least to 1830, the date of Dickinson's birth. St. Armand contends that "Emily Dickinson had already explored most of the ideas about a domestic heaven and a spiritual love beyond the grave which were embodied in *The Gates Ajar* by the time that this pot-boiler was first published in . . . 1868."[7] But this historical gloss does not account for the poem's tone. Because the speaker is unable to project herself imaginatively into a redeemed future scene, the poem's mode is neither sentimental nor domestic, but agonistic. Here, Dickinson has married the reality of sexual rage, which she unconsciously associates with the destruction of her womanhood. This explains why, having indulged herself in the fantasy of virility which is presented as a punishment in stanza one, she goes on to introduce the element of shame in stanza two—an element that is otherwise inexplicable within the terms of the story she tells. At some level of consciousness, she asks herself, Why would anyone persist in such strict adherence

7. Barton Levi St. Armand, "Paradise Deferred: The Image of Heaven in the Work of Emily Dickinson and Elizabeth Stuart Phelps," *American Quarterly* 29 (Spring 1977): 56.

to a discipline of pain? One of the answers Dickinson provides is that she does not conceive of this love as hopeless, that, on the contrary, she looks forward to a reconciliation with her lover after death. The emotional logic of her stance is more accessible if we assume that, in some measure, she already has what she wants: to perpetuate the power of secrets and, in so doing, to control her rage.

The object of this rage is not obviously or simply her archetypal "husband." Certainly, the poem suggests that the affections of actual wives are untrustworthy. It does not specify that wives become disaffected because they are oppressed by their husbands, though this is a reasonable extension of her line of thought. Perhaps this is the secret Dickinson chooses not to acknowledge to herself and the source of the sexual rage against which her masochism defends her. In any event, she perceives the sexual climate of her environment as oppressive. In response to this oppression, Dickinson oppresses herself. Consciously, she attributes her pain to her lover's absence. Unconsciously, her vision of marriage is unredeemable. The actual wife she imagines may be a furiously castrating virago, as her secret wife is not. Thus Dickinson does indeed rearrange a wife's "affection," although it is not clear for whom she martyrs herself; her loyalties appear perhaps equally divided between *her* requirements, those of her "husband," and those of his typically disaffected wife. Because the manuscript is missing, there is no way of dating this unsettling poem with any certainty. Presumably it postdates the remaining marriage poems I shall discuss, but it is particularly useful, as endings often are, in illuminating origins.

Let us return to the birth of Dickinson's bride. She makes her first appearance in 1860 with the blunt declaration,

> I'm "wife"—I've finished that—
> That other state—
> I'm Czar—I'm "Woman" now—
> It's safer so—
>
> How odd the Girl's life looks
> Behind this soft Eclipse—
> I think that Earth feels so
> To folks in Heaven—now—
>
> This being comfort—then
> That other kind—was pain—
> But why compare?
> I'm "Wife"! Stop there!   (199)

Dickinson presents an absolute cleavage between the girl's life and the woman's, is unambiguous in associating marriage and power ("I'm Czar—I'm 'Woman' now—"), but attaches highly qualified values to this abrupt transformation in status which is preceded neither by courtship rituals nor by a sensuous awakening. The tone of the poem is not precisely ironic, yet the quotation marks around "wife" and "Woman" suggest that the speaker is still resisting these terms. Amazed to discover herself so different from the vulnerable creature she had been, she calls her new life "safer," compares it to being in heaven—comfortable, but perhaps boring. Marriage, a "soft Eclipse" of the unregenerate self, represents stoppage, not process. The absence of perfect rhyme for ten lines, an unusually long suspension, reinforces the closural effect of the concluding couplet, just as it provides an auditory articulation of her theme: her loyalty to the odd, unclosed girl's life undercuts the marriage fiction she creates for herself and a fuller comparison of the old self and the new might reveal that they have more in common than she cares to admit here. The lines themselves are unusually short, their limited rhythmic sweep interrupted even further by dashes and by two- and three-word sentences. Thus the sound conveys constriction rather than expansion, since what the poem examines best is not marriage (for where, after all, is her husband?) but the speaker's need to defend herself against her original social context.

Again, this situation is a highly suggestive one. As an unmarried woman, Dickinson is peculiarly vulnerable to others. She has no husband, for example, to defend her against influential parents. To escape from her old home, she needs a new one. This escape is impeded by the attitudes toward marriage and toward sexual experience she has acquired, in part, by observing the interactions of her biological progenitors. Fantasy provides a way out; however, to the extent that fantasy gratifies her, as it clearly does within the poem just cited, it also locks her in, since she stops there.

Escaping into fantasy, Dickinson's virginal and saintly wife imposes upon herself the martyr's burden of sexual repression. Dickinson's vision of saintliness was grounded, however, in no steady religious belief, and she does not always conceive of marriage in society and in nature as an unredeemable experience. The degree of her unfocused sexual rage fluctuates. Thus many poems suggest that her loss of sexual experience was not a voluntary sacrifice but an accidental bereavement, an unwilled crucifixion she struggles to endure. For example, in the following poem as "Empress of Calvary," she is "Betrothed—without the swoon / God sends us Women." Having been "Born—Bridalled—Shrouded— / In a Day," she strokes words whose sexual implications she has yet to master. Her attitude toward this lost experience ricochets back and forth from line to line, from phrase to phrase, from word to word, and I shall examine the poem in more detail shortly. But for the moment, let us note that one of its themes is that to be both married and unmarried sunders body and spirit, and that the speaker's words are designed to reunite them:

> Title divine—is mine!
> The Wife—without the Sign!
> Acute Degree—conferred on me—
> Empress of Calvary!
> Royal—all but the Crown!
> Betrothed—without the swoon
> God sends us Women—
> When you—hold—Garnet to Garnet—
> Gold—to Gold—
> Born—Bridalled—Shrouded—
> In a Day—
> "My Husband"—women say—
> Stroking the Melody—
> Is *this*—the way?   (1072)

Similarly, in a poem whose language aligns it closely with others of her marriage group, she continues to emphasize that her status involves both an affirmation and a negation. A revelation or "Sign" has been granted her which nullifies her sense of having been cheated, robbed, stolen from. Although the manner of the revelation is obscure, the feeling stimulated by it is not: "Mine." "Mine." "Mine." "Mine." "Mine." "Mine—long as Ages steal!"

> Mine—by the Right of the White Election!
> Mine—by the Royal Seal!
> Mine—by the Sign in the Scarlet prison—
> Bars—cannot conceal!
>
> Mine—here—in Vision—and in Veto!
> Mine—by the Grave's Repeal—
> Titled—Confirmed—
> Delirious Charter!
> Mine—long as Ages steal!   (528)

Why all this concern with titles, charters, seals, contracts? Such words distance the experience of marriage while attempting to legitimize the speaker's right to it. Dickinson, however, refuses to reveal the history that has legitimized her, for fear that it may be robbed of her. The language teases us with a vision of communicability that is simultaneously vetoed. If this is a poem about being married to "God," as Charles Anderson has suggested, He speaks to her alone.[8] This imbalance between a referential language of experience and a nonreferential language of language camouflages the delirious egoism the poem cannot conceal. God expands as nature recedes; the persona becomes godlike in an empty universe. The last speaker in history's scarlet prison, she is the first emigrant to ecstasy's unbloodied shores. In this respect, He may also be She. The speaker herself may be God.

Dickinson's attitude toward the death of her natural universe, a death occasioned by the suppression of her sexual rage, varies from poem to poem and indeed from moment to moment within particular texts. For example, in "Title divine—is mine!" the opening line is an unqualified endorsement of her own titular divinity. Line two, "The Wife—without the Sign!" both specifies what kind of title she has and indicates that something is missing. Line three, "Acute Degree—conferred on me," takes up the theme of emptiness or pain and thus contradicts the attitude initially expressed. It also causes us to wonder who conferred this by now remarkably problematic status on her. Lines four and five come closest to unifying the antagonistic feelings she is expressing toward the state in which she finds herself, a state of simultaneous marriage and divorce: "Empress of Calvary! / Royal—all but the Crown!" Lines six through nine measure her distance from the tribe, from other women, and introduce an agent. I am, however, reluctant to conclude that this agent, "God," can now be comprehended as the missing actor of line three or, rather, that the speaker herself had come to this conclusion at that point in the poem. That "God" legitimizes double-ring ceremonies and permits women to enjoy sexual pleasures once they are officially married need not imply his accountability for her predicament in line three. Lines ten and eleven introduce a new element into the story for

8. After tracing the biblical sources of its language through several pages of dense textual analysis, Charles Anderson concludes that the poem is "an imaginative projection of what it would be like to be betrothed to God." See *Emily Dickinson's Poetry: Stairway of Surprise* (New York: Holt, Rinehart and Winston, 1960), pp. 183–87.

which the poem has not adequately prepared us: the speaker was "Born—Bridalled—Shrouded— / In a Day." The poem has prepared us for the association of her titular marriage and death, but it has not provided us with the information we need to understand why the day of her birth is also the day of her death. Marriage ceremonies happen in a day, crisis conversions may happen in a day, but someone who is "Empress of Calvary!" has a history behind her and must have done something to earn that "Title divine" to which she lays claim in the opening line. From other poems, we may infer that she has extinguished "the Girl's life," that she has died or renounced the world in order to be [re]born. That information is presented in the passive voice here, nor is it plausible that all this could have happened in a day. The danger of backsliding is too great. In addition, the word "Bridalled," with its suggestion of being reined in like a horse, is a curious choice given the sacred implications of her language. Since the speaker is now dead, or dead to the world, the poem might be expected to end here or to rise to the level of retrospective summary.[9] Instead, in the last three lines the emphasis is more exclusively focused on the speaker's desire to imitate the language and the experience of other women. These lines underscore the difficulty of sustaining a relationship that is deprived of appropriate context, or audience. We are then left with a question that directs us back into the poet's unfinished life, rather than into the completed realm of transpersonal myth.

Since Dickinson turns to others at the conclusion of this discourse asking, "Is *this*—the way?" let me take up the challenge. The marriage she is describing is incomplete. Is this its virtue or its tragic flaw? No one but the speaker can answer this question, but her distance from any lover (whether husband or God) prevents her from evaluating how she would feel were partnership at issue. As "Empress of Calvary," Dickinson already has an identity, that of an artist who wants to be God, to complete herself, and to have us watch her doing so. She wants us to be present at the creation and to stand back herself and admire her handiwork; since what she has created is herself, this is love begotten by despair upon impossibility. She also wishes not to be God; crowns weigh heavily on human heads. Thus she seeks a husband who might share her burden or who

9. An alternate version sent to Sue inserts an extra line, the adjectival phrase "Tri Victory," at this point.

might usurp her privilege. The poem incorporates both the hope and the fear. It cannot tell us what outcome she foresees, for the text emerges out of her ambivalence toward the death of imperial selfhood.

In poems where she sacrifices her ambition to be God, Dickinson establishes a more convincing case for her lover's omnipotence:

> I got so I could hear his name—
> Without—Tremendous gain—
> That Stop-sensation—on my Soul—
> And Thunder—in the Room—
>
> I got so I could walk across
> That Angle in the floor,
> Where he turned so, and I turned—how—
> And all our Sinew tore—
>
> I got so I could stir the Box—
> In which his letters grew
> Without that forcing, in my breath—
> As Staples—driven through—
>
> Could dimly recollect a Grace—
> I think, they call it "God"—
> Renowned to ease Extremity—
> When Formula, had failed—
>
> And shape my Hands—
> Petition's way,
> Tho' ignorant of a word
> That Ordination—utters—
>
> My Business, with the Cloud,
> If any Power behind it, be,
> Not subject to Despair—
> It care, in some remoter way,
> For so minute affair
> As Misery—
> Itself, too great, for interrupting—more—   (293)

The alternate word choices provide a somewhat sharper indication of the episode to which the second stanza alludes, for which it provides such precise geography. "Where he turned so, and I turned—how— / And all our Sinew tore—": "Where he turned so, and I let go— / And all our Sinew tore." Once, her resistance crumbled and her love was physically consummated. Once, "Formula, had failed," once "Filament—had failed." Once, the "single Hair," the "filament," the "law," the "Cobweb—wove in Adamant," the "Battlement—of Straw" collapsed (398). Another reading is possible here, since the language also suggests rending, parting, divorce. In either case, what has never been joined cannot be torn asunder. At some time, in some way, these characters were one flesh, even if only in her imagination of their mutual excruciation. Riveting us with her emphasis on where events occur ("on my Soul," "in the Room," "That Angle in the floor," "the Box— / In which his letters grew," "that forcing, in my breath") Dickinson nevertheless admits this essential ambiguity: she may have let go of herself or of her lover; she and he may have turned toward or away from each other; a turning toward may also be a turning away. Now, having been abandoned by her lover after having abandoned herself to him, she turns toward the vast amorphous "It" unacquainted with grief, grief that can neither arrest itself nor be arrested by a God who has never himself been subjected to despair. Within this poem, Dickinson's lover probably knows such despair. He, however, is not ignorant of the sacred word "That Ordination—utters." He, as I attempted to show in chapter 3, was an ordained minister. As she seeks to identify the power behind nature's cloud, "If any Power behind it, be," Dickinson spells out the difficulty of transferring her loyalty from a godlike man to an inhumane deity and concludes that this transference cannot be effected. Although the Bible tells us that "None see God and live—" (1247), Dickinson tells us that none who have seen a god incarnate can live without him. As a principle of cosmic justice, "God" exists in this poem only to reveal the futility of the speaker's quest for order.

A number of critics have remarked on the poem's movement from confidence to despair.[10] This movement is, however, thoroughly

10. R. P. Blackmur cites it as an example of Dickinson's "technical and moral confusion" in "Emily Dickinson: Notes on Prejudice and Fact," *Southern Review* 3 (1937); reprinted in *The Recognition of Emily Dickinson: Selected Criticism since 1890*, ed. Caesar R. Blake and Carlton F. Wells (Ann Arbor: University of Michigan Press, 1964), pp. 221–23. David Porter, in *The Art of Emily Dickinson's Early Poetry* (Cambridge: Harvard University Press, 1966), pp. 173–74, calls it a work of "consummate artistry" which brings "emotional disturbance under control." He concludes that "the vision is a tragic one: even if God is attentive to individual anguish, He is effectually indifferent." Sharon Cameron, in *Lyric Time: Dickinson and the Limits of Genre* (Baltimore: Johns Hopkins University Press, 1979), p. 60, argues that "the disjunction between the two parts of 'I got so I could take his name' is revelatory of narrative breakdown, not of controlled narrative transformation."

comprehensible within the terms of the story she sets forth. When she is most firmly identified with her lover, she experiences the greatest degree of personal integration. This identification depends initially on the language she associates with him and subsequently on his physical presence. Because the poem turns on his visit to her room, which destroyed the more controlled text of their prior communication, Dickinson's memory of that decisive turning is followed by what appears to be a turning away from her story. In perpetuating the religious vocabulary she associates with her lover, however, Dickinson continues to perpetuate her identification with him. Beginning with stanza four, she attempts to place her loss within a less personal context: "Could dimly recollect a Grace— / I think, they call it 'God'— / Renowned to ease Extremity— / When Formula, had failed." This effort to align personal experience with religious theory necessarily proves ineffectual. What kind of "Formula" could account for "That Stop-sensation—on my Soul— / And Thunder—in the Room," or for an imagination this attentive to what must be risked to secure "Tremendous gain"? Although "A nearness to Tremendousness— / An Agony procures—" (963), a distance from tremendousness produces nothingness.[11]

"I got so I could hear his name—" may have been written in 1861, the year following Charles Wadsworth's visit to Amherst, probably to Dickinson's room, and perhaps to the "Room" of her body. That is, Dickinson's poems, including the sexually suggestive text just cited, establish a somewhat more convincing case for her knowledge of "Master's" body than her relationship with Wadsworth is likely to have yielded. "I live with Him—I see His face—" has been attributed to 1862. Certainly, however, this poem is psychologically later. Dickinson's memories of her lover's physical presence are less acute; consequently, her anger at having been deserted by him—anger which, in "I got so I could hear his name," she had projected onto an inhumane deity—is also less intense. Nevertheless, her ability to dis-

11. The heavily emended text of this poem, as photographed in *The Manuscript Books of Emily Dickinson*, ed. R. W. Franklin, 2 vols. (Cambridge: Harvard University Press, 1981), 1: 231, suggests that Johnson may have misread line one of the first stanza, which perhaps reads, "I got so I could hear his name—think—*take*—". Johnson proposed "think" and "take" as alternatives for "hear." Franklin's facsimile also suggests an additional line at the poem's conclusion: "Supremer than—Superior to—". Were these changes to be adopted, the first would seem to amplify Dickinson's meaning, the second to weaken an already problematic ending. Clearly, Johnson misread the verb "called" in stanza four. Finally, line three, stanza two, may read, "Where he turned so, and I turned—how—let go—".

tinguish effectively between physical absence and emotional presence is undercut by her inability to distinguish between unreciprocated love and death. Dickinson has progressed beyond bitterness, but she has not progressed so far beyond it as to have shaken herself free from an unappeased hunger for her lover's physical presence. Hence the poem zigs out of shape in the second stanza when she attempts to distinguish between the solitude of her life and the solitude of her anticipated death:

> I live with Him—I see His face—
> I go no more away
> For Visiter—or Sundown—
> Death's single privacy
>
> The Only One—forestalling Mine—
> And that—by Right that He
> Presents a Claim invisible—
> No Wedlock—granted Me—
>
> I live with Him—I hear His Voice—
> I stand alive—Today—
> To witness to the Certainty
> Of Immortality—
>
> Taught Me—by Time—the lower Way—
> Conviction—Every day—
> That Life like This—is stopless—
> Be Judgment—what it may—   (463)

As the poem builds to the concluding stanza, the speaker testifies to the power of any emotion that outdistances its cause, usurps the present, and expands to include the whole of life. How can we evaluate, how does the speaker evaluate, an experience of this sort, for this matter of "Judgment," of psychological and moral perspective, cannot be dismissed by attacking a theological structure that is also represented as out of touch with "Time—the lower Way." The poem suggests that "stopless" experiences or the obsessions that occasion them preclude judgments. Judgments depend on a distance from experience; obsessions depend on the absence of this distance. In attacking a theological structure that has distanced reality, Dickinson, perhaps unconsciously, attacks herself as well. Thus the ambiguity persists: her lover is both alive and dead, as is the speaker. Similarly, although she states categorically "No Wedlock—

granted Me," some kind of wedlock is clearly hers. Sacred marriage and death marriage in one, this relationship effectively neuters both characters. This self-neutering is the tragic end toward which her finest achievements as a poet of love's loss are directed.[12] The insanity of this conclusion is such that she herself resists it:

> I cannot live with You—
> It would be Life—
> And Life is over there—
> Behind the Shelf
>
> The Sexton keeps the Key to—
> Putting up
> Our Life—His Porcelain—
> Like a Cup—
>
> Discarded of the Housewife—
> Quaint—or Broke—
> A newer Sevres pleases—
> Old Ones crack—
>
> I could not die—with You—
> For One must wait
> To shut the Other's Gaze down—
> You—could not—
>
> And I—Could I stand by
> And see You—freeze—
> Without my Right of Frost—
> Death's privilege?

12. No aspect of Dickinson's love poetry has provoked more discomfort among critics than her intermittent praise of a fleshless interior marriage over a more recognizable erotic union. If Cody and Griffith have been quick to label her attitudes neurotic, Charles Anderson makes the more restrained assertion that "in her poetry spiritual ecstasy burns with a purer incandescence than amorous joy, and it creates better poems." See *Emily Dickinson's Poetry*, p. 190. George Monteiro seeks to overcome this difficulty with the observation, "She reached the conviction that immortality gained would enable, not a meeting of disembodied beings forever spiritualized and abidingly discrete, but the happy union of two lovers, physically and sensually joined at last and for eternity." Though Dickinson never reached this conviction, Monteiro anticipates my argument. See "Love & Fame Or What's A Heaven For?: Emily Dickinson's Teleology," *New England Quarterly* 51 (March 1978): 106. Since religious conversion and marriage are so closely intertwined linguistically throughout Dickinson's bridal group, William R. Sherwood believes that she is describing the Puritan experience of grace. Dickinson, he argues, dedicated herself to God alone in 1862, following a failed attempt at human love. See *Circumference and Circumstance: Stages in the Mind and Art of Emily Dickinson* (New York: Columbia University Press, 1968).

Nor could I rise—with You—
Because Your Face
Would put out Jesus'—
That New Grace

Glow plain—and foreign
On my homesick Eye—
Except that You than He
Shone closer by—

They'd judge Us—How—
For You—served Heaven—You know,
Or sought to—
I could not—

Because You saturated Sight—
And I had no more Eyes
For sordid excellence
As Paradise

And were You lost, I would be—
Though My Name
Rang loudest
On the Heavenly fame—

And were You—saved—
And I—condemned to be
Where You were not—
That self—were Hell to Me—

So We must meet apart—
You there—I—here—
With just the Door ajar
That Oceans are—and Prayer—
And that White Sustenance—
Despair—   (640)

Arguing with herself, Dickinson considers three major resolutions for the frustrations she is seeking to define and to resolve. Each of these resolutions is expressed in negative form: living with her lover, dying with him, and discovering a world beyond nature. Building on this series of negations, Dickinson advances a catalogue of reasons for her covenant with despair, which are both final and insufficient. Throughout, she excoriates the social and religious authorities that impede her union, but she remains emotionally unconvinced that she has correctly identified her antagonists.

In stanzas four and five, Dickinson considers and rejects a suicide pact, yet the reasons she advances as a deterrent simply underscore the ambivalence behind her statement "I could not die—with You." Why "You—could not—" wait to close her eyes were she to predecease him is unexplained. Perhaps at this point, in stanza four, she fantasizes her lover's immortality. If so, this fantasy is immediately rejected and countermanded by stanza five. Under the circumstances she is describing, there is no particular reason why a corpse needs to have its eyes closed, unless she is implying that she needs help with dying and that her lover would be incapable of murder.[13] However one interprets these lines (one critic believes she is alluding to an age difference between them), stanzas four and five are internally coherent only if one assumes that the real problem is not her inability but her unwillingness to die herself or to cause her lover to do so.[14] If we answer the rhetorical question of stanza five by responding "No," suicide provides her with the resolution she is seeking, but this resolution has already been foreclosed by the initial power of the negative, "I could not die—with You." Stanzas six and seven develop the emotional logic of this death-wish, but they do so in language permeated with the promise of Christian redemption. Interposing her lover's face between herself and Jesus, she chooses her human lover over his divine rival but is unwilling to renounce the promise of a new life. Consequently, there is a further development of this conflict between religious authority and Dickinson's experience of it.

Stanzas eight through eleven, while they may allude to her lover's ministerial vocation, certainly allude to the only source of conflict between them: his piety as contrasted with her unbelief. Judged by the standards of sexton and housewife (this is not absolutely a two-person human universe), their love is illegitimate, perhaps because he is already married, perhaps because he has already dedicated himself to Christ, as she has not. Yet this conflict comes to rest, finally, not between the lovers or between the lovers and the society to which they are marginally attached. Rather, it is positioned within the speaker's blasphemous and devotional modes of seeing. Her love for him has blocked her earlier vision of paradise. He is now her paradise, what she saw previously only "sordid excellence." Because

---

13. See "Promise This—When You be Dying—" (648) for an occasion when the persona, in closing her lover's eyes, participates in a deathbed ritual that is emotionally convincing.

14. Cameron, *Lyric Time*, p. 81.

he lives by the values she appears to have renounced, her attachment to him perpetuates her need for legitimate religious authority.
Whether or not he represents such authority she has no way of
telling: whether he "served Heaven" or merely "sought to" she does
not know. Nor does she understand the relationship between the
attempt to serve heaven, in which she claims not to have participated, and the end product, grace. Thus it might happen that she
should be saved, he lost, or that he should be saved and she condemned to be where he was not. In either case, "That self—were
Hell to Me." Though the concluding six-line stanza does not succeed
in identifying a comprehensive cause for this still insufficiently motivated suffering, it does succeed in identifying a comprehensive end.
Like houses on two discrete continents, these lovers "meet apart
. . . With just the Door ajar / That Oceans are—and Prayer— / And
that White Sustenance— / Despair." In abandoning the power of the
negative, Dickinson frees herself to admit that, as a consequence of
her terminal loneliness, symbols of linkage are by now indistinguishable from symbols of separation.

Although Dickinson's religion of love is also a religion of despair,
the extent to which her most ecstatic love poems depend on a religious vocabulary that distances nature is no mere accident. Much as
some poems protest against her loss of erotic experience, Dickinson's imagination when it soars successfully invokes a world elsewhere and thus reaches beyond the limits of human sexuality as we
know it. A poem such as the following, for example, although structured around the conceit of flying which in Freudian terms we may
understand as a dream metaphor for sexual intercourse, is primarily
concerned with leave-taking as a mode of transcendence. Rising
above "this mortal noise" as did Elijah in his chariot, a journey to
which she alludes explicitly in poem 1254, Dickinson describes an
experience of such unnatural tranquility that "No Seasons were to
us— / It was not Night nor Morn— / But Sunrise stopped upon the
place / And fastened it in Dawn":

> It was a quiet way—
> He asked if I was his—
> I made no answer of the Tongue
> But answer of the Eyes—
> And then He bore me on
> Before this mortal noise
> With swiftness, as of Chariots

And distance, as of Wheels.
This World did drop away
As Acres from the feet
Of one that leaneth from Balloon
Upon an Ether street.
The Gulf behind was not,
The Continents were new—
Eternity it was before
Eternity was due.
No Seasons were to us—
It was not Night nor Morn—
But Sunrise stopped upon the place
And fastened it in Dawn. (1053)

Similarly, in Dickinson's best-known love poem, she is "Rowing in Eden," where human sexual antagonisms have ceased to matter.[15] The concluding image, "Might I but moor—Tonight— / In Thee!" is freed from its physical connotations in order to convey the quiet, even regressive aftermath of orgiastic release. Her journey into Eden hearkens back to the oceanic bliss of a prior time:

Wild Nights—Wild Nights!
Were I with thee
Wild Nights should be
Our luxury!

Futile—the Winds—
To a Heart in port—
Done with the Compass—
Done with the Chart!

Rowing in Eden—
Ah, the Sea!
Might I but moor—Tonight—
In Thee! (249)

Again, the following poem employs the eternally regressive sea imagery of "Wild Nights." Perpetuating a Christian North, it introduces a Jewish and a pagan South as well. A gentled paternal touch once transformed Dickinson into a ravished, royal self. The concluding stanza, however, acknowledges that her transfiguration has been

15. For a brief but illuminating discussion of sexual envy in Dickinson, see Judith Fetterley, *The Resisting Reader: A Feminist Approach to American Fiction* (Bloomington: Indiana University Press, 1978), p. ix.

a partial one. After this single encounter with "her imperial Sun,"
she is still baffled, even crucified, by her distance from him:

> He touched me, so I live to know
> That such a day, permitted so,
> I groped upon his breast—
> It was a boundless place to me
> And silenced, as the awful sea
> Puts minor streams to rest.
>
> And now, I'm different from before,
> As if I breathed superior air—
> Or brushed a Royal Gown—
> My feet, too, that had wandered so—
> My Gipsy face—transfigured now—
> To tenderer Renown—
>
> Into this Port, if I might come,
> Rebecca, to Jerusalem,
> Would not so ravished turn—
> Nor Persian, baffled at her shrine
> Lift such a Crucifixal sign
> To her imperial Sun.   (506)

Poems such as these which admit physical tenderness are rare
achievements for a sensibility which is most deeply committed to the
theme of sexual adversity. Emily Dickinson's love poems were never
conceived as impersonal experiments in a conventional lyric genre.
If their association of lover and father-God is "too persistent to be
dismissed,"[16] their association of sex and death and of male on-
slaughts and female deaths is equally pronounced:

> Struck, was I, nor yet by Lightning—
> Lightning—lets away
> Power to perceive His Process
> With Vitality.
>
> Maimed—was I—yet not by Venture—
> Stone of stolid Boy—

16. In *The Tenth Muse: The Psyche of the American Poet* (Cambridge: Harvard University Press, 1975), pp. 241–42, Albert Gelpi argues persuasively that "love was for her
an experience which had something to do with man and something to do with
God. . . . The association of the amatory and (in a loose sense) the mystical—as God
becomes lover-bridegroom or lover manifests praeternatural or deific qualities—is
too persistent to be dismissed."

Nor a Sportsman's Peradventure—
Who mine Enemy?

Robbed—was I—intact to Bandit—
All my Mansion torn—
Sun—withdrawn to Recognition—
Furthest shining—done—

Yet was not the foe—of any—
Not the smallest Bird
In the nearest Orchard dwelling
Be of Me—afraid.

Most—I love the Cause that slew Me.
Often as I die
It's beloved Recognition
Holds a Sun on Me—

Best—at Setting—as is Nature's—
Neither witnessed Rise
Till the infinite Aurora
In the other's eyes.   (925)

At first maimed by an unnatural rapist, Dickinson emerges from this experience hungry for further wounds. She claims to have had an experience that she likens to a physical attack, to robbery, and to death, to have salvaged her "Power to perceive His Process," and then to enjoy the repetition of her dyings. Punished for her unnatural strength, which she explicitly denies in the fourth stanza, she has also been rewarded for it. Though chilled by the absence of her lover, whom she compares to the sun, Dickinson is electrocuted by his presence. As he withdraws from her, his power diminishes and she recognizes in his waning the occasion of her rebirth.

In telling the story of her unnatural devotion to a lover who persistently slays her, Dickinson attempts to reconcile her fear of male dominance with her passion for its power. Because these attitudes toward male sexual aggression are fundamentally incompatible, eventually she views time itself as her enemy: it prolongs her sexual vulnerability and impedes her spiritual rebirth. Consequently, she concludes that "Spirit cannot be moved by Flesh—It must be moved by spirit—" (PF44). If she and her lover are both disembodied, spirit may be moved by spirit. Dickinson, however, recognizes the perilous or morbid implications of this resolution and strives to control her sexual nature, rather than to eradicate it.

The psychological serenity Dickinson associated with an atemporal sexual utopia continued to elude her; her heavenly homecomings, in which spirit is moved by spirit, are transacted in the future or conditional tense.[17] Nevertheless, poems that draw heavily on a religious vocabulary which arrests nature at its most perfect or harrowing moment are generally more successful than poems where her lover is, in some immediate sense, more recognizably human. One sees this even in the wonderful poem just cited, "Struck, was I, nor yet by Lightning," in which Dickinson violates the logic of her Sun God metaphor in the concluding three lines. As each figure becomes the dawn or aurora, she introduces a new mutuality into the unequal relationship she has been depicting. With the Sun God now as dependent on her as she is on him, he is more nearly just a man, hungry for human affection. But it was the poem's scrupulous attention to modes of male dominance and female submission, extended throughout the subordinate metaphors even to the schoolboy with the stone, that engendered its climax, "Most—I love the Cause that slew Me," surely as perfect a resolution of the conflicts we have been examining as any single line Dickinson ever wrote.

To terminate the uncertain journey. To breathe superior air. To achieve an inner harmony that obviates the need for language. To escape from earth's limitations into that unbounded sea of love. Positing these transcendent goals, Dickinson locates them beyond time and beyond the gates of imprisoning human space of which the body is the pattern prison, the unfilable chain, reiterating imperiously, impatiently, "What if":

> What if I say I shall not wait!
> What if I burst the fleshly Gate—
> And pass escaped—to thee!
>
> What if I file this Mortal—off—
> See where it hurt me—That's enough—
> And step in Liberty!
>
> They cannot take me—any more!
> Dungeons can call—and Guns implore
> Unmeaning—now—to me—

17. An exception to the statement about tenses is "'Twas a long Parting—but the time / For Interview—had Come—" (625), which does not employ a first-person speaker. "Of Tribulation—these are They" (325) could describe either a psychological triumph over suffering or posthistorical sainthood.

As laughter—was—an hour ago—
Or Laces—or a Travelling Show—
Or who died—yesterday! (277)

This poem, like so many others, derives its power from Dickinson's shocking swerve away from the expected associations of freedom with life and of imprisonment with death. Yet even as she flaunts the boldness engendered by her despair, fantasizing a spirit-body which can choose its element, which her language has already caused us eerily to see, she resists that final step into the undiscovered country from which no traveler returns. Although the last two stanzas are grammatically present tense, they are aligned emotionally not with the "thee" who lured her on, provided her with an audience, provoked her ruthless "enough," but with her past. Recalling what she may lose, what she claims she has already lost—laughter, frivolous material pleasures, artful diversions, the capacity for grief which validates the meaning of human relationships—she is no longer the one who died, was dying yesterday. "Unmeaning—now—to me—": this too is the boundless place, liberated even from her memory of the wraithlike "thee." What if, indeed.

ANTI-QUEST,

OR THE AWFUL VACUUM

I

When her sacred marriage fails, Dickinson's death marriage
takes its place:

> Because I could not stop for Death—
> He kindly stopped for me—
> The Carriage held but just Ourselves—
> And Immortality.
>
> We slowly drove—He knew no haste
> And I had put away
> My labor and my leisure too,
> For His Civility—
>
> We passed the School, where Children strove
> At Recess—in the Ring—
> We passed the Fields of Gazing Grain—
> We passed the Setting Sun—
>
> Or rather—He passed Us—
> The Dews drew quivering and chill—
> For only Gossamer, my Gown—
> My Tippet—only Tulle—
>
> We paused before a House that seemed
> A Swelling of the Ground—
> The Roof was scarcely visible—
> The Cornice—in the Ground—

Since then—'tis Centuries—and yet
Feels shorter than the Day
I first surmised the Horses Heads
Were toward Eternity— (712)

Naive, blank-faced, repelling thought and emotion, the speaker permits herself to be transported to worlds unknown. The first step is easy. The gentleman-caller she calls Death is kindly, civil. The threesome is cozy, he does what she cannot do, the unexamined space of the carriage arouses no anxiety in her, the journey is a leisured one, and she has no sense of unfinished business: "'My Business but a Life I left— / Was such remaining there?'" (609) Because she is unable to decide whether earth's the right place for love and is not even aware of asking herself this question, she feels no need to choose between love and death, fused as they are in her imagination of them. She has all the time in the world, and in other worlds besides. Remarking on the presence of a third figure, Immortality, she cannot stop to ask herself what this barely personified abstraction, the shard of a disintegrated religious tradition, signifies. Wholly engrossed as she is by her deceptive double, she cannot afford to question whether beneath the smooth, seductive surface his intentions are equally decorous. What she has done is to yield herself up to the power of a dominant obsession. What this obsession is we do not know absolutely. The poem invokes a reason only to dismiss it: "Because I could not . . . He." Thus, although the idea of suicide is implicit in its denial, so too is the idea of controlling this death-wish by displacing it onto another character who is initially capable of masking the deception motif the poem is designed to reveal. In limited terms, perhaps this obsession may be described as the compulsion to repress the anxiety that the circumstances of her life have aroused in her. In its broadest terms, perhaps this obsession may be described as her fear of mortality itself.[1]

The speaker deceives herself into believing that it is possible to

1. In *Heaven Beguiles the Tired: Death in the Poetry of Emily Dickinson* (University: Alabama University Press, 1966), Thomas W. Ford explains Dickinson's obsession with this theme as follows: "Though there were many possible reasons for her great concern with death, at the heart of her preoccupation was a religious motivation. . . . Because she was deeply concerned with religious values, she was equally anxious to investigate every attitude toward death. It may be that Man's ability to foresee death is at the core of religion in general" (pp. 18–19). Clearly, I find this approach psychologically unsophisticated. At the heart of her preoccupation with death was an experience of social powerlessness which was both reinforced and assuaged by the religious myths of her culture.

renounce her past while sustaining a belief in progress, but her powers of observation are nevertheless acute. In contradistinction to her lack of interest in the life she is leaving behind, once the journey is under way she notices both human and natural actions, indeed she notices them so intently that she imagines "Fields of Gazing Grain," attributing to these fields the quality which, for better or for worse, continues to define her point of view: her intense interest in everything exterior to her—her anxiety about where she has been and where she may be headed having been thoroughly repressed. This anxiety begins to erupt at the start of stanza four, when she is forced to correct herself. Volition becomes compulsion as she remarks that nature has its own dynamic: "We passed . . . We passed . . . We passed . . . Or rather—He passed Us." The climate of the poem grows more ominous and she goes on to comment on her clothing, which might be the costume of a bride. This feminine imagery is extremely effective in suggesting the fragility of her body, her ego, and her psychic defenses. It justifies her nascent suspicion that, in taking her leave from the environment that shaped an interior perspective on the self, she may have gotten more than she bargained for. Her unfathomable companion is, of course, untroubled by this human frailty.

And so they ride on together, pausing before "a House that seemed / A Swelling of the Ground— / The Roof was scarcely visible— / The Cornice—in the Ground." A grave? Perhaps. But it looks enough like a grave or a buried home (in her end is her beginning) so that her companion takes his leave at this point, abandoning her to a single chilling thought: that she is to ride on forever toward an inconceivable place, "Eternity," that she is never to reach it, and that the experience of stopping, controlling, or arresting the uncivil, savage, quivering emotion that engendered this quest for an ending is never to be hers. At the poem's conclusion, the "Horses Heads" know at least as much about where she is headed as she does; perhaps more.

As long as human life has any meaning, the impulse to sum up the episodes of a concluded life-plot after death has done its work of fictionalizing presence will persist. Writing her own obituary, Dickinson summons up the resources of a religious tradition which, in its mid-Victorian incarnation, insisted on the moment of dying as a test of faith. The challenge a poem such as the one just cited hurls at the intriguing notion of a death-bed revelation about what, if anything, exists beyond the borders of the grave is evident. Allen

Tate, for example, remarks that "she has presented a typical Christian theme in its final irresolution, without making any final statements about it." He calls it "One of the perfect poems in English," but also observes that "the content of death in the poem eludes explicit definition."[2] While I agree wholeheartedly with his assessment of the poem's merit, I disagree with this latter contention. Death, for Dickinson, is to be deprived of or to accede to the loss of those experiences that have the potential to order meaning. "Because I could not stop for Death—" enacts the death of her quest motif, which pivots on actions of inclusion and exclusion. At the conclusion of this perfectly realized fantasy, no further actions are possible, since nothing remains to be resisted. Dickinson shapes the crucial event of dying from within in order to suggest that life contains many such deaths. The self is a function of its relationships, and once these relationships have been extinguished, there emerges a concept of being without essence. The poem is a flawless working-out of this insight, as is its companion piece which hums with even more shocking violations of mimetic plausibility:

> I heard a Fly buzz—when I died—
> The Stillness in the Room
> Was like the Stillness in the Air—
> Between the Heaves of Storm—
>
> The Eyes around—had wrung them dry—
> And Breaths were gathering firm
> For that last Onset—when the King
> Be witnessed—in the Room—
>
> I willed my Keepsakes—Signed away
> What portion of me be
> Assignable—and then it was
> There interposed a Fly—
>
> With Blue—uncertain stumbling Buzz—
> Between the light—and me—
> And then the Windows failed—and then
> I could not see to see—   (465)

Beginnings, as Edward Said reminds us, are marked points of departure from what is past, entries into what is present, and deter-

---

2. Allen Tate, "Emily Dickinson," *Collected Essays* (1932); reprinted in Richard B. Sewall, ed., *Emily Dickinson: A Collection of Critical Essays* (Englewood Cliffs, N.J.: Prentice-Hall, 1963), pp. 21–22.

minants of what is to come.[3] Nothing could be more ordinary in its proper time and place than this most ordinary event (hearing a fly buzz). Nothing could be more startling than this interposition of banality at the center of this climactic occasion. Nothing, that is, except the persona's flat, laconic statement that she has heard the sound of death, coolly witnessed her own demise, and survived to tell the tale. Dickinson thus begins by hurling emphatically contradictory demands in the reader's face: that we believe in the simultaneity of her persona's life and death. Much of the esthetic pleasure of the poem devolves from our interest in how she will resolve this extreme tension between subject matter and tone, subject matter and point of view, whether she will get away with it and, if so, how. Initially, she has induced in us the condition of suspense to which her character is also subjected as she waits in tense anticipation for that final heave of storm which will, for all time, insulate her from the menacing literalism of a life cut off from its hopeful beginnings.

What is inherently shocking here, however, is not the postmortem perspective on life (the epitaph for the self has been a traditional literary form at least from the time of the Greeks on through to the present day) but the insistence on deception this deliberately gimmicky opening statement reveals. Were this final pronouncement whose closural effect is reinforced by its syntactic completion the climax rather than the beginning of the speaker's discourse, the effect would be significantly less jarring. Were the clauses themselves reversed, the finality of this single-sentence introduction would be significantly weakened: When I died—I heard a fly buzz. The opening line, then, implicitly insists that when phenomena are perceived makes all the difference. In reading the poem, we learn that, on the contrary, time has no capacity to instruct us. The more of it we get, the more we will find that our expectations are continuously betrayed. Because the initial ugly shock is the ultimate reality, the irrational hiatus between the two clauses of the introductory declamation can never be resolved.

After such a beginning, Dickinson sets out to persuade us that she herself resisted this punishing conclusion with every ounce of energy available to her, that she too believed she might be instructed by the future, but that after is now. She does her work of preparing us for this tear in the fabric of her belief so successfully that many

3. Edward Said, *Beginnings: Intention and Method* (Baltimore: Johns Hopkins University Press, 1975).

discussions of the poem suggest a source in her direct observation of New England deathbed scenes. Though we recall the depressing effect on her of a visit to her terminally ill friend Sophia Holland in 1844, there is no evidence that Dickinson had ever witnessed a death as such before writing this poem. She had, however, witnessed the literary representation of deathbed scenes in which the dying "I" discloses to the mourners assembled, as at a theatrical spectacle, "what it be / 'Twere blessed to have seen—" (547). She had read her *Uncle Tom's Cabin* and could not have overlooked the death of the secular evangelist Little Eva, the sinless child, who, after having distributed her golden ringlets to the grieving slaves surrounding her and throwing her arms around the neck of her dear papa, expired in a decorative set piece so dear to the hearts of Victorian novel readers as follows:

> The child lay panting on her pillows, as one exhausted, the large clear eyes rolled up and fixed. And, what said those eyes, that spoke so much of heaven? Earth was past, and earthly pain; but so solemn, so mysterious, was the triumphant brightness of that face, that it choked even the sobs of sorrow. They pressed around her, in breathless stillness.
> "Eva," said St. Clare, gently.
> She did not hear.
> "Oh, Eva, tell us what you see! What is it?" said her father.
> A bright, a glorious smile passed over her face, and she said, brokenly, —"Oh! love,—joy,—peace!" gave one sigh, and passed from death unto life!

Even down to the distribution of keepsakes, Dickinson's poem may be read as a harshly ironic inversion of this sentimental tradition of a beautiful death consoling to the beholders.[4] Although literary experience has prepared us both for an oracular vision of the soul's flight

4. For a discussion of Dickinson's relationship to Stowe, see Karl Keller's chapter, "Morning Has Not Occurred: Emily Dickinson and Harriet Beecher Stowe," in *The Only Kangaroo among the Beauty: Emily Dickinson and America* (Baltimore: Johns Hopkins University Press, 1979), pp. 97–124. He describes their mutual indebtedness to Puritan culture, "with very different results."
Stowe visited Amherst in 1851 and in 1853 and spent the summer of 1872 visiting her daughter Georgiana (the wife of the local Episcopalian rector, Henry F. Allen) in Amherst, but there is no record of any meeting with Dickinson. Susan Dickinson describes her conversations with Stowe in 1872, without mentioning Dickinson. See her manuscript, "The Annals of The Evergreens," in Houghton Library, Harvard University, Cambridge, Mass. Though the Dickinson and Beecher-Stowe families had other contact both directly and through mutual acquaintances, Dickinson's only reference to Stowe occurs in an 1853 letter (113) to Austin, which I discuss in the next chapter. It implies a favorable assessment of *Uncle Tom's Cabin.*

from earth and for a dignified summation of the history of a particular life or set of lives ("Both rob'd of aire, we both lye in one ground, /
Both whom one fire had burnt, one water drownd"),[5] it has not
prepared us for an absurd terminal destiny, recognized by the speaker as such, and manifestly true. Thus it has not prepared us for
Dickinson's representation of death as an ending that refuses to
conclude. Because her consciousness is ultimately located in no conceivable space in either this poem or in "Because I could not stop for
Death," because the speaker of both poems is transported from a
more or less recognizable locale into nothingness, again there
emerges a concept of negative identity, of dying in perpetuity, which
forever violates the speaker's expectations of rebirth. Conceived as a
separation rite "When Sense from Spirit—files away— / And Subter-
fuge—is done—" (664), death has, in both of these poems, done its
work imperfectly. While the job has been botched, the poems are not.
The theme of both of these poems is fraud, and Dickinson tells us that
fraud is not merely the essence of life, it is the essence of death as well.
Anyone who looks to the future, as she herself so often did, to resolve
the ambiguities of the present will find, in the end, only more of the
same. Eternity is memory.

What the buzzing of the fly means we cannot with any finality say.
We can say what it is not. Set up like the persona for an apocalyptic
drama, "For that last Onset—when the King / Be witnessed—in the
Room," we find only drama's antithesis: a perpetual subjunctive, a
hyphen which will never yield to a period. Whether the fly portends
the body's decay and is thus the type of which death is the failed
antitype; whether the fly is, in a proleptic Kafkaesque turn, the king;
whether, as seems more likely, the fly has no office as a messenger
from another world and simply represents nature in its most trivial,
demeaning, and least glorious manifestation; the king as King fails
to show. The mourners have fulfilled their function. The intensity
of whatever grief they may have felt has already passed. The speaker has done her part, willing away whatever it is of herself she still
has left to give. She has set her house in order, she is ready to go,
resolute, firm: "and then it was / There interposed a Fly— / With
Blue—uncertain stumbling Buzz— / Between the light—and me— /
And then the Windows failed—and then / I could not see to see."

5. The lines quoted are John Donne's epigram "Hero and Leander," as quoted in
Barbara Herrnstein Smith, *Poetic Closure: A Study of How Poems End* (Chicago: University of Chicago Press, 1968), p. 204.

Within this scene, an incoherent death implies an incoherent life, a life in which the fly's uncertain, stumbling anti-quest is the symbol of her own. Once Dickinson's emblem of masculine authority withholds his presence, she loses all contact with the possibility of either spiritual illumination (if the king is God) or with a natural ending (if the king turns out to be Death, the eradicator of all senses, including the sense of memory). Instead, she is subjected to the cruel immortality of an eternal present, although she has been stripped of the mythic trappings available to a character such as Tennyson's Tithonus, who was damned by the gods with the gift of eternal life without the gift of eternal youth. There remains a voice forever condemned by memory to rehearse one fragment of its past, a voice confessing to its own impotence of vision, a rational voice that has been irrevocably violated by a profoundly irrational fate. Retrospectively, we may infer that the final show of concern of "The Eyes around," themselves disconnected from their usual corporeal envelope, is itself a last-gasp mockery rather than a logical extension of the circumstances of her life. The undispersed attention she commands together with her resort, in the end, to a legal ritual which appears to control her fears of abandonment and of having nothing beyond her keepsakes to leave behind, are themselves frauds perpetrated by the poem on the reader, perpetuated by her culture on the speaker, and perpetuated by her participation in the hollow rituals of this culture by the speaker on her self.

When Dickinson finds that, like the central character in Henry James's *The Beast in the Jungle,* she is the personage to whom nothing is destined ever to happen, the drama of this suspension of passion "Between the Heaves of Storm—" is brought to its perfect anti-dramatic conclusion. She need not bother to tell us what she surmises, as she does in "Because I could not stop for Death." By showing us what happens within a sentence that skips across stanzas and whose grammatical swell underscores the disintegration of meaning, she renders any further commentary superfluous. "Between the Heaves of Storm—" is exactly where she remains, at the point of maximum instability between that heave anterior and then posterior to the text.

The discipline Dickinson imposes on that betrayal of passion which is also self-betrayal is literally breathtaking, and generations of readers have properly responded to "I heard a Fly buzz—when I died—" as the single most powerful protest poem she ever wrote.

Only an artist who had staked her all on resolving the incomprehensible hiatus between her past and her future could have written such a poem. In what follows, I hope not to betray her original expectation that the passage of time may illuminate endings that are perceived as incoherent in a static present lengthened into infinity.

If "Death" represents a separation rite, what her speaker absents herself from, as well as the direction in which she believes herself to be or is in fact headed, makes all the difference. Exploring her poems on death in life within this framework will bring us significantly closer to the heart of Dickinson's imagination of suffering than attempting to distinguish between the physical and psychological components of her experience of the void. Whatever the occasion, Dickinson is always concerned with the impact of death on consciousness. Moreover, what she anatomizes best is the relationship between disease and cure: the relationship between those experiences of separation that disorganize her personality and those that reintegrate her ego. Her strongest protests are directed, as we have seen, against "Death" conceived as a separation rite which has done its work imperfectly. The self-criticism implicit in this focus is immediately apparent.

Protecting herself against social relationships by withdrawing herself from them, Dickinson also drew on a major cultural myth (the mythology of death as a necessary yet triumphant interlude in the life of the soul) to exorcize her experience of the world as an insufficient or actively menacing place. To the extent that this strategy of withdrawal intensified her despair as, one gathers, it horrendously did, she found herself unable to credit her own audacious claims to self-reliance. In selecting her own society, she had also selected the society of someone who could assert, joylessly, in 1864, "the World is dead" (L296). As misread by Dickinson, Puritan and transcendental typology encouraged the death of the social self, a self defined in and through its finite historical relationships. Ideally, this death would precipitate the rebirth of a self-consciousness "suspended / Above Mortality—" (1260), a consciousness that had transcended its anxiety of social powerlessness by projecting further ends. When, in her own life, Dickinson discovered that "Morning has not occurred" (13), she also discovered the inadequacies of American idealism:

> To die—without the Dying
> And live—without the Life

> This is the hardest Miracle
> Propounded to Belief.   (1017)

Though this convergence of her personal predicament with the predicament of certain aspects of her culture was of inestimable value for her art, Dickinson had not the freedom from self-preoccupation to perceive herself as that urgently mandated poet, Woman Thinking. Having sacrificed or witnessed the defeat of her social ambitions, ambitions which, in her fatal arrogance, she also viewed as unworthy of her, Dickinson, or so it seemed to her in certain moods, had paid the price in personal morbidity for her "Eden" without reaping the reward of it. From this postcontextual, posthedonic point of view "After great pain" (341), she developed a vocabulary whose attentiveness to the workings of the maladjusted mind remains unsurpassed. And yet, as I have suggested elsewhere, the line between Dickinson's analysis of this condition and her revelation of it is sometimes difficult to determine:

> Severer Service of myself
> I—hastened to demand
> To fill the awful Vacuum
> Your life had left behind—
>
> I worried Nature with my Wheels
> When Her's had ceased to run—
> When she had put away Her Work
> My own had just begun.
>
> I strove to weary Brain and Bone—
> To harass to fatigue
> The glittering Retinue of nerves—
> Vitality to clog
>
> To some dull comfort Those obtain
> Who put a Head away
> They knew the Hair to—
> And forget the color of the Day—
>
> Affliction would not be appeased—
> The Darkness braced as firm
> As all my stratagem had been
> The Midnight to confirm—
>
> No Drug for Consciousness—can be—
> Alternative to die
> Is Nature's only Pharmacy
> For Being's Malady—   (786)

The severe service this speaker has taken it upon herself to perform is the work of drugging consciousness by subjugating herself to a disciplined regimen designed to extinguish her memory of loss. The opening word is especially interesting because it implies that hers was already a life of severe service. The strategy she employs to control her feelings is nothing new but rather an extension of the course on which she was already set. This was someone whose ego had always made extraordinary demands upon her id. Initially, she speeds herself up to slow herself down. It looks, at least for the moment, as though this may be a battle she can win, knowing as she does that she has nothing to fear but the leisure in which feeling will erupt to paralyze her will. Perhaps Dickinson stayed up late at night writing. Perhaps she redoubled her attention to household chores. Within the poem, however, *where* this experience transpired does not matter. It blanks out the importance of scene, just as it ultimately reduces all times to midnight. Nor does the specific form of the tasks she is compelled or that she compels herself to perform matter. The stunning image "I worried Nature with my Wheels / When Her's had ceased to run—" suggests just the right degree of contact with her environment, just the right degree of machinelike resistance to it. Since no one literally has wheels, exactly what she does is unknown, and she transfers our attention from the task performed to the agitation that motivates her. Sensing that nature is already dead, since a part of her has already died, she does not yet know whether nature's cycle of death and rebirth has been temporarily or permanently arrested. "Nature," then, serves primarily to indicate her failure to receive the response she needs from the "You" who constitutes her link to an environment that works for her. In stanza two, however, she does not yet know this, as the antithesis of the subsequent image, "When she had put away Her Work / My own had just begun," implies. Thus it would be an exaggeration to assert that nature has no objective function, since her ability to project her inertia onto some force beyond herself whose reality she credits stimulates her frenetic activity.

Casting about for vital signs, this projective faculty, initially directed toward "You," then toward "Nature," is by stanza three unable to sustain itself and is thus directed inward toward the effect she seeks rather than outward toward cause so that there is no longer any preservation of her concept of a specific task. Striving "to weary Brain and Bone," she says nothing here about that convenient division of body and soul on which her fiction of a kindly immortality is predicated. Her language moves even further away from an actual representation of her objective mission, as her efforts to fatigue her "glittering Retinue of nerves—" prove ineffectual. Here, Dickinson's point of view undergoes a subtle transformation. We expect the phrase "Vitality to clog" to be followed by an indication of how actions are being performed, carrying out the pattern established in the preceding stanzas. We expect to hear the word "through" or "by" or some connective such as "when" which will admit an equivalent example. Instead, she again describes the effect she is seeking, as well as the head, hair, and color she is trying to forget, which she has to some extent successfully repressed since she does not imagine the "Head," "Hair," or "color of the Day" in any sensuous detail. The degree of her forgetting is somewhat obscured, however, by her allusion to the grief of others rather than to her own. Moreover, while stanzas one and two complete sentences, with the word "clog" the sentence structure skips across stanzas and fails to supply an independent verb so that the effect is that of a loss of linguistic and perceptual control. The speaker is still too alive to the connection she makes between forgetting "the color of the Day" and forgetting the "You" whom she addressed directly in stanza one, whom she represented through "Nature" and through her own nature in stanzas two and three and whom she represented as anyone lost to the "Those" of stanza four.

Returning exclusively to her own situation, she states unqualifiedly, "Affliction would not be appeased— / The Darkness braced as firm / As all my strategem had been / The Midnight to confirm." The even more emphatic conclusion extends what she has discovered in her own life into a law of nature. "You" represents life, which, in the end, either is or is not. No shadings between light and darkness exist, so that the experience "You" represents must be presumed to be obscure to the speaker and to have been obscured before the first line of her discourse. The "awful Vacuum" may now be interpreted as the anterior failure of this specific projective or identifying power which might have been accrued in the presence of the "You" whom she has never, as it turns out, intimately known. The pervasiveness of this generalized condition is indeed "Being's Malady," although I question whether the speaker herself intends this meaning. "You" is pretext rather than subtext, and it is in poems where this pretext has already been jettisoned or more thoroughly integrated into the progressions she traces that Dickinson schools her emotions more patiently in the discipline of esthetic control.

Given its comparative brevity, the poem attempts to do too much. It talks directly to "You," closes with a universalized maxim applied to her own condition and then with a universalized maxim that is maximally comprehensive, and in its middle sections trails off into a consideration of how other mourners have sought to extricate themselves from despair. However brilliant the parts, the effect of the whole is that of a significant problem addressed by a significant sensibility which just falls short of absolute mastery of its theme.

The following poem adopts the same postexperiential perspective, but it is more willing to compress the first of these styles, the direct evocation of "You," more willing to abandon the quest for role models, and more economical in its recourse to a closural generalization. As a consequence, although the plight that it depicts is even more extreme, the speech is significantly more unified:

> I tie my Hat—I crease my Shawl—
> Life's little duties do—precisely—
> As the very least
> Were infinite—to me—
>
> I put new Blossoms in the Glass—
> And throw the old—away—
> I push a petal from my Gown
> That anchored there—I weigh
> The time 'twill be till six o'clock
> I have so much to do—
> And yet—Existence—some way back—
> Stopped—struck—my ticking—through—
> We cannot put Ourself away
> As a completed Man
> Or Woman—When the Errand's done
> We came to Flesh—upon—
> There may be—Miles on Miles of Nought—
> Of Action—sicker far—
> To simulate—is stinging work—
> To cover what we are
> From Science—and from Surgery—
> Too Telescopic Eyes
> To bear on us unshaded—
> For their—sake—not for Our's—
> 'Twould start them—
> We—could tremble—
> But since we got a Bomb—
> And held it in our Bosom—
> Nay—Hold it—it is calm—

> Therefore—we do life's labor—
> Though life's Reward—be done—
> With scrupulous exactness—
> To hold our Senses—on— (443)

This is one of the longest poems Dickinson ever wrote, and it contains more journalistic detail about the range of her nonliterary activities than do her shorter, more severely selective self-portraits.[6] We see her here as one of Them, as having been coopted by the enemy: fussing with her clothes, keeping herself neat and clean, filling a vase with flowers, throwing the old ones away, rejecting nature insofar as it impinges on her body, performing "Life's little duties" precisely, even though she is busy about nothing. After this preamble, her statement that "Existence—some way back— / Stopped—struck—my ticking— through—" stands out in bold relief. Experiencing herself as a broken clock, she expresses her next thought through a plural pronoun that generalizes her plight and that is designed to repel the suicidal impulse the previous admission has engendered in her. The narrative changes abruptly here as she abandons her first-person-singular point of view. Again, as in "Severer Service of myself," we have been led to expect an explanation of either how or why this fragmentation occurred. But as we have already seen, one of Dickinson's major concerns is her need to eradicate the specific pain of memorial detail. Thus she draws herself up short with an emphatic prohibition against suicide while reiterating that she is already dead to pleasure. Her existence was designed to fulfill a unique purpose which, from the perspective of "the aftermath," she now views as an "Errand," as a matter of slight yet infinite importance.[7]

Within the context of the poem as a whole, it is impossible to say

---

6. In *The Editing of Emily Dickinson: A Reconsideration* (Madison: University of Wisconsin Press, 1967), pp. 40–46, Ralph Franklin suggested that the last nine lines were never intended by Dickinson to form part of this poem, but *The Manuscript Books of Emily Dickinson*, ed. R. W. Franklin, 2 vols. (Cambridge: Harvard University Press, 1981), 1:553–55, does not fully support this contention.

7. David Porter has written that "the crucial affair for her . . . is living after things happen. [The elementary experience] is a preoccupation with afterknowledge, the living in the aftermath. . . . The vision repeatedly angles out of psychic voids that follow crisis, where in 'larger—Darknesses— / Those Evenings of the Brain,' . . . unfolds the frightful leisure in which to seek what will suffice. . . . Afterward is the condition of the best known poems of physical and psychic death." See "The Crucial Experience in Emily Dickinson's Poetry," *ESQ: A Journal of the American Renaissance* 20 (Fourth Quarter 1974):280. *Dickinson: The Modern Idiom* (Cambridge: Harvard University Press, 1981), pp. 9–24, contains a revised version of this essay.

whether the end toward which her existence was directed has already been accomplished or whether she has failed to achieve her goal. A hasty reading of the poem might suggest that she failed to complete her mission, particularly since she expresses no pleasure in accomplishment. Yet her language insists that "the Errand's done." Perhaps these two possibilities can be reconciled if we assume that at this point in the poem she is exclusively preoccupied with an aimless present rather than with the past. *What* happened no longer matters. Outwardly, her life ticks on even though her mainspring is broken; her mind continues to function, but it contemplates the death of ambition. Probably the speaker attributes her spirit's death to the loss of someone who once appeared to symbolize her psychological salvation. But even if her spirit's death was not self-induced, her depression is self-perpetuating. Her subjective morbidity cannot be arrested by her objective perception that she is still capable of performing trivial tasks. Subjectively, time is meaningless to her; objectively, it continues to organize her behavior.

The next sentence, "There may be—Miles on Miles of Nought— / Of Action—sicker far—" causes us to expect a conclusion along the line of "And yet," to expect another example of her inauthentic, law-abiding behavior. Instead, she turns her attention to the energy required to perform those actions she characterizes as "sicker far." Attempting to conceal her morbidity is "stinging work," but she also implies that she does not wish to be found out because she is unwilling to be treated as a patient or to excise the feelings she associates with her body. Her characterization of "Science" and "Surgery" as "Too Telescopic Eyes / To bear on us unshaded" has a quality of hysteria to it, as the sexual paranoia she is seeking to repress through syntactic parallels begins to bulge out of the frame that has been established. The word "Too" sustains the sound pattern of "To simulate . . . To cover," a pattern reestablished with the infinitive "To bear," but repetition where the sound does not fit the meaning to the expected sense causes us to revise our expectations about the psychological significance of audible emphasis. By directing our attention to an illogical aural identity, the repetition which is particularly marked in the section beginning "There may be—Miles on Miles of Nought—" takes on an even more disturbed, compulsive quality. The speaker feels like a split personality: hence her emphasis on "two." This split was occasioned by her loss of an erotic relationship: hence also her emphasis on "two." From a domestic or social perspective, the "Errand" she was predestined to execute was illicit; from her perspective what may be illicit about it is that it is over but not done with.

At this point it is reasonable to ask whether the speaker herself knows what this errand was and to answer yes and no. She knows what she thinks it was, but she also has some residual feeling that she may be self-deluded and that were she to examine herself more closely, her pain would be infinitely magnified. Here it seems that this wonderful poem falters slightly when she avers to altruism ("For their—sake—not for Our's") as her motive. However, the emotional logic of this rationalization emerges clearly in the lines that follow, when Dickinson describes her buried fury: " 'Twould start them— / We—could tremble— / But since we got a Bomb— / And held it in our Bosom— / Nay—Hold it—it is calm." "Start" may signify "startle," but it also implies that she fears to "start" or provoke her oppressors. Were she to be subjected to the homicidal onslaught, whether verbal or physical, she is imagining, she too would tremble. These lines effectively conceal who would be the killer, who the victim, and it is only in the intensity of their shared fury that "I," "We," "Man," "Woman," and "them" coalesce.

The poem ends with what appears to be a law-abiding epigram as Dickinson acknowledges that there is indeed a further deterioration to which her ego might be subjected were she to abandon the "scrupulous exactness" to duty which, we now surmise, she once abandoned and which engendered in her such an unremitting sense of guilt. The hypocrisy structuring her outward behavior also has its inner use: it is helping to keep her sane. It would, however, be fatuous to suggest that sublimation triumphs once and for all in either our minds or the speaker's. In some way, in some time or place, the bomb in her bosom is bound to explode. Our experience of Dickinson's plural pronoun has by now been significantly altered. We have encountered two characters. The passion of one is social order, the passion of the other the destruction of that order the poem both confirms and undermines. If we peer more closely at the final quatrain, we observe that lines three and four qualify the authority of lines one and two. If life's reward is done, reasons are superfluous. If it is necessary to reveal how and why actions are performed, labor still has some value. While the lid is tightly sealed on her imagination of pleasure, her imagination of subsequent terrors is wide open. Thus Dickinson's tendency to make emphatic assertions whose superficial logic she contradicts but whose emotional logic is reinforced by the fact of the contradiction persists throughout. Contradiction is the poem's point.

Once the element of political protest disappears from Dickinson's style as the other characters who populate the worlds of "Because I could not stop for Death," "I heard a Fly buzz—when I died," "Severer Service of myself," and "I tie my Hat—I crease my Shawl—" vanish, she extinguishes the possibility of projecting her anxieties onto other figures whom she invests with varying degrees of power to relieve her from the burden of a false self system. Blanking out the exterior scenes within which these personae manifest themselves, she blanks out the escapes from fraud which Death and King initially appeared to represent in "Because I could not stop for Death—" and "I heard a Fly buzz—when I died—" and from the anxiety imperfectly deflected by her compulsive industry in "Severer Service of myself" and "I tie my Hat—I crease my Shawl." This projective faculty had already been strained to its limit in "I tie my Hat—I crease my Shawl," since the other figures she imagines impose inauthenticity on her even as they appear to provide her with a means to control her fears of insanity. That is, there is no single character invested with unique messianic potential and this switch from character to characters corresponds to the disintegration of her imagination of a regenerated self. The errand she came to flesh upon is already conceived as over, and the only goal she sets herself is that of sustaining some minimal hold over her functioning. Once these other characters are eliminated, the bomb in the bosom explodes, but the victim turns out to be herself. She then proceeds to describe states of alienation in which unconscious processes have even greater dominion over the suspended lives whose "Hour of Lead" she anatomizes.

II

In one of her most perfect definition poems, the voices of passion and dispassion we observed arguing with themselves in "I tie my Hat—I crease my Shawl—" come together to shape a consciously detached perspective on the passion of involuntary suffering:

> After great pain, a formal feeling comes—
> The Nerves sit ceremonious, like Tombs—
> The stiff Heart questions was it He, that bore,
> And Yesterday, or Centuries before?

The Feet, mechanical, go round—
Of Ground, or Air, or Ought—
A Wooden way
Regardless grown,
A Quartz contentment, like a stone—

This is the Hour of Lead—
Remembered, if outlived,
As Freezing persons, recollect the Snow—
First—Chill—then Stupor—then the letting go—   (341)

After the apocalypse, which it would be absurd to try to distinguish as *either* physical *or* psychic trauma since grief of this magnitude swallows all nice distinctions between body and soul and fuses them into a horrific whole, impassioned struggle cools to "formal feeling": to automatic modes of response to time and space, those fundamental executors of identity which have ceased to register on the consciousness of a self entombed by its past. The "stiff Heart," unable to recognize itself as belonging to a larger organism, has lost all sense of time's variety. "Yesterday, or Centuries before" are equally meaningless to a self dissociated from its vital center, centered on despair, asking "was it He," unable to say "I," let alone what passion it bore or suffered. Splintering off parts of the body ("Nerves," "Heart," "Feet") to represent the missing "I," the self capable of relationship to otherness and hence of the totality of vision the poet alone sustains, Dickinson describes a heart so bruised by defeat that it exists in the absolute zero, the "Ought" of total self-absorption.

Thus the only sign of intellectual life the anonymous subject of "After great pain" manifests is to ask a question perhaps of itself, perhaps of no one or no thing in particular (that we cannot make this distinction is very much to the point) which is in no way answered, since there is no one on the scene to hear it. Nor is there any scene: the only limited spatial marker ("like Tombs") is an analogy for a ritualized state of being rather than a reference to a particular place. The other spatial markers ("Of Ground, or Air, or Ought— / A Wooden way") are even more general and serve to indicate the absence of identity rather than to create it through contact with a particular environment. This creation is foreclosed by the failure of environment to manifest itself.

The poet who can speak elsewhere of "A perfect—paralyzing Bliss— / Contented as Despair—" (756) employs a wondrously strange figure here to describe the relationship between suffering and narcissism. Even this condition is not totally devoid of pleasure: it has its "Quartz contentment, like a stone," a perfected imperviousness to external stimuli such as a stone might feel, were it capable of feeling at all. While the idea is in itself startling, this simile subverts the normal function of analogy which is, as Samuel Johnson observed, to yoke disparate elements together. Dickinson's figure comes close to likening stone to stone. This redundancy is barely avoided since she compares an abstraction to a mineral both in the initial phrase where "Quartz" functions adjectivally and in the conclusion which moves from subtype to type. This subversion of analogic function is, however, a stylistic representation of the subject's plight. Analogy-making depends on the ability to perceive difference. When pain expands or "contracts—the Time" to an eternal present, the imagination collapses under the weight of a perpetual now.

The conclusion reached, "This is the Hour of Lead—" picks up the heavy sound of the trochaic opening line, after an intervening pattern of iambic beginnings. Indeed, in contrast to the monotonous timelessness of unconscious obsession with which the subject is freighted, the entire poem is unusually varied rhythmically. After an initial decasyllabic quatrain, introduced by an opening line with six strong stresses, Dickinson reverts to her more usual combination of eights and sixes, the "short meter" of her hymnal. But she breaks up the potential third line of stanza two into two lines of iambic dimeter, thereby creating a five-line stanza. Lines three and four of the concluding quatrain are again decasyllabic, while the concluding line with its initial spondees has seven climactic stresses, producing one of the most heavily accented lines Dickinson ever wrote. Similarly, the rhyming sounds are unusually flexible. Beginning with an instance of consonantal rhyme ("comes-Tombs") Dickinson moves to a complete end rhyme ("bore-fore"), to a linkage of the next end sound with an interior word ("round-Ground"), through a series of approximate vowel rhymes ("Ought-way-grown"), back to a full rhyme with "grown-stone," to the consonantal dissonance of "Lead-lived," and then to the final instance of full rhyme ("Snow-go") with which the poem concludes.

The "Hour of Lead," the feeling she likens to the densest metal, lends itself to interpretation only after it has been outlived, as it may not be. It will be remembered, she tells us, "As Freezing persons, recollect the Snow— / First—Chill—then Stupor—then the letting go—": the latter a symbolic equivalent of death—perhaps the release of total unconsciousness—for the self still connected through its numbness to its original "great pain," the disruptive emblem of negative interaction between self and world.

Purged of the circumstances that enable us to speak of personality, this condition is represented as what would happen to Any Person subjected to a comparable degree of stress. That is, perhaps Dickinson's major psychological insight into the symptomatology of suffering is that rebirth necessitates the death of a rigid set of impulses grown comfortable and familiar; that pain signifies a loyalty to frustrated aspirations which is both heroic and dysfunctional; and that the unconscious is the unwitting conservator of personal history. For this reason she likens the pain of rebirth to death itself. Because some form of separation from the past is a necessary yet not sufficient condition for growth, the pain of rebirth may be indistinguishable in process from a death throe, as it is here. This character no longer has the power to set its sights on any form of conscious renunciation. Whatever happens, nature or the passage of time is to determine its fate. If this condition is outlived, sequence, with its possibilities of change, will be reintroduced into its perspective. The poet possesses this consciousness of change; her character does not.

What Dickinson means by "letting go" is partially clarified by another poem which examines the functionality of "Trance" or "Swoon," agents of a merciful forgetting, to rescue the self from a present it can no longer endure:

> There is a pain—so utter—
> It swallows substance up—
> Then covers the Abyss with Trance—
> So Memory can step
> Around—across—upon it—
> As one within a Swoon—
> Goes safely—where an open eye—
> Would drop Him—Bone by Bone.   (599)

Extreme pain, Dickinson believes, destroys the memory of its occasion. This destruction creates an "Abyss" which may be successfully evaded by some further repression of consciousness. The soul cannot bear too much reality and commands a variety of amnesiac responses which blank out pain, all of which prefigure that ultimate amnesiac, death. Thus, while in a poem previously cited Dickinson asserts "No Drug for Consciousness—can be— / Alternative to die / Is Nature's only Pharmacy / For Being's Malady," in "There is a pain—so utter—" nature's pharmacy includes types of death in life. They are, she tells us, life preservers when reality is literally unbearable. Partial interments of consciousness are preferable to an open-eyed fall, "Bone by Bone," into psychosis. Similarly, poem 859 exalts "A merciful Mirage / That makes the living possible / While it suspends the lives":

> A Doubt if it be Us
> Assists the staggering Mind
> In an extremer Anguish
> Until it footing find.
>
> An Unreality is lent,
> A merciful Mirage
> That makes the living possible
> While it suspends the lives.

When reality is unalterable, the self must adjust to those "larger—Darknesses— / Those Evenings of the Brain—" by adopting a defensive posture of strategic withdrawal. In time, "Either the Darkness alters— / Or something in the sight / Adjusts itself to Midnight— / And Life steps almost straight" (419). In short, Dickinson proposes to survive her "Hour of Lead" by succumbing to it for some undetermined period of time; in the extreme case, psychosis is preferable to suicide. When the self has been dehumanized by pain, physical or psychological, nature sometimes comes to the rescue. "Anguish has but so many throes," she wrote in an undated prose fragment, "then Unconsciousness claims it" (PF67). "Letting go," with its connotations of giving up and giving in, while tonally antiheroic, is the only heroism left to a self defeated by its past. To know when to quit, when to withdraw, not to fight on after the battle has been lost—this is the sanity nature and its ally unconsciousness impose on the heart stiffened by despair. Dickinson explained to Mrs. Holland in a letter of 1878, "I suppose there are depths in every Consciousness, from which we cannot rescue ourselves—to which none can go with us—which represent to us Mortally—the Adventure of Death—" (L555). "Letting go," sinking down to the ground floor of volitionless being, is one such annihilating adventure.[8]

8. In *Disease, Pain & Sacrifice: Toward a Psychology of Suffering* (Chicago: University of Chicago Press, 1968), David Bakan observes that death may be the consequence of

"After great pain" earns its stoic conclusion. It moves from a withheld occasion which formalizes feeling to the loss of a sense of exterior time and space to a final silence. Because the "subject" or figure in the poem is so fragmented from the outset, this subtle, progressive deterioration is clarified only by the poem's last line. The "Hour of Lead" is defined by the deepening introversion of a self no longer embedded in various or variable or perceivable contexts. The poem rises to an occasion with the concluding simile which may move us into a confrontation with psychosis, as one critic suggests, but which also moves us back toward nature and death.[9] The concluding lines remind us that whether in fact as from actual freezing or in imagination, "such moments are," but that it is only retrospectively that separation rites in either their ultimate or foreshadowing forms can be ethically appraised.

Although Dickinson occasionally tosses off a salvo at the dionysiac approach to mental deviance ("Much Madness is divinest Sense— / To a discerning Eye—" [435]), because she views reality as profoundly unreasonable, the question to which she returns unerringly is the value of consciousness itself.[10] The following poem, for example, ends with another one of those "merciful" forgettings which make "the living possible / While it suspends the lives." Thus the text's most ambiguous element is less the hazardous action with which it concludes than Dickinson's moral evaluation of it. The final

---

internal defense mechanisms which while initially successful in warding off the threat of annihilation to the organism become overstimulated and self-injurious: "Freud wrote that 'the instincts of self-preservation, of self-assertion and of mastery . . . are component instincts whose function it is to assure that the organism shall follow its own path to death, and to ward off any possible ways of returning to inorganic existence other than those which are immanent in the organism itself.' . . . But it is this very response itself, self-induced, as it were, by the organism, that is the real and dangerous disease" (p. 26). I am suggesting that Dickinson, a brilliant self-clinician, anticipates some of the work of Freud and his followers on the relationship between defense mechanisms and disease processes.

9. John Cody, *After Great Pain: The Inner Life of Emily Dickinson* (Cambridge: Harvard University Press, 1971), pp. 328–29.

10. In "Romanticism and 'Anti-Self-Consciousness,'" in Harold Bloom, ed., *Romanticism and Consciousness: Essays in Criticism* (New York: W. W. Norton, 1970), Geoffrey Hartman explains: "The Romantic poets do not exalt consciousness *per se*. They have recognized it as a kind of death-in-life, as the product of a division in the self. . . . It is consciousness, ultimately, which alienates them from life and imposes the burden of a self which religion or death or a return to a state of nature might dissolve" (p. 51).

Margaret Homans, in *Women Writers and Poetic Identity: Dorothy Wordsworth, Emily Brontë, and Emily Dickinson* (Princeton: Princeton University Press, 1980), explores Dickinson's resistance to "a return to a state of nature." She argues that "Mother Nature is not a helpful model for women aspiring to be poets" (p. 13).

word "then" returns her speaker to the condition of penultimate "knowing" that characterized her funereal tension at the poem's inception. The lesson she learns as consciousness is progressively interred is a simple one: that she has collided and will always collide with any conceivable world. If this be madness, it is the madness to which poets as simple separate persons have always committed themselves initially, although few lyric speakers have rendered this knowledge with such stark finality:

> I felt a Funeral, in my Brain,
> And Mourners to and fro
> Kept treading—treading—till it seemed
> That Sense was breaking through—
>
> And when they all were seated,
> A Service, like a Drum—
> Kept beating—beating—till I thought
> My Mind was going numb—
>
> And then I heard them lift a Box
> And creak across my Soul
> With those same Boots of Lead, again,
> Then Space—began to toll,
>
> As all the Heavens were a Bell,
> And Being, but an Ear,
> And I, and Silence, some strange Race
> Wrecked, solitary, here—
>
> And then a Plank in Reason, broke,
> And I dropped down, and down—
> And hit a World, at every plunge,
> And Finished knowing—then—   (280)

As reason is progressively interred, "That Sense was breaking through—" takes on a dual meaning. The temporal and spatial order that causes funerals *not* to occur in the brain has already been irrevocably violated, but sense is also erupting. A breakdown is also a breakthrough. What begins as ritual mourning as the persona witnesses her own funeral ends in even greater solitude. Reason links her to a human community and to a ritual designed to exorcise the disorder inherent in the solitude of death. The introversion of this ritual is also a perversion of its affective power; real funerals acknowledge, they do not anticipate, the fact of death. The mourners may be viewed as resisting this perversion. They are the bearers of her dead hopes; as such, they violate her psyche's instinct for peace. The persona does not, however, acknowledge that she is both subject and object, witness to and participant in her own funeral. She causes us to see that this is so, but *a* funeral is not *my* funeral, *a* service not *my* service, *a* box not *my* box, nor is a plank in reason a plank in *my* reason. This lack of recognition is perhaps the most brilliant stroke in this superbly organized poem. The irony of her statement that she "Finished knowing" causes us to creak across the fact that she never consciously acknowledged what was happening to her. The reality that it is *her* funeral she is being forced to witness is too painful, even from the opening line, to be admitted into consciousness directly.

The dissociation this suppression of etiology induces in her causes her to describe herself as two entities bizarrely conjoined: as "I, and Silence, some strange Race / Wrecked, solitary, here." Unconsciously, she already knows all she needs to know. When the bottom falls out as it must, since this recognition that irrevocable solitude and death are indistinguishable is insupportable, the persona plunges away from this thought. Returning from this psychotic journey to speak to us, she returns to the work of knowing which both links her to us and condemns her to the recognition that "Consciousness" is "Captivity" (384). Once an unremittingly hostile environment has been thoroughly internalized, the split between self and world on which the poem is, predicated can never be adequately resolved. Viewing herself as subject and object in no way alters her condition. When she is forced to witness what she is powerless to avert, Dickinson's language is enlisted in the service of moral nihilism.

In organizing the progressively denser burden of this schizophrenic condition, Dickinson relieves us of the uncontrollable tension to which her character is insanely subjected. Her final plunge, following the withdrawal of mourners and heavens, induces in us a feeling of exhilaration. It is the only action the speaker herself performs in a poem where all motion is siphoned off to other figures. Throughout the poem, she forces us to witness her emotional paralysis by means of the precision with which she notes repetitive physical gestures. This precise notation is grotesquely mirrored by her repetitive syntax: "And Mourners . . . Kept . . . till . . . And when . . . Kept . . . till . . . And then . . . And creak . . . Then Space . . . And Being . . . And I, and Silence . . . And then . . . And I . . . And hit . . . And . . . then." These fated sounds, culminating in her drop "down and down" as she hits "a World, at every plunge," are reinforced even further by an extraordinary sequence of internal and end-sound doublings. Given the nature of the experience she is describing, as we see her "breaking" we wish to see her "broke." When the mourners are seated, which might signal the end of their imposition on her, a service "like a Drum" begins. When she hears them lift a box (the only upward-bound gesture in the poem) and "creak across [her] Soul," space begins to toll. When she is wrecked in a here which is nowhere, "Being" being exterior to her, "a Plank in Reason" breaks. The pattern Dickinson has established implies that every conclusion shall be followed by an even more tortuous beginning. The concluding line both confirms this pattern and satisfies our desire to know no more. "Which Anguish was the utterest— then— / To perish, or to live?" (414).

Dickinsonian schizophrenia is both personal and ontological: personal because her persona's isolation prevents her from identifying its social causes, ontological because this preclusion generalizes her paradigm of a divided self.[11] Again and again, she is compelled to observe interior actions that arise unbidden and that have their own inexorable progressions. "Postponeless Creature[s]" in that madhouse that is the universe, they are like biological dyings in their moral impenetrability, unlike such dyings in their perpetuation of neurotic terror. Because the mere passage of time has yielded, in many poems, no further knowledge of what happened or why, Dickinson returns obsessively to this scene in which "It was not Death," a scene in which her alienation from the authority of events also signals her negation of a categorical distinction between the living and the dead:

> It was not Death, for I stood up,
> And all the Dead, lie down—
> It was not Night, for all the Bells
> Put out their Tongues, for Noon.
>
> It was not Frost, for on my Flesh
> I felt Siroccos—crawl—
> Nor Fire—for just my Marble feet
> Could keep a Chancel, cool—

---

11. In *The Politics of Experience* (New York: Ballantine, 1967), p. 130, R. D. Laing reminds us that, etymologically, schizophrenia means broken-heartedness.

In "Irony, Literature and Schizophrenia," *New Literary History* 12 (Autumn 1980): 107–17, Rolf Breuer defines schizophrenia, "the symbolic disease of an era of alienation," as "the abandonment of contact between outer and inner worlds."

And yet, it tasted, like them all,
The Figures I have seen
Set orderly, for Burial,
Reminded me, of mine—

As if my life were shaven,
And fitted to a frame,
And could not breathe without a key,
And 'twas like Midnight, some—

When everything that ticked—has stopped—
And Space stares all around—
Or Grisly frosts—first Autumn morns
Repeal the Beating Ground—

But, most, like Chaos—Stopless—cool—
Without a Chance, or Spar—
Or even a report of Land—
To justify—Despair. (510)

When the Dickinsonian self, trapped within a temporal and spatial void, has lost the memory of a personal past, it cannot explain *why*. Unable to explain *why*, her speaker cannot explain *what*. The loss of origins frustrates communication with self and world, themselves problematic constructs for the isolate. Yet without some memory, however depleted of joy, her speech could not occur: intelligible communication depends on an intelligible prior context which enables the self to interpret its emotions. Dickinson draws on rudimentary physical sensations and on the suffocating ritual of burial to pierce the unnamable. Although desperately bewildered, she describes her living death in a flat, apathetic monotone drained of outrage or self-pity. Her dark night of the soul excludes such emotions.

Despair, as Dickinson interprets it in this poem, depends on an awareness of its opposite: on the knowledge that someone somewhere has sighted "Land," which symbolizes hope or salvation. This report of "a Chance, or Spar" is inaudible to the drowning soul, flooded by the "Chaos" of its unconscious life. Dickinson's speaker is locked into an almost inconceivable hopelessness: "The old words are *numb*—and there *a'nt* any *new* ones—" (L252). She recognizes that appropriate language depends on common experience, whereas her alienation is an uncommon doom. Language mediates between self and world; when this connection is all but sundered, emotional reality must be approached obliquely. Thus she explains herself at first through a series of negative definitions ("It was not Death . . . It was not Night . . . It was not Frost . . . Nor Fire") before returning to formulations that had been nominally rejected: "And yet, it tasted, like them all . . . As if my life were shaven . . . And 'twas like Midnight, some." Unable to reach conclusions about her condition, she cannot commit herself to any formulation that implies some ideal of order. Her search for the apt negation or analogy or word is the only residual evidence of the personality she explicitly denies, for the poem is predicated on the assumption "It was not I." As she seeks to explain herself to herself, negative definitions and imperfect analogies provide her with an approach to meaning. Linguistic order cannot gratify her desire for a life that is filled with motion, warmth, color, and rounded forms; yet it is all this marginal speaker has left. As the figures of stanza three suggest, she views her life as split off from herself and feels as though she has ingested death.

Without any awareness of the thwarted passion that has reduced her to this state, she exists in an uninterrupted middle. Her death has neither beginning nor bourn. The absence of terminal rhyme (there is but one instance of full rhyme in the entire poem, which is suspended until the penultimate stanza) conveys this inability to come to closure. Death at least is not chaos. It has a name and the "Specific Grace" Dickinson describes elsewhere as "Capacity to Terminate" (1196). Memory, that vital resource of the romantic spirit, summons up only corpses. The speaker's appetitiveness, partitioned off to "Bells," putting out "their Tongues, for Noon," has been narrowed to her quest for a mode of telling. As she stares into the void of negative identity, Dickinson creates "the fiction of disorientation while rescuing the reader from the fact of it."[12] Because she has no exterior context against which to justify or defend herself, the poem ends before the speaker completes her self-definition, although from the reader's perspective the poem completes its definition of despair. For Dickinson, the loss of a sense of an ending is the paradoxical center of a living death. This loss emerges from her prior inability to distinguish the "Me" from the "Not-Me."

Until the breakthrough to the final word "Despair," a word that is tonally anticlimactic, there is significant ambiguity throughout the poem about the focus of the speaker's language. Is she attempting to

12. Sharon Cameron, *Lyric Time: Dickinson and the Limits of Genre* (Baltimore: Johns Hopkins University Press, 1979), p. 49.

locate an exterior cause ("It") that is the source of her feeling or is she attempting to describe that feeling itself? Because "It" exists within and without, she cannot consistently designate either an exterior source or an internal effect. The inconsistency of her focus is reflected in the development of her examples. Stanzas one and two establish what appears to be a logical syntactic pattern. There are four concise negative definitions; each is followed by an inappropriate response were the definition true; each consists of two lines. The parallelism is further heightened by the repetition of the "It was not" construction, followed by a variable noun. This pattern is sustained by the lucid ellipsis of the fourth example, "Nor Fire." However, the second example in stanza one, "Night," violates the psychological order of the progression: the speaker's response, which is presented in the other three cases as the conclusive and dismissive counterexample, is withheld. Instead, we are told that "all the Bells / Put out their Tongues, for Noon." After the synesthesia at the start of stanza three ("And yet, it tasted, like them all") we expect an illustration of the sensation of tasting death, night, frost, and fire. Instead, we are presented with a visual memory which is not accessible to the sense of taste: "The Figures I have seen / Set orderly, for Burial, / Reminded me, of mine." This memory leads to an abandonment of the "It" formula, and the speaker now uses the words "my life." Subsequently, in stanza four she continues to describe how she feels (stripped, stretched, suffocated) and to attribute this unnatural effect to a natural cause ("Midnight"). The abstraction "Chaos" in stanza six is presented as having infinite duration ("Stopless") and temperature ("cool"), as metaphysical and physical, as what she feels and where she is, as a feeling and a place extending into infinity, so that even the body as a fundamental executor of identity has ceased to demarcate the difference between the "Me" and the "Not-Me." The speaker is both exterior to and part of a landscape of death, an "It" and an observer of "It." As I have suggested, the speaker's fragmentation is reflected in her mode of telling. She sets out a confused pattern of thought; each of her observations makes sense, but their coherence is fundamentally flawed.

III

When the center does not hold, the speaker sometimes attributes her psychological suffering to a religious source. This attribution tends to neutralize her fear of insanity and revitalize her conscious-

ness of limited selfhood, as it struggles to define itself against injustice. In many of her most characteristic utterances, however,
Dickinson invokes a theological structure only to dissociate herself
from it. Pain that has no comprehensible objective source has no
unambiguous subjective end:

> There's a certain Slant of light,
> Winter Afternoons—
> That oppresses, like the Heft
> Of Cathedral Tunes—
>
> Heavenly Hurt, it gives us—
> We can find no scar,
> But internal difference,
> Where the Meanings, are—
>
> None may teach it—Any—
> 'Tis the Seal Despair—
> An imperial affliction
> Sent us of the Air—
>
> When it comes, the Landscape listens—
> Shadows—hold their breath—
> When it goes, 'tis like the Distance
> On the look of Death—   (258)

Light is a traditional symbol of spiritual illumination. As such, it
oppresses the speaker who feels threatened by it, perhaps because
traditional symbols remind her of her dissociation from God, as do
"Cathedral Tunes." A vertical shaft angled in the season of despair,
afternoon sunlight precipitates her awareness of unrectified emotions that preceded its coming, which she attributes to its presence.
Projecting her despair into the natural world, Dickinson appropriates the language of the Book of Revelation to describe the absence
of revelation. The "Seal Despair" seals in a present that ends neither
in damnation nor in salvation. Hers is an "imperial affliction," in
that it recalls a heroic past when "Those—dying then, / Knew where
they went— / They went to God's Right Hand—" (1551). Hers is a
morally impenetrable psychological landscape, in that her immediate self-scrutiny heightens her awareness of an inscrutable end.
Rather than discovering the divinity of human nature, the speaker
discovers a secular obsession with "internal difference, / Where the
Meanings, are." Her individuality is the source of her suffering.

Referring to herself as "We" throughout the poem, Dickinson implies that individuality is the source of all human suffering. Nevertheless, "a certain Slant of light" or the burden of consciousness it symbolizes continues to weigh her down. It scars her spirit without laying a finger on her. Associating subjectivity with death, she is unable to associate death with rebirth or to redeem a solitary moment lengthened into infinite confusion.

Within the randomness of this "design" she finds a glimmer of hope. Such moments come, and such moments go. They may end either in death or in distance from death; the future cannot be inferred from the past. Dickinson expresses a passionate desire to reconstitute a natural universe predicated on a stabilizing relationship between the self and God. The poem describes the frustration of that desire, as nature reminds her of herself. But in an incoherent universe, no emotion and no suffering, however intense, need be construed as permanent.

Certainly the poem's most unexpected statement is the curtly dismissive formula at the beginning of stanza three: "None may teach it—Any." Who but Dickinson would desire to instruct "a certain Slant of light," to teach it something, anything? Who but Dickinson would cut the word in half as if to emphasize the hopelessness of her quest for a unified sensibility? What might the speaker teach it, what might anyone teach it, if "a certain Slant of light" were willing to be instructed? Perhaps she would teach it that, as she once wrote, "No part of mind is permanent. This startles the happy, but it assists the sad" (L362). Perhaps she would teach it that, as she also wrote, in her terror of premature endings, her dread of permanently arrested development, "All but Death, can be Adjusted—" (749). Or perhaps she would teach it what her language teaches us: that morally impenetrable psychological conditions may serve to dramatize the interpretive inadequacy of an inherited vocabulary of belief, but that to abandon a common vocabulary of forms, however inadequate it may be, is to risk verbal autism. Dickinson suggests that the despair she associates with "a certain Slant of light" cannot be communicated. However we interpret the elliptical line "None may teach it—Any," it reflects her transitory belief that "split lives—never 'get well'" (L246).

Although the light is "certain," the speaker is uncertain about its ethical function. Finally, it is "like the Distance / On the look of Death." This is a blank image that cannot be visualized, although it alludes to the sense of sight.[13] Its interpretive power is further distanced by analogic form. Thus to conclude that the cause of her despair is the fact of mortality oversimplifies the complexity of the poem's ending.[14] Death reminds the speaker of an inexpressible emotion, unanchored by an adequate cause. To some readers the concluding figure has suggested the vacant or hostile stare of a corpse, but the image is significantly more abstract and obscurantist: the personification is an approximate one.[15] The preceding lines describe a stimulus and a response: "When it comes, the Landscape listens— / Shadows—hold their breath." In the final lines, the response is apparently attributed to the stimulus itself: "When it goes, 'tis like the Distance / On the look of Death." Or can it be that when "the Seal Despair" departs, the speaker is literally wiped out? Unless restricted contextually, the noun "look" signifies both a glance and an appearance. Perhaps the parallelism is carried out obliquely through the fusion of the stimulus, death, and the respondent, the speaker. Evidently, if we knew how she felt about the transformation of despair into death, the concluding lines would be clarified. Dickinson is fascinated by death's dreaded invasion and repelled by it. Because of the moral ambiguity of her stance, the figure withholds its meaning.

In "There's a certain Slant of light," the speaker admits no memory of a usable personal past. Her memory of an archaic religious myth intensifies her suffering. "When it goes," when pain departs, she is released into a future space that is genuinely unknown. In dissociating herself from God, Dickinson dissociates herself not only from pain, which at first confers identity on her, but also from a coherent system of natural signs. Clark Griffith argues,

> Where the Emersonian held Nature to be deliberately benevolent, Emily Dickinson agrees that Natural processes are indeed deliber-

13. David Porter has examined Dickinson's "Strangely Abstracted Images" in *Modern Idiom*, pp. 25–36. See also Archibald MacLeish, "The Private World: Poems of Emily Dickinson," *Poetry and Experience* (1961); reprinted in *Emily Dickinson*, ed. Sewall, pp. 152–54.

14. And so "We do not think enough of the Dead as exhilirants—they are not dissuaders but Lures—Keepers of that great Romance still to us foreclosed—while coveting . . . their wisdom we lament their silence. . . . The power and the glory are the post mortuary gifts" (PF50).

15. When Dickinson wants to refer to the eyes of the dead, she employs a much more straightforward vocabulary: "The Eyes glaze once—and that is Death—" (241); "The Forehead copied Stone— / The Fingers grew too cold / To ache—and like a Skater's Brook— / The busy eyes—congealed—" (519).

ate—but deliberately treacherous and unpredictable. In her poetry, Nature is capable of conferring moments of great ecstasy. But the moments prove fleeting and transitory. They tantalize the observer, lull her into feelings of false security. Suddenly they pass, to be followed by periods when Nature glares back with a chilling hostility. With the Emersonian contention that Nature is rich with symbolic significance, Emily Dickinson again concurs: she never doubts for one moment that all Natural phenomena are intensely meaningful.[16]

But she does. That is the modernist despair at the heart of "There's a certain Slant of light": nature may signify nothing at all.[17] The speaker who attributes her "Heavenly Hurt" to "the Air" is unable to formulate a coherent account of the relationship between nature and her consciousness of it. Were it not for the ballast of a religious vocabulary that structures the speaker's passionately frustrated quest for meaning, the poem would not be what it is—a controlled expression of the nature of moral confusion—but an example of the deterioration of language under the pressure of such confusion.

Bereft of origins, Dickinson's speaker is also bereft of ends. Within this antiautobiographical style, personal desires can no longer be immediately apprehended. Many of her finest poems are genuinely despairing in that they argue against retrospective interpretations of the significance of suffering. They are life-affirming in that they articulate what cannot be understood and thereby retard the annihilation of consciousness that is anticipated by a poem such as "There's a certain Slant of light." To master despair, she looks for a relationship between her interior and exterior worlds; sunlight in a winter afternoon reminds her of death. To master death, Dickinson looks it in the face; she discovers nothing but a distant shadow. Once she removes the scar tissue of the past, there is no landscape, she is the landscape, and the only sound is silence.

16. Clark Griffith, *The Long Shadow: Emily Dickinson's Tragic Poetry* (Princeton: Princeton University Press, 1964), p. 25.

17. In "When the Soul Selects: Emily Dickinson's Attack on New England Symbolism," *American Literature* 51 (November 1979): 349–63, E. Miller Budick suggests that "Dickinson was hostile to the use of symbolic forms, and that in this hostility she was reacting against specific details of New England's history of idealization and symbolism, the gigantic Platonization of experience which characterized her Puritan and Transcendentalist forebears both." Contending that Dickinson's tropes often fail to bridge the "'gap between outer existence (the world) and inner meaning,'" she views this failure as an expression of Dickinson's literary radicalism.

"SOME—WORK
FOR IMMORTALITY—":
THE FEMALE ARTIST
AS PRIVATE POET

Dickinson's refusal to publish her poems during her lifetime has been subjected to a number of interpretations, none of which is wholly satisfactory. Although some nineteenth-century observers were puzzled by her stubborn adherence to a private vocation, they tended to accept her public silence as the natural analogue to her seclusion. Moreover, they knew that she refused repeated requests to publish her poems, that she had constructed her own audience of intimates in conjunction with her extensive correspondence, and that there were significant pressures on women writers to protect their personal lives from public scrutiny. Twentieth-century commentators, particularly since the publication of the Johnson editions of poems and letters in 1955 and 1958, have had access to primary materials that have enabled them to investigate, in greater detail, the development of Dickinson's life and art. Although her 1862 correspondence with Higginson, the literary critic she approached for advice and support, is generally understood as a turning point in her tentative effort to achieve recognition as an artist during her lifetime, the debate persists. Why would a poet who simultaneously announces and protests "This is my letter to the World / That never wrote to Me—" (441) refuse to share the not-so-simple "News that Nature told—" with the "Sweet—countrymen—" whose approval she craved and resisted, even as she commanded and implored, "Judge tenderly—of Me." By placing her initially ambivalent but ultimately steely choice of a private vocation in the context of certain widely shared assumptions about why women wrote in mid-century Victorian America, I hope to elucidate the mystery of her public silence and to clarify some of the problematic features of her poems on art and fame. I shall restrict my examples to poems and letters in which she confronts the relationship between artist and audience most directly.

There was a vigorous female literary subculture in mid-century Victorian America which Dickinson knew and which she gave some thought to joining. During the summer of 1861, she rewrote the second stanza of "Safe in their Alabaster Chambers—" (216) in an unsuccessful attempt to please her closest friend and sister-in-law, Susan Gilbert Dickinson. When Sue responded negatively to this revision, she again rewrote stanza two, and then replied to Sue's praise, "Could I make you and Austin—proud—sometime—a great way off—'twould give me taller feet—" (L238). The tone of their exchange at this time suggests that this process of criticism and revision may not have been a unique occurrence. When "Safe in their Alabaster Chambers—" appeared in the *Springfield Republican* on 1 March 1862, Sue sent an excited note across the lawn inquiring, "*Has girl read Republican?* It takes as long to start our Fleet as the Burnside."[1] It was with Sue's backing, and, if her own story is to be believed, the backing of the two *Republican* editors, both close family friends, that Dickinson approached Higginson six weeks later asking,

Mr Higginson,
    Are you too deeply occupied to say if my Verse is alive?
    The Mind is so near itself—it cannot see, distinctly—and I have none to ask—
    Should you think it breathed—and had you the leisure to tell me, I should feel quick gratitude—
    If I make the mistake—that you dared to tell me—would give me sincerer honor—toward you—
    I enclose my name—asking you, if you please—Sir—to tell me what is true?
    That you will not betray me—it is needless to ask—since Honor is it's own pawn— (L260)[2]

1. Jay Leyda, *The Years and Hours of Emily Dickinson*, 2 vols. (New Haven: Yale University Press, 1960), 2:48.
2. In her second letter to Higginson, Dickinson explained, "Two Editors of Journals came to my Father's House, this winter—and asked me for my Mind—and when

"Safe in their Alabaster Chambers—" was one of the four poems she enclosed for his inspection.

Her choice of Higginson was to some extent fortuitous. A *Republican* editorial had praised his "Letter to a Young Contributor" in the April issue of the *Atlantic Monthly*, and Higginson, a Unitarian minister who had renounced his pulpit, was a well-known supporter of liberal causes, including feminism.[3] His "Letter to a Young Contributor," a superficial pastiche of practical and moral advice, was intended to encourage unknown writers to submit manuscripts to editors who were, he blandly assured them, always hungry for new talent. The opening paragraph of his "Letter" made it clear he included "young ladies" in his avuncular embrace and that he was sensitive to their anxieties about entering the literary marketplace in a society that had defined their proper sphere of influence as the home. Alluding to the artist-heroine of a recent novel by Theodore Winthrop, he deftly acknowledged, "Many are the Cecil Dreemes of literature who superscribe their offered manuscripts with very masculine names in very feminine handwriting." He then cited the example of Harriet Beecher Stowe, the most celebrated American woman writer of the day, by way of further encouragement.

Although Dickinson's choice of Higginson was in part accidental, it also exemplifies an alliance between literary women and liberal clergymen documented by Ann Douglas in *The Feminization of American Culture*.[4] For Dickinson, as for other women writers, clergymen

---

I asked them 'Why,' they said I was penurious—and they, would use it for the World—" (L261). This seems to me an unmistakable reference to Samuel Bowles and J. G. Holland, the only editors Dickinson knew. Ruth Miller contends, however, that "between 1858 and 1862 Emily Dickinson had besieged her friend Samuel Bowles, editor of the *Springfield Republican*, with poems and with pleas on their behalf but failed to move him." See *The Poetry of Emily Dickinson* (Middletown, Conn.: Wesleyan University Press, 1968), p. 4. In *The Life of Emily Dickinson*, 2 vols. (New York: Farrar, Straus and Giroux, 1974), Richard B. Sewall supports this view, but with significant qualifications.

3. Higginson has been the subject of four book-length biographies. See Anna Mary Wells, *Dear Preceptor: The Life and Times of Thomas Wentworth Higginson* (Boston: Houghton Mifflin, 1963); Howard N. Meyer, *Colonel of the Black Regiment: The Life of Thomas Wentworth Higginson* (New York: Norton, 1967); Tilden G. Edelstein, *Strange Enthusiasm: A Life of Thomas Wentworth Higginson* (New Haven: Yale University Press, 1968); and James W. Tuttleton, *Thomas Wentworth Higginson* (Boston: Twayne, 1978).

4. In *The Feminization of American Culture* (New York: Alfred A. Knopf, 1977), Ann Douglas argues that liberal clergymen, their power eroded by the "disestablishment" of the Protestant Church during the post-Revolutionary years, aligned themselves with a newly emergent class of women writers in the Northeast, between about 1820 and 1875. Conservative politicians and businessmen such as Edward Dickinson opposed the "sentimental sabotage" of this coalition.

were strategic supporters, as well as potential antagonists. Since Dickinson's relationship with Higginson was the central literary friendship of her life, it is worth pursuing the implications of his attitude toward literary women, as reflected in "Letter to a Young Contributor," somewhat further.

Who, then, was Cecil Dreeme, Higginson's prototype for a female "Young Contributor"? "Dreeme" is the pseudonym of a woman disguised as a man, a recluse who goes out on solitary walks only at night, and a woman with a sensational secret. Her art is the direct expression of her fear and loneliness. Spurning fame, "Cecil Dreeme," née Clara Denman, has narrow brushes with suicide and madness and is estranged from her family, who have betrayed her finer nature. The uncanny closeness of these conventionalized materials to the stuff of the Dickinson legend is immediately apparent.[5] Much of Winthrop's novel is concerned with the growing intimacy between Dreeme and the male narrator, who perceives her as a man with a woman's refinement and sexual allure. Unwittingly but inevitably, "Dreeme" threatens the narrator's sexual self-confidence; her transvestism arouses his homosexuality. Both of these sexual crossings are situational, but the novel's achievement is its ability to turn this situation to prurient advantage. The original model for Dreeme was William Hurlbut, a close friend of Higginson's early manhood. According to Higginson, Hurlbut was "so handsome in his dark beauty that he seemed like a picturesque oriental." Higginson recalled the relationship by explaining, "I never loved but one male friend with passion—and for him my love had no bounds—all that my natural fastidiousness and cautious reserve kept from others I poured on him; to say that I would have died for him was nothing."[6] At best, Cecil Dreeme is a problematic prototype; at worst, she is a hostile one. Dickinson, refusing the mask of a male pseudonym, was to adopt the even more extreme disguise of invisibility.

After the initial passing reference to "Mrs. Stowe," Higginson proceeded to establish his authority by referring to some sixty writers. Only two of them are women: "Miss Burney" and one of "the

5. Like Dickinson's poetry, Theodore Winthrop's novel *Cecil Dreeme* (Boston: Ticknor and Fields, 1861), was posthumously published by the author's family. He died in June 1861 in the battle of Big Bethel. Dickinson identified with martyred artists; Winthrop was considered a military martyr by his contemporaries, as Daniel Aaron points out in *The Unwritten War: American Writers and the Civil War* (New York: Alfred A. Knopf, 1973), pp. 162, 353.
6. Edelstein, *Strange Enthusiasm*, pp. 313, 64.

Brownings." Thus "Mrs. Stowe" is the only American woman writer mentioned by Higginson, Elizabeth Barrett Browning the only poet, and she functions as part of a couple, as to a lesser degree does "Mrs. Stowe." All his generalized references to literary professionalism employ male pronouns. While underrepresenting the contributions of women to literature, Higginson employed figures of speech such as the following which emphasized the social and domestic aspects of female identity:

> Far from me be the wild expectation that every author will not habitually measure the merits of a periodical by its appreciation of his or her last manuscript. *I should as soon ask a young lady not to estimate the management of a ball by her own private luck in respect to partners.*
>
> Of course no editor is infallible, and the best magazine contains an occasional poor article. Do not blame the unfortunate conductor. He knows it as well as you do,—after the deed is done. The newspapers kindly pass it over, still preparing their accustomed opiate of sweet praises, so much for each contributor, so much for the magazine collectively,—*like a hostess with her tea-making, a spoonful for each person and one for the pot.*
>
> Do you expect him [an editor] to acknowledge the blunder, when you tax him with it? Never,—he feels it too keenly. He rather stands up stoutly for the surpassing merits of the misshapen thing, *as a mother for her deformed child; and as the mother is nevertheless inwardly imploring that there may never be such another born to her,* so be sure it is not by reminding the editor of this calamity that you can allure him into risking a repetition of it.[7]

Such feminine comparisons democratize the profession of authorship, but Higginson's specific descriptions of functional femininity privilege childhood, courtship, marriage, and motherhood, together with housekeeping and, in one instance, letter-writing: "How few men in all the pride of culture can emulate the easy grace of a bright woman's letter!" Intellectual authority is implicity viewed as a male prerogative.

Higginson's latent sexual anxieties determine the essay's true subject: a justification of the manliness of a literary life, even in times of national emergency. Benignly looking to the future to heal the wounds of the present, he imposed a rhetorical conclusion on his

---

7. Thomas Wentworth Higginson, "Letter to a Young Contributor," *Atlantic Monthly* 9 (April 1862): 401–02. Italics mine.

vocational anxieties which was prophetic for his Amherst correspondent:

> Yet, if our life be immortal, this temporary distinction is of little moment, and we may learn humility, without learning despair, from earth's evanescent glories. Who cannot bear a few disappointments, if the vista be so wide that the mute inglorious Miltons of this sphere may in some other sing their Paradise as Found? War or peace, fame or forgetfulness, can bring no real injury to one who has formed the fixed purpose to live nobly day by day. I fancy that in some other realm of existence we may look back with some kind interest on this scene of our earlier life, and say to one another,—'Do you remember yonder planet, where once we went to school?' And whether our elective study here lay chiefly in the fields of action or of thought will matter little to us then, when other schools shall have led us through other disciplines.[8]

Four months later, Higginson volunteered for action in the Union Army, where he distinguished himself as the commanding officer of its first black regiment. Recapitulating her private history a number of years later, Dickinson wrote him, "Of our greatest acts we are ignorant—You were not aware that you saved my Life" (L330).

Although Higginson's letters to Dickinson no longer exist, his attitude toward the poems she sent him in April 1862 can be inferred from her letters to him. His response was both encouraging and discouraging. He praised her poems but made suggestions for improving them which she described as "surgery . . . not so painful as I supposed" (L261). He chastised her for stylistic obscurities and formal irregularities, but the language of his second letter was so fulsome that she answered, "Your letter gave no Drunkenness, because I tasted Rum before—Domingo comes but once—yet I have had few pleasures so deep as your opinion, and if I tried to thank you, my tears would block my tongue—" (L265). In response to questions about herself, she misled him with the statement, "I made no verse—but one or two—until this winter—Sir—" (L261). Thus the nub of this exchange, his advice that she "delay 'to publish'" (L265), was conditioned by her specific misstatement and by her more general misrepresentation of the duration and seriousness of her literary apprenticeship. Higginson, who was preparing for wartime service, had no way of knowing that his correspondent was no longer

8. Higginson, "Letter to a Young Contributor," pp. 410–11.

especially young (she was thirty-one years old); that she had already
written hundreds of poems; and that the *Springfield Republican* had
first published one of them ten years previously with a cordial pref-
ace inviting her to initiate a "more direct" correspondence.

In her second letter (261) Dickinson described a "terror—since
September" which had not yet been exorcised, alluded to a recent
illness from which she had not yet recovered, and exhibited other
signs of nervousness. Higginson might reasonably have questioned
the wisdom of launching a demanding enterprise at that time, especially since the publication of a volume of Dickinson's poems was
bound to affront the sensibilities of some readers. There was also the
risk that Dickinson's poetry, which appeared to ignore political issues, might be ignored by a nation in the throes of Civil War. Dickinson herself may have suspected that her apparent indifference to
contemporary issues could be turned to her advantage, judging by
the somewhat escapist poems she originally sent him: "Safe in their
Alabaster Chambers—" (216), "I'll tell you how the Sun rose—"
(318), "The nearest Dream recedes—unrealized—" (319), and "We
play at Paste—" (320). The mild rebuff she suffered at Higginson's
hands only confirmed her in the "White Election" of a private vocation toward which she was already strongly impelled: "I smile when
you suggest that I delay 'to publish'—that being foreign to my
thought, as Firmament to Fin—If fame belonged to me, I could not
escape her—if she did not, the longest day would pass me on the
chase—and the approbation of my Dog, would forsake me—then—
My Barefoot-Rank is better—" (L265). And there she let the matter
rest.

Although there is some reason to believe that if Higginson had
hailed her at the beginning of a great career and urged her not to
"delay 'to publish'" Dickinson might have been prevailed upon to
yield up some of her least obviously autobiographical poems to public view, there is more reason to believe that no external pressure,
even of a favorable sort, could have persuaded her to take up the
public vocation of poet. One of her cousins recorded that, some
years later, "When urged to publish her verses, she said, 'I would as
soon undress in public, as give my poems to the world.' "[9] Nor can
there by any doubt that when Thomas Niles of Roberts Brothers
Publishers solicited a volume of verse in 1882 and again in 1883, at

9. Leyda, *Years and Hours of Emily Dickinson,* 2:482.

the urging of Helen Hunt Jackson, Dickinson unmistakably rejected his advances, just as she had those of the unidentified Miss P (perhaps Elizabeth Stuart Phelps), who had approached her in 1872.[10] Dickinson wrote to her cousin Louise Norcross at that time, "Of Miss P—-I know but this, dear. She wrote me in October, requesting me to aid the world by my chirrup more. Perhaps she stated it as my duty, I don't distinctly remember, and always burn such letters, so I cannot obtain it now. I replied declining. She did not write to me again—she might have been offended, or perhaps is extricating humanity from some hopeless ditch" (L380).

"'I would as soon undress in public, as give my poems to the world.'" Can Dickinson have believed that female modesty was inconsistent with print; that men were to carry on the business of literature, women to write for themselves or for the elect few possessing "the rare Ear / Not too dull—" (842) when she wrote

> Publication—is the Auction
> Of the Mind of Man—
> Poverty—be justifying
> For so foul a thing
>
> Possibly—but We—would rather
> From Our Garret go
> White—Unto the White Creator—
> Than invest—Our Snow—
>
> Thought belong to Him who gave it—
> Then—to Him Who bear
> It's Corporeal illustration—Sell
> The Royal Air—
>
> In the Parcel—Be the Merchant
> Of the Heavenly Grace—
> But reduce no Human Spirit
> To Disgrace of Price— (709)

Dickinson's equation of publication with the reduction of the human spirit to the "Disgrace of Price" is a carefully disguised expression of hostility from writer to reader. Instead of addressing herself to cultural taboos against careers for women, the speaker

10. For Dickinson's correspondence with Niles and Jackson, see *The Letters of Emily Dickinson,* ed. Thomas H. Johnson, vols. 2 and 3 (Cambridge: Harvard University Press, 1958).

suggests that publication automatically destroys the integrity of any writer. Her language and tone are obviously defensive. Instead of addressing herself to the conflict between female social and professional identity, Dickinson manipulates economic metaphors to suggest that chastity is a precondition for any unsullied art. The implied alternative is prostitution. Thus she barricades herself behind her "feminine" refusal to barter with a corrupt world and announces that she is not for sale. As a normative expression of Dickinson's attitude toward the availability of books or toward other women writers (her interest in their art and lives was inveterate), the poem is nonsense. "Publication—is the Auction / Of the Mind of Man—" nevertheless demonstrates that Dickinson's private vocation was motivated by a profound distrust of her audience, coupled with an equally profound distrust of the legitimacy of her thoughts.

The poem is an unconscious travesty on mid-Victorian sex-role norms. Economic deprivation justifies careers for some women. Absent such justification, the speaker who calls herself "We" identifies "Publication" with male sexual power. A categorical distinction between masculinity and femininity informs the text, but Dickinson finds it necessary to delete the specifically female component from her justification of economic deprivation as the rationale for a literary career. Dickinson had a rich and, in certain respects, indulgent father; thus this rationale is not available to her. Her thought-disturbance is most apparent in stanza three, in which she suggests that thought belongs to God the Father, a proposition that generalizes her biographical dilemma. The second and third lines of this stanza are exceptionally difficult because of the barely intelligible phrase "Corporeal illustration," which further identifies "Him" in line one. To a significant degree, the poem pivots on this identification. This linguistic breakdown indicates an unintegrated, agitating thought. Describing the spirit's impregnation by an original source, presumably God, Dickinson associates an immaculate conception with the birth of a legitimate, male child of God. She appears to suggest that thinkers or writers in the Jesus tradition—those uncorrupted by their materialistic, secular society—are also men. Presumably Dickinson's unintegrated thought is an awareness of herself as an illegitimate daughter.

Thus behind the legal nicety of such statements as "Thought belong to Him who gave it— / Then—to Him Who bear / It's Corporeal illustration" lies a conviction that the woman poet's strength is a theft from the father, the "White Creator," the "Merchant / Of the Heavenly Grace" who parsimoniously parcels out the "Royal Air." A number of Dickinson's weaker poems attempt to conceal this aggressive knowledge from her implied audience and from herself. Disenfranchised because of her sex, she merely tidies a house littered by others with more important work to do:

> I was a Phebe—nothing more—
> A Phebe—nothing less—
> The little note that others dropt
> I fitted into place—
>
> I dwelt too low that any seek—
> Too shy, that any blame—
> A Phebe makes a little print
> Upon the Floors of Fame— (1009)

The singing bird is a conventional romantic emblem of the artist's harmonious relationship to nature's text, but the punishment motif, together with the emphasis on abstinent marginality—on shyness, smallness, voraciousness denied—is specifically Dickinsonian. This poem reflects Dickinson's struggle not merely with her culture's vocabulary of "true womanhood" but also with her need "to offset and deny—or even disguise—her actual dimensions as she must have experienced them."[11] Since the poem was transcribed in 1865 at the close of her major period, it also suggests that this aversion to "her actual dimensions as she must have experienced them" was not eradicated by the astonishing achievement of those turbulent years, but was, instead, one of its core elements.

What emotional logic impelled the writer who described herself as a "Loaded Gun" to describe herself as a "Phebe"? Dickinson sought to control her aggression by adopting a feminine persona, but the character she creates is excessively feminine. The common element uniting both of these personae, "Loaded Gun" and "Phebe," is the extravagance of their divergence from a social norm. Both personae express her self-distrust, which emerges in response to her hostility toward the sexual norms of her environment. Dickinson was excep-

11. Adrienne Rich, "Vesuvius at Home: The Power of Emily Dickinson," *Parnassus* 5 (Fall-Winter 1976): 49–74; reprinted in *Shakespeare's Sisters: Feminist Essays on Women Poets*, ed. Sandra M. Gilbert and Susan Gubar (Bloomington: Indiana University Press, 1979), p. 106.

tionally skillful at defending herself against aggression. Irony is one
such defense. Hers is nevertheless a poetry of experience, which
describes social conflicts she was unable to resolve except by withdrawing herself from them. Thus the resolutions she conceived
were overdetermined by her history. Hence the strain, which sometimes takes the form of excessive receptiveness to her second-class
status, and which sometimes takes the form of excessive rebellion
against it.

Dickinson's poems, then, are compacted by the pressure of an
internal and an external censor. Straitened by hymn meters and the
conservative sexual morality of the woman in white, the voice of the
poet reclaims those buried components of consciousness hidden by
her veil of civilized rectitude. Identifying the poet's powers of creation and destruction as a theft from an inscrutable male deity and
his sons, Dickinson was deeply ambivalent about her achievement.
By sacrificing her ambition for recognition during her lifetime, she
freed herself to usurp the privilege of strong creation from the
archetypal male figure who was "Burglar—Banker—Father" (49).
Reinforced by the tenets of Protestant individualism and Emersonian self-reliance, she broke with the popular wisdom of American
women's poetry in defining her sphere of freedom as her inner
world, the house of "Possibility" she so insistently contrasted with
the house of "Prose" (657). Yet she also knew that she was fated to
live out in her art the crisis of sexual and human identity she could
not resolve in her life. Torn between her desire to submit herself to
the transforming power of a male-lover-God and her desire to *be* the
power she courted, she could never risk the open identification with
maleness that a public vocation represented to her. Thus Dickinson's
practice as poet exploring the alien underworld of the female psyche
is often curiously at odds with her extravagant tributes to the poet as
invulnerable superman:

> This was a Poet—It is That
> Distills amazing sense
> From ordinary Meanings—
> And Attar so immense
>
> From the familiar species
> That perished by the Door—
> We wonder it was not Ourselves
> Arrested it—before—

Of Pictures, the Discloser—
The Poet—it is He—
Entitles Us—by Contrast—
To ceaseless Poverty—

Of Portion—so unconscious—
The Robbing—could not harm—
Himself—to Him—a Fortune—
Exterior—to Time—   (448)

However vigorous, a subculture is still a subculture. Dickinson's
anxiety about the legitimacy of her powers was unusual in degree
but not in kind. There *was* an antipublication cult in nineteenth-
century America that was part of a larger pattern of cultural unrest
about the departure of women from their proper sphere of influence, the home. This conflict between the profession of "true womanhood" and the profession of authorship can be located with particular clarity in a thesis novel by one of the *Springfield Republican's*
editors and in the reaction of Edward Dickinson to literary women.

J. G. Holland, self-styled "lay preacher to a nation," was the husband of Dickinson's close friend Elizabeth and coeditor of the
Springfield Republican, which published six of the eight Dickinson
poems appearing (all of them anonymously) during her lifetime.[12]
His gloriously symptomatic novel, *Miss Gilbert's Career: An American
Story* (1860), describes the development of a successful female novelist whose mother is dead and whose proud papa is ambitious for her.
At the height of her fame, she sees the error of her ways and renounces her selfish aspirations for personal renown in favor of marriage to an emasculated clergyman. Her conversion experience occurs while she holds a deformed child who dies in her arms, in a
scene that the *Atlantic Monthly* reviewer (Higginson) singled out as
"one of the most beautiful and touching pictures ever yet presented."[13] Fanny Gilbert, the "new woman," is converted back into a
self-sacrificing "true woman." She is reborn as the carrier of conser-

12. In "Another Dickinson Poem Published in Her Lifetime," Karen Dandurand
adds "Nobody knows this little Rose—" (35) to the previous list of seven that had been
established by Johnson and others. The poem appeared in the *Springfield Republican*
on 2 August 1858. It was, according to the paper, "Surreptitiously communicated,"
presumably by someone other than the author. See *American Literature* 54 (October
1982): 434–37.
13. Thomas Wentworth Higginson, "Miss Gilbert's Career," *Atlantic Monthly* 7 (January 1861): 126.

vative family values in an industrializing society inimical to the preservation of a rural, pastoral ideal of Christian community. Holland
places the blame for Fanny Gilbert's misguided ambition (money is
never an issue) squarely on the doorstep of her father, Dr. Gilbert,
portraying him as a traitor to his sex and class.

Holland, a shrewd businessman, acceded to reality as editor of the
Republican, opening its columns to women writers while continuing
to suggest from time to time that "happy marriage and rest from
doubt and scandal take the passion out of women geniuses."[14] *Miss
Gilbert's Career* was a rearguard action by a self-made literary man
hoping to deflect his female competition into a convenient sociologi-
cal backwater.[15] It was also based on the widely shared assumption
that the woman writer's desire for professional success was a displacement of her natural desire for husband and children or a com-
pensation for their absence. These pre-Freudian views of art as sub-
limated sexuality generated attacks on women writers accusing them
not only of mannishness but also of joylessness or even self-imposed
martyrdom. Thus the distinction between a secret sorrow and a
morbid, masochistic temperament was often blurred by a critical
literature that associated female creativity with female suffering.

The response of Edward Dickinson to an encounter with the celebrated novelist Catharine Maria Sedgwick in 1826 typifies New England's ambivalence toward its women writers. In a letter to his
fiancée Emily Norcross he explained,

> I passed Tuesday evening, of this week, in company with Miss Sedg-
> wick, the Authoress of "Redwood" & "New England Tale", at a party
> at Judge Lyman's. She had an interesting countenance—an ap-
> pearance of much thought, & rather masculine features. And I feel
> happy at having an opportunity of seeing a female who had done so
> much to give our works of taste so pure and delicate a character—
> and a conscious pride that women of our own country & our own
> state, too, are emulating not only the females but the men of En-
> gland & France & Germany & Italy in works of literature—

14. "Books, Authors and Art" column announcing George Eliot's new novel, Feb-
ruary 1862; reprinted in Leyda, *Years and Hours of Emily Dickinson,* 2:47.
15. For a more enthusiastic analysis of Holland's career, see Harry Houston
Peckham, *Josiah Gilbert Holland in Relation to His Times* (Philadelphia: University of
Pennsylvania Press, 1940). In "J. G. Holland's Moral Politics," *Journal of Popular
Culture* 12 (Summer 1978): 127–37, Jonathan Morse argues that *Miss Gilbert's Career*
exemplifies Holland's interest in the Whig ideal of the Christian gentleman, which
Morse associates with "the politics of [female] subordination."

Progressive patriotism notwithstanding, he concluded

> Tho' I should be sorry to see another Mme. de Stael—especially if any one wished to make a partner of her for life. Different qualities are more desirable in a female who enters into domestic relations— and you have already had my opinions on that subject—[16]

His opinions on that subject were "Females, also . . . have a sphere of action, which, tho' different entirely in its kind from that of the other sex, is no less important."[17] He lectured the diffident Emily Norcross repeatedly on this ethic throughout their protracted courtship.

Perhaps because of the constant vigilance required to suppress his own passionate nature, Edward Dickinson was an old-fashioned Puritan in his suspicion of "fictions—vain imaginations to lead astray foolish young women" (L31). "He buys me many Books," Dickinson told Higginson in 1862, "but begs me not to read them—because he fears they joggle the Mind" (L261). That same year and month (April 1862) Edward Dickinson presented his daughter with a copy of *Letters to a Daughter, on Practical Subjects,* by the Reverend William B. Sprague. Sprague cautions against random reading, suggests that Shakespeare should be read only under the supervision of a tutor, and advises young ladies to be diligent in spelling and handwriting. A typical passage is the following: "I hardly need say that you can lay no claim to the character of an accomplished scholar, until you can speak and write with correctness your own language. And in order for this, you must gain a thorough knowledge of English grammar and Rhetoric."[18] The daughter to whom *Practical Subjects* is nominally addressed cannot be more than fifteen or sixteen years old. A gift of this sort to the thirty-one-year-old poet implies a shocking distance between her bold inner life and her father's aspirations for her. This set of *Letters,* interestingly enough to a "motherless daughter," is one of only two books in the Harvard collection inscribed to the poet by her father after 1859. The other, *Christian Living and Believing* by the Reverend F. D. Huntington, attacks "soft" poetry. Given the critical vocabulary of the period, which associated exces-

16. Sewall, *Life of Emily Dickinson,* 1:49.
17. Sewall, *Life of Emily Dickinson,* 1:48.
18. William B. Sprague, *Letters to a Daughter, on Practical Subjects* (Albany, N.Y.: E. H. Pearse, 1851), p. 49.

sive emotion and insufficient thought with the stereotypical woman writer, the words "soft" and "feminine" are interchangeable.[19]

Dickinson concealed much of her literary activity from the members of her family. The cozy scene in William Luce's popular play *The Belle of Amherst,* where Edward Dickinson acknowledges and indulges his daughter's nighttime hours, has no basis in recorded fact. Dickinson's attitudes toward the intellectual aggression she identified with male sexual behavior were deeply influenced by her relationship with her father, just as this relationship was informed by the patriarchal religious culture of the Connecticut Valley. Although he predeceased her by twelve years, throughout her adult life she was locked into a convoluted, thoroughly internalized power struggle with him she could afford neither to lose nor to win.[20] Because of the unspeakable rage and love with which this struggle was charged, Dickinson equated her independence with her father's destruction. Poised between rebellion and submission, "Vesuvius at Home" and "little Girl," she was unable to challenge his authority as the representative of the Dickinson family in the world of public affairs. As the "Representative of the Verse," she identified with him but concealed this identification within a private vocation:

> I have a King, who does not speak—
> So—wondering—thro' the hours meek
> I trudge the day away—
> Half glad when it is night, and sleep,
> If, haply, thro' a dream, to peep
> In parlors, shut by day.
>
> And if I do—when morning comes—
> It is as if a hundred drums
> Did round my pillow roll,

19. F. D. Huntington, *Christian Living and Believing* (Boston: Crosby, Nicholas, 1860).

20. As Joanne Feit Diehl observes in "'Come Slowly—Eden': An Exploration of Women Poets and Their Muse," *Signs* 3 (Spring 1978): 578, "Threat of dependence foments rebellion; by casting off her Precursor, she fears that she may be relinquishing her muse as well. In the process of exorcising her Precursor, she may banish the source of her art. In her late poems, Dickinson asserts her independence of any master, yet she remains haunted by the possibility that she may have been robbed of his potency and power. Her poems vacillate between these two poles—the conflict remains unresolved and so must be reenacted in poem after poem." The other poets she considers are Elizabeth Barrett Browning and Christina Rossetti. Her statement about the chronology of Dickinson's development is, however, an oversimplification.

And shouts fill all my Childish sky,
And Bells keep saying 'Victory'
From steeples in my soul!

And if I dont—the little Bird
Within the Orchard, is not heard,
And I omit to pray
'Father, thy will be done' today
For my will goes the other way,
And it were perjury!   (103)

To the casual observer, no two people could have been more dissimilar than this "Nobody" poet and her "Somebody" father. Yet to the instructed eye, Edward Dickinson—not as he was, but as he might have been—was her most formidable precursor. Within the poem just cited, his silence activates her voice.

Dickinson played out this drama within the haunted chambers of her mind, but in the life where she encountered a significantly less oneiric figure, it was otherwise. Richard Sewall undoubtedly is correct: like Ahab, Edward Dickinson " 'had his humanities.' "[21] There *were* good times, laughter, and gaiety in the house on Pleasant Street and in the Homestead. No ogre could have commanded the loyalty this stalwart figure evoked not just in the poet but in all the members of his immediate family. Nevertheless, Edward Dickinson's opposition to the feminization of American culture was unmistakable. Dickinson told Higginson, " 'My father only reads on Sunday—he reads *lonely* & *rigorous* books' " (L342a). Higginson recorded after their 1870 interview,

> Her father . . . did not wish them to read anything but the Bible. One day her brother brought home Kavanagh hid it under the piano cover & made signs to her & they read it: her father at last found it & was displeased. Perhaps it was before this that a student of his was amazed that they had never heard of Mrs. [Lydia Maria] Child & used to bring them books & hide in a bush by the door. They were then little things in short dresses with their feet on the rungs of the chair. After the first book she thought in ecstasy "This then is a book! And there are more of them!" (L342b)

While this story may contain apocryphal elements, it reflects Dickinson's belief that her father disapproved of her literary interests,

21. Sewall, *Life of Emily Dickinson,* 1:44.

which undermined the authority of this parent on whom she relied not only for financial but also for emotional sustenance.

Edward Dickinson's opposition to the feminization of American culture also took the form of denigrating what he knew of his daughter's writing, which was apparently not much: "Father, too busy with his Briefs—to notice what we do" (L261). His silent disapproval is especially marked in contrast to his extravagant praise for Austin Dickinson's efforts. "Father says your letters are altogether before Shakespeare, and he will have them published to put in our library," she wrote in 1851 (L46). He was so pleased by Austin's unenthusiastic account of a concert by Jenny Lind in Boston that he considered having it published in the local paper (L44). When Austin criticized one of Emily's letters, she recorded with apparent good humor that "[Father] told me you'd 'hit me off nicely'" (L128). Nowhere is there any indication of any paternal praise for Dickinson's poetry. "*Her sister* [italics mine] is proud of her," William Stearns, the president of Amherst College, remarked to Higginson in 1870.

Following Edward Dickinson's death in 1874, the poet told her Norcross cousins, "I dream about father every night, always a different dream, and forget what I am doing daytimes, wondering where he is" (L471). This letter was written in the summer of 1876, more than two years after his death. Yet in 1873 she was already describing herself as an orphan, writing to Mrs. Holland, "She [Vinnie] has no Father and Mother but me and I have no Parents but her" (L391). Dickinson's account of her last afternoon with her father reflects her desire to please him, her ability to do so on a contrived occasion, and her wariness of his pleasure:

> The last Afternoon that my Father lived, though with no premonition—I preferred to be with him, and invented an absence for Mother, Vinnie being asleep. He seemed peculiarly pleased as I oftenest stayed with myself, and remarked as the Afternoon withdrew, he "would like it to not end."
> His pleasure almost embarrassed me and my Brother coming—I suggested they walk. Next morning I woke him for the train—and saw him no more.   (L418)

Given this set of cultural pressures intimately lived, it is no wonder that Dickinson cast many of her clearest acknowledgments of her own imaginative powers in an ironic, negative, and self-deprecating mode. In many of her poems on poets, on books, and on reading,

Dickinson employs an androcentric model, represents the female speaker as an enthusiastic admirer who never writes a line, or describes the poet's function as the creation of ideal images whose contrast with reality torments the reader. Thus one of the major dramatic tensions these poems incorporate depends on the contrast between the speaker's insistent confessions of her own limitations and the transcendent power of the antithetical other, the artist-poet whose freedom from nature and from human society she celebrates. The wonder is that this renunciatory stance could release the "Glee" of perfect self-possession. In stanzas two, three, and four of the following poem, she whirls away the paralysis of obscurity in a dazzling fantasy of public acclaim:

> I cannot dance upon my Toes—
> No Man instructed me—
> But oftentimes, among my mind,
> A Glee possesseth me,
>
> That had I Ballet knowledge—
> Would put itself abroad
> In Pirouette to blanch a Troupe—
> Or lay a Prima, mad,
>
> And though I had no Gown of Gauze—
> No Ringlet, to my Hair,
> Nor hopped for Audiences—like Birds,
> One Claw upon the Air,
>
> Nor tossed my shape in Eider Balls,
> Nor rolled on wheels of snow
> Till I was out of sight, in sound,
> The House encore me so—
>
> Nor any know I know the Art
> I mention—easy—Here—
> Nor any Placard boast me—
> It's full as Opera—   (326)

When Dickinson states, slyly, "I cannot . . . No Man instructed me," she also means that she refused such instruction as was offered her, or wished to. Staking out this position of extreme ignorance, she cuts herself off from one kind of knowledge, for example the knowledge that "among my mind" is a bizarre construction. Similarly, she cuts herself off from an audience that has received such instruction, for example the knowledge that a terminal rhyme sound such as "Here . . . Opera" does not sound "full." Because she has received enough instruction to perceive herself, somewhat grotesquely, as hopping "for Audiences—like Birds, / One Claw upon the Air," an image that is both parodic and self-parodic, she lacks the unself-conscious ignorance of the authentic primitive: it "possesseth" her not. For one perfect moment, a civilized unself-consciousness is achieved, in stanza four, as Dickinson floats "out of sight, in sound," buoyed up by an acclaim that enables her to lose herself within it. Nevertheless, Dickinson's uncompromising repression of the exhibitionism this poem so beautifully expresses heightened her sense of competitiveness with other women artists. Thus, when Dickinson describes herself as performing "In Pirouette to blanch a Troupe— / Or lay a Prima, mad," she also means that she has exorcised her jealousy of other gifted women, women less fundamentally gifted with her "gift of Screws—" (675).[22]

In her ardent tributes to other women writers, Dickinson simultaneously undercut and praised their powers, which is to say that Charlotte Brontë, George Eliot, and Elizabeth Barrett Browning are absorbed into the vortex of her own self-conception.[23] Except in a single instance where she portrays Barrett Browning as the purveyor of illicit experience (593), as witch and magician, she adopted the eulogy as her mode, emphasizing even in poem 593, charged as it is with the excitement of a first discovery, that "Magicians be asleep."[24] She denied them an audience and cast them in the "mar-

22. This poem is widely glossed within the context of her correspondence with Higginson, to whom she sent it in August 1862, asking, "Are these more orderly?" Charles Anderson and others consider it a satire on the artificiality of his poetic conventions, which she likens to those of the classical ballet. In *Emily Dickinson's Poetry: Stairway of Surprise* (New York: Holt, Rinehart and Winston, 1960), pp. 21–23, Anderson demonstrates that Dickinson does indeed possess "Ballet knowledge," though she may never have seen a performance, and glosses the concluding word, "Opera," as an obvious synonym for "Opera house." This gloss reemphasizes my point that the poem's conclusion reintroduces a problem: something is missing. Though this absence is the mother of modernist invention, it is still perceived as a loss.

23. Dickinson wrote two eulogies for Charlotte Brontë, "All overgrown by cunning moss," and "Gathered from many wanderings." Both are numbered 148 by Johnson, although they are two separate poems. The three poems for Barrett Browning are "Her—'last Poems'—" (312), "I went to thank Her—" (363), and "I think I was enchanted" (593).

24. In "Dickinson, Poe, and Barrett Browning: A Clarification," *New England Quarterly* 54 (March 1981): 121–24, I describe this poem's original occasion. Dickinson knew some of Barrett Browning's work by August 1854, when she wrote letter 171 to Henry Emmons.

tyr poet" tradition, even when this lack of public recognition was patently untrue. If in her letters she writes, "'What do I think of *Middlemarch?*' What do I think of glory," (L389) when she evaluated Eliot's achievement ten years later, what emerges is a poem beginning "Her Losses make our Gains ashamed—" in which a contextless punishment motif again figures strongly:

> Her Losses make our Gains ashamed—
> She bore Life's empty Pack
> As gallantly as if the East
> Were swinging at her Back.
> Life's empty Pack is heaviest,
> As every Porter knows—
> In vain to punish Honey—
> It only sweeter grows. (1562)

Perpetuating her stance as eager reader, she implicitly denied her own poetic vocation, particularly in the eulogies for Barrett Browning, who was the strongest female influence on her style. To many mid-nineteenth-century American readers, Barrett Browning's career seemed to validate the humanitarian mission of the female artist. According to the writer of her obituary in the *Atlantic Monthly* (Higginson), "Her life was one long, large-souled, large-hearted prayer for the triumph of Right, Justice, Liberty. . . she . . . lived for others . . . . wife, mother, and poet, three in one, and such an earthly trinity as God had never before blessed the world with." Even on her deathbed, he concluded, "Her thoughts were not of self."[25] Dickinson, however, describes this precursor as an inimitable or death-dealing poet, before projecting herself into the role of a bereaved bridegroom. In the process, she transformed her envy of Barrett Browning into an emotion more acceptable to her, an "easy wo":

> Her—'last Poems'—
> Poets—ended—
> Silver—perished—with her Tongue—
> Not on Record—bubbled other,
> Flute—or Woman—
> So divine—

25. Thomas Wentworth Higginson, "Elizabeth Barrett Browning," *Atlantic Monthly* 8 (September 1861):368–76.

> Not unto it's Summer—Morning
> Robin—uttered Half the Tune—
> Gushed too free for the Adoring—
> From the Anglo-Florentine—
> Late—the Praise—
> 'Tis dull—conferring
> On the Head too High to Crown—
> Diadem—or Ducal Showing—
> Be it's Grave—sufficient sign—
> Nought—that We—No Poet's Kinsman—
> Suffocate—with easy wo—
> What, and if, Ourself a Bridegroom—
> Put Her down—in Italy?   (312)

This transformation of jealousy into grief is among the most fundamental gestures of Dickinson's psyche. Consequently, hers is grief with a vengeance, and on many levels this style is a covertly vindictive one. For example, the line "Gushed too free for the Adoring—" disengages itself, sardonically, from the text. Within a context of praise, the line is virtually unintelligible. Reconstructing its tortuous syntax is a tortuous process: Not unto its summer morning [did] [any] robin utter half the tune [which] gushed too free[ly] for the adoring [public] from the Anglo-Florentine [for us to adore robins]. Consciously, Dickinson is saying something like this: Elizabeth Barrett Browning expressed herself too freely for us to be able to admire the songs of summer robins. That is, she defeated nature; robins competed against her ineffectually. Unconsciously, Dickinson is saying something more interesting: Elizabeth Barrett Browning gushed too freely for an uncritical audience; Dickinson does not form part of this audience and cannot adore her. Within a context of praise, the line is woefully underdetermined. Disengaged from it, it stands as a witty "Put . . . down" of Barrett Browning's verbosity. Dickinson's dissent from a convention of praise is underscored by her grammatical dissent as she withholds, superbly, the expected adverbial ending. Consciously, Dickinson expresses the thought that Barrett Browning's achievement preempts utterance. Unconsciously, Dickinson expresses the thoughts, "Barrett Browning's legacy is a sterile one; I cannot claim her as a foremother; her audience is not mine."

Hers is, then, the freedom to withhold, which depends on her ability to withhold certain thoughts from herself. More specifically, she denies the fact that the freedom to withhold is only half a freedom. But Dickinson knew this:

I'd so much joy—I told it—Red—
....
I felt it publish—in my Eye—
....
I put my pleasure all abroad—
I dealt a word of Gold
To every Creature—that I met—
And Dowered—all the World— (430)

The character who is not put down is Robert Browning, whose grief is sincere because it is distinguishable from envy. And it is with Robert Browning that Dickinson begins to identify within the last four lines, an identification that transpires within a context of blocked competition. Saying "what if," Dickinson also says "What, and if," a conditional locution interrupted rather than coordinated by its superfluous conjunction. Thus Dickinson's unconscious hostility toward Barrett Browning is inappropriate on two counts. First, Dickinson's conscious intention is to magnify rather than to denigrate Barrett Browning's achievement. Second, Dickinson's envy of Barrett Browning is also displaced hostility toward Robert Browning. He represents both a masculine poetic tradition and a long line of proprietorial husbands. Dickinson's relationship to Barrett Browning is thus complicated by the sexual ambivalence of its focus.[26] Stating that Barrett Browning has had the last word while making it impossible for her to have done so, Dickinson also has the *first* word for those critics, including myself, who have investigated Dickinson's indebtedness to her and who believed her when she wrote,

I think I was enchanted
When first a sombre Girl—
I read that Foreign Lady—
The Dark—felt beautiful— (593)

Within poem 312, grief-stricken because it is an elegy, grief-stricken because it is a half-song written out of anger programmatically suppressed, Dickinson's vocabulary of praise is derivative and belated. Such praise refuses to complete itself because it is suffocated

26. In *The Anxiety of Influence: A Theory of Poetry* (New York: Oxford University Press, 1973), Harold Bloom discusses the relations between modern or post-Enlightenment male poets. He argues that "as poetry has become more subjective, the shadow cast by the precursors has become more dominant." Bloom's strong poets are depicted as "father and son . . . though some of the fathers . . . are composite figures" (p. 11).

by another set of attitudes. Thus, for example, the thought-line "Diadem—or Ducal Showing—" is unable to sustain itself. Such derivative or belated praise, she tells us, " 'Tis dull—conferring." That Barrett Browning cannot hear it is unremarkable. That Dickinson finds it dulling to deny her anger is worth recording and "on Record."

As I have suggested, the examples of Elizabeth Barrett Browning, Charlotte Brontë, George Eliot, and other exceptional women posed particular problems for Dickinson. On the one hand, she identified with them; on the other hand, she perceived herself as competing, perhaps ineffectually, against them. She found it easiest to identify with their failures which, given Dickinson's transformation of failure into nonbeing, meant their deaths. Thus Charlotte Brontë is not the author of *Jane Eyre;* instead, she is "All overgrown by cunning moss, / All interspersed with weed" (148). George Eliot is not a prodigiously fecund author nor the lover of George Henry Lewes; instead, "She bore Life's empty Pack . . . gallantly." Nor is Helen Hunt Jackson a person to be cherished in her own right; instead, her effect is derivative: "Because He loves Her / We will pry and see if she is fair" (1229). These judgments have, of course, their own audacity, but I am less interested in Dickinson the literary critic than in Dickinson the artist coming to terms with one aspect of her fate: socially unrewarded work, which she described as "The Service without Hope—" (779). All of Dickinson's poems on other women writers contain more generous elements, and "The Service without Hope" is also the service without despair, but my point is a simple one: when Dickinson states of Eliot, "Her Losses make our Gains ashamed," she also means, "Her gains make me ashamed of my losses." This pattern also exists in Dickinson's eulogies for women whose vocation is not art but death. Within the wonderful poem "The last Night that She lived," grief begets jealousy. But when Dickinson writes, "A Jealousy for Her arose / So nearly infinite," she also means, "My jealousy *of* her is now finite because I have killed her into art."

It is now possible to provide a denser context for the contextless punishment motif that erupts so unexpectedly within the poems I have been examining. Dickinson's "I cannot" or "I'm Nobody" stance emerges in response to an emotion or an environmental threat she pretends not to credit. This stance, in varying degrees, unblocks her identification with poetic power, which she perceives within an essentially masculinist tradition. This association also arouses her fears of sexual transgression. Thus she is haunted not only by the guilt of her desires but also by the guilt of her denial of them. Dickinson's punishment motif, with its attendant shames and blames, expresses her fear that she will be punished for unwomanly behavior, her determination to risk such punishment, her fear that she is unwilling to risk such punishment, her desire to punish the punishers, and, finally, her confusion as to whether it is possible to identify the distinguishing characteristic of this class of persons. Her identification of power with the dominant masculine element in her culture suggests an easy and sexist solution to the problem of its abuse, so that

> He fumbles at your Soul
> As Players at the Keys
> Before they drop full Music on—
> He stuns you by degrees—   (315)

Since she herself participates in this power, as do certain women, she is unable—quite wonderfully—to persuade herself that abuses of power are a male prerogative:

> She dealt her pretty words like Blades—
> How glittering they shone—
> And every One unbared a Nerve
> Or wantoned with a Bone—   (479)

Participating in this power, she finds it illogical to deny herself the reward of it: the fame she associates with love. This association in turn raises the question of what form this love is to take and, more specifically, what its sexual component is to be. If she has, in fact, usurped male power, how much of it has she usurped? Because this conflict remains unresolved, she denies herself an audience.

Deeply obsessed by the theme of fame in both its mortal and supernatural manifestations, Dickinson compensated in her art both for fear of her own transforming power—her "terror of vocation"[27]—and for her lack of an audience by insisting repeatedly that

27. The phrase is Inder Nath Kher's, in *The Landscape of Absence: Emily Dickinson's Poetry* (New Haven: Yale University Press, 1974). He writes, "Dickinson's terror of vocation—which is poetry—is consistent with her idea of what poetry is. . . . One always fears what one truly loves. One is struck with wonder in its presence. Emily Dickinson's love is poetry; therefore she fears poetry" (p. 16).

Fame of Myself, to justify,
All other Plaudit be
Superfluous—An Incense
Beyond Necessity—

Fame of Myself to lack—Although
My Name be else Supreme—
This were an Honor honorless—
A futile Diadem—   (713)

The Beggar at the Door for Fame
Were easily supplied
But Bread is that Diviner thing
Disclosed to be denied   (1240)

As her thought-lines contract in response to the threat she pretends not to credit, Dickinson maintains that generous audiences, uncritical and lavish, are (like lovers) to be had for the asking. Seeing beneath and beyond them, she is intent either on her own self-assessments or on some elemental sustenance "Disclosed to be denied." When she discovers that the "Bread" or immutable love she craves is unattainable, she negates her sense of loss by deflating the significance of human relationships. Negating the significance of human relationships, she negates the significance of her historical frustrations, as in the "I cannot" or "I'm Nobody" poem which is one of her recurrent types. Thus she describes herself as less artful and more accomplished than the members of her potential audience. As I have already suggested, still another way in which Dickinson discharges the anxiety expressed by these inverse images of a dislocated self is through her identification with a socially unconditioned power, a mastering principle as in the "King" poem previously cited, or the paradigmatic poem of this type, "My Life had stood—a Loaded Gun." This identification with a biographically neutral principle of spontaneous power can occur as she responds to an exceptional occurrence in nature:

Of Bronze—and Blaze—
The North—Tonight—
So adequate—it forms—
So preconcerted with itself
So distant—to alarms—
An Unconcern so sovreign
To Universe, or me—

Infects my simple spirit
With Taints of Majesty—
Till I take vaster attitudes—
And strut upon my stem—
Disdaining Men, and Oxygen,
For Arrogance of them—

My Splendors, are Menagerie—
But their Competeless Show
Will entertain the Centuries
When I, am long ago,
An Island in dishonored Grass—
Whom none but Daisies, know.   (290)

Observing the northern lights, the aurora borealis in their sov-
ereign unconcern "To Universe, or me," the speaker, momentarily
infected by "Taints of Majesty," takes "vaster attitudes" and struts
upon her "stem—": "Disdaining Men, and Oxygen, / For Arrogance
of them." But because Dickinson's response to nature is so thoroughly preconditioned by her response to the pressures of her immediate culture, this identification is undermined and then broken
by the staccato urgency of death, "the Hyphen of the Sea—"
(1454).[28] Her immortality fiction, here the dream of having outlived
the need for love, is corrected by an ironic perspective on the hubris
of her momentary afflatus. Mortality, Dickinson suggests, is more
typically an experience of inadequacy, anxious proximity to alarm,
concern with reputation, with physical needs, and with the ultimate
terror of irreversible anonymity. The poem momentarily reverses
this terror, becoming itself the caravan of splendors which "Will
entertain the Centuries / When I, am long ago, / An Island in dishonored Grass— / Whom none but Daisies, know." Her alternate
word choice for "Daisies" reads "Beetles."

Ideally, the Dickinsonian artist is unviolated by death: solitary
insights are permanent, social judgments ephemeral. For example,
in "Some—Work for Immortality," Dickinson initally views her poetic identity as a function of her relationship to her employer, "Immortality." Others may work for "Time," a male figure whom she

28. Roy Harvey Pearce is helpful here. In *The Continuity of American Poetry* (Princeton: Princeton University Press, 1961), he states that "she discovers only the power of
the sensibility to 'use' its world in order to discover itself. We may observe that the
transaction in which nature 'told' Emily Dickinson this 'simple News' is an involved
one, since she told it to nature first" (p. 179).

associates with "Fame," but her sexually indeterminate paymaster "Checks—on Fame." "Immortality" compensates a deserving few slowly. "Immortality" also "Checks—on Fame" in the sense that the reputations of "The Chiefer part" are transitory. Eventually, "Immortality" rectifies temporal injustice. Untransformed by Dickinson's language, the idea is a cliché: easy come, easy go.

Liberating herself from the temptation to personify "Immortality" and to specify its gender, in stanza two Dickinson implies that she is endlessly patient in her pursuit of amorphous goals. Her quest nevertheless enables her to reject "The Bullion of Today—" because of her avidity for "the Currency / Of Immortality." Her cynicism toward "the Broker's insight," which she continues to identify with ephemeral masculine values in stanza three, to some extent defines her aim. Finally, "Immortality" signifies the psychological autonomy of a gifted female mind. Dickinson distances her claim to such autonomy by avoiding the first-person-singular pronoun and by stressing the impoverished social status of any discerning "Beggar," but the poem appears to have been written in an exceptionally self-congratulatory mood, in 1862. Thus, even in 1862, Dickinson's desire for a contemporary literary reputation was checked by her allegiance to a habit of thought that confirmed the immediate and future value of her private vocation:

> Some—Work for Immortality—
> The Chiefer part, for Time—
> He—Compensates—immediately—
> The former—Checks—on Fame—
>
> Slow Gold—but Everlasting—
> The Bullion of Today—
> Contrasted with the Currency
> Of Immortality—
>
> A Beggar—Here and There—
> Is gifted to discern
> Beyond the Broker's insight—
> One's—Money—One's—the Mine—   (406)

Carrying her conception of deferred rewards even further, in one poem Dickinson explicitly identified herself with "Martyr Poets" whose inconclusive search "in Art—" for "the Art of Peace—" is finally valuable to some members of a future generation.[29] Describing her implied audience as yet unborn, Dickinson asserts that the artist who confesses herself to her contemporaries diffuses her commitment to her craft. The poet, or any artist, must sacrifice an audience in the present for an audience in the future; hence her unexplored competition with her poetic or biological precursors compels her to neglect her contemporaries.[30] The poem's conclusion is apparently imperfectly motivated: a stoical sublimation of grief into language is rapidly reformulated as a perpetual vow of silence. Dickinson's vulnerability to criticism probably explains this vow. The members of her immediate social circle arouse her "anxiety of influence," and she projects a larger, contemporary audience in their image:

> The Martyr Poets—did not tell—
> But wrought their Pang in syllable—
> That when their mortal name be numb—
> Their mortal fate—encourage Some—
>
> The Martyr Painters—never spoke—
> Bequeathing—rather—to their Work—
> That when their conscious fingers cease—
> Some seek in Art—the Art of Peace—   (544)

When she is most self-confident, however, Dickinson thrives on adversity. Whether spoken by others or by herself, as she explained to her suitor Judge Otis Lord in 1878, "'No' is the wildest word" in the English language (L562). Dissociating herself as a user of words from the feelings that inspired them, she also associated peace of mind with psychological and therefore artistic impotence. In "I would not paint—a picture," a self-consciously feminine speaker de-

29. This identification was encouraged not only by Dickinson's biographical experience but also by Barrett Browning's reinterpretation of Keats, "these were poets true, / Who died for Beauty as martyrs do / For Truth—the ends being scarcely two." See Elizabeth Barrett Browning, "A Vision of Poets," *The Poetical Works of Elizabeth Barrett Browning* (Boston: Houghton Mifflin, 1974), lines 289–91. According to Harriet Waters Preston, "She explained that the object of the poem was to indicate 'the necessary relations of genius to suffering and self-sacrifice'" (p. 128).

30. In letters 444a and 937a, Helen Hunt Jackson accused Dickinson of wronging her "day and generation" by refusing to "sing aloud." She warned, "When you are what men call dead, you will be sorry you were so stingy." She asked to be Dickinson's literary executor, but predeceased her.

scribes herself as "Enamored—impotent—content," luxuriates in the feigned despair of her sumptuous passivity, and finally acknowledges the "awful yes in every constitution" (PF79). On this rare occasion, Dickinson almost internalizes the stunning masculine license she associates with natural and erotic violence and with the bruising impact of an alien language. Even as it threatens to annihilate, this almost irresistible masculine force promises to complete her nature. Since Dickinson associated psychological completion not only with marriage but also with death, her poetry depends on her power to sustain the complexity of an unsurrendered life:

> I would not paint—a picture—
> I'd rather be the One
> It's bright impossibility
> To dwell—delicious—on—
> And wonder how the fingers feel
> Whose rare—celestial—stir—
> Evokes so sweet a Torment—
> Such sumptuous—Despair—
>
> I would not talk, like Cornets—
> I'd rather be the One
> Raised softly to the Ceilings—
> And out, and easy on—
> Through Villages of Ether—
> Myself endued Balloon
> By but a lip of Metal—
> The pier to my Pontoon—
>
> Nor would I be a Poet—
> It's finer—own the Ear—
> Enamored—impotent—content—
> The License to revere,
> A privilege so awful
> What would the Dower be,
> Had I the Art to stun myself
> With Bolts of Melody!   (505)

INDEX OF POEMS

The first lines of Dickinson poems cited are listed below. Poem numbers from the 1955 Johnson variorum edition appear in parentheses.

GENERAL INDEX

255

Library of Congress Cataloging in Publication Data

POLLAK, VIVIAN R.
   Dickinson, the anxiety of gender.

   Includes index.
   1. Dickinson, Emily, 1830–1886.   2. Poets, American—
19th century—Biography.   3. Sex roles in literature.
4. Sex (Psychology) in literature.   5. Identity
(Psychology) in literature.   I. Title.
PS1541.Z5P58   1984   811'.4 [B]   83–45941
ISBN 0–8014–1605–1